From Mogadishu to Dixon

From Mogadishu to Dixon

The Somali Diaspora in a Global Context

edited by

Abdi M. Kusow and Stephanie R. Bjork

The Red Sea Press, Inc.
Publishers & Distributors of Third World Books
RSP
P. O. Box 1892
Trenton, NJ 08607
P. O. Box 48
Asmara, ERITREA

The Red Sea Press, Inc.
Publishers & Distributors of Third World Books

P. O. Box 1892
Trenton, NJ 08607

P. O. Box 48
Asmara, ERITREA

First Printing 2007

Book and Cover design: Saverance Publishing Services
Cover Photo: Hassan Adan, Toronto, Canada

Library of Congress Cataloging-in-Publication Data

From Mogadishu to Dixon : the Somali diaspora in a global context / edited by Abdi M. Kusow and Stephanie R. Bjork.
p. cm.
Includes bibliographical references and index.
ISBN 1-56902-285-2 (hard cover) -- ISBN 1-56902-286-0 (pbk.)
1. Somalis--Africa--Social conditions--Case studies. 2. Somalis--Europe--Social conditions--Case studies. 3. Somalis--North America--Social conditions--Case studies. 4. African diaspora. 5. Somalia--Emigration and immigration. 6. Somalia--History--1991- I. Kusow, Abdi. II. Bjork, Stephanie R.
DT403.F76 2007
305.89'354--dc22

2007029529

IN MEMORY of the late Professor Nur Abdi Hussen, a pioneer of the Somali diaspora in the United States, without whose support and wealth of information, many Somali immigrants and refugees in Columbus, Ohio would have had a much harder road to travel and less knowledge of the American urban landscape to draw upon.

CONTENTS

ACKNOWLEDGMENTS

I like to thank my wife, *Alangti Umur Mad Aliyow*, for her unconditional love; and my children, Karima, Omar, and Abbas for being the wonderful children they are. A special and a deep sense of appreciation and love go to both my mother *Ina Cabdi Semed Aw Muxumed* and my mother in-law, *Alangti Aw Nurow Emed.*

—Abdi M. Kusow

I thank my parents Thomas and Jacqueline Bjork and husband Thinh Le, MD for their continued support.

—Stephanie R. Bjork

Introduction

THE SOMALI DIASPORA IN A GLOBAL CONTEXT

Abdi M. Kusow and Stephanie R. Bjork

For nearly two decades, and particularly since the civil war, Somali men, women, and children have left the country in droves. Some sought refuge amongst long-established Somali communities in the Horn of Africa, the former colonial powers of England, France, and Italy, and the Middle East. Others journeyed to new destinations. Today, Somali communities are found in nearly every corner of the world from small rural towns like Barron, Wisconsin and Lewiston, Maine in the United States, to cities like Cairo, Johannesburg, Sydney, Rome, Helsinki, Minneapolis, and last, but not least, the famous Dixon high-rises in Toronto. Diasporic Somalis are just as likely to speak Afrikaans or Finnish as they are to speak Somali.

The name Dixon in the title is not a coincidence. It represents the first significant destination of the Somali diaspora in North America. During the first influx of Somali refugees in Canada, Dixon--pronounced as *Diksan* in Somali--was known in refugee camps in Ethiopia, Kenya, and Yemen. Dixon was the Somali refugee dream city from 1988 to 1997. Even Somali immigrants who could obtain legal entry to the United States in the late 1980s often opted for resettlement in Canada.

In the physical sense, Dixon is simply the name for a community of six high-rise buildings located at the intersection of Dixon and Kipling in Etobicoke, a city in the northern suburb of Toronto. The six buildings have a total of 18,000 units designed for a population of roughly 4,000, but soared to 5,800 residents as a result of the arrival of Somali refugees who fled the Somali civil war in the early 1990s.

The arrival of the Somali refugees coincided with Transport Canada's decision to allow planes taking off from Pearson Airport to fly over the Kingsview Village where the Dixon buildings are located. This decision apparently increased jet noise, and in turn forced many residents to move out, consequently lowering the value of the neighborhood. By 1995, Somali refugees accounted for 50% of the Dixon community. Social scientists in the United States refer to this phenomenon as *white flight*.

White flight is an urban American condition in which poor black working class families--one family after another family--move into a predominantly white neighborhood. This process initiates a reactive out-movement of the white residents and results in a predominately black neighborhood. This process occurred in the Dixon high-rises--the more Somali refugees moved into the complex, the more white Canadian residents moved out of the complex. Today, Dixon is predominantly inhabited by Somalis and it has qualities that are stereotypical of other poor urban neighborhoods in North America, particularly sub-standard elementary and primary education.

Socially, however, Dixon represents a deeper and a more complicated Somali diaspora story. It represents the first major culture clash between the Somali diaspora and the Canadian society, and North America in general. This encounter initiated stereotypes and counter stereotypes between Somali refugees and white Canadian residents. Canadian residents implicitly accused the new Somali community of disrespecting tenant rules and overcrowding, spreading tuberculoses, and engaging in welfare fraud. Moreover, other residents accused Somali residents of painting anti-white graffiti on the swimming pools and parking structures. The culture clash between the new Somali community and other residents of the complex led the Canadian Broadcasting Corporation (CBC) to produce *A Place Called Dixon*, a documentary which immortalized this encounter.

Dixon also represents the epicenter of Somali diaspora cultural production and the articulation of tension and conflict that characterize the Somali diaspora around the globe. The Somali community in Toronto initiated the reproduction of clan identities in the form of community associations in the diaspora. By 1995, there were scores of Somali associations in Toronto. Each association was managed by a particular Somali clan. This process is the modus operandi for Somali associations throughout the Somali diaspora from Helsinki, Finland to Durban, South Africa. This process has now elevated into a situation where some cities in Europe and North America have different clan concentrations. Dixon also experienced the first consequences of transformed gender relations among the Somali diaspora. Moreover, Somalis in Dixon also started to show a more pronounced devotion to Islam and Islamic values and identities. Dixon residents also exhibited a total obsession with the political dynamics of Somalia. In some cases, this obsession took the form of active political engagement where Somalis sent financial support to respective clan lords through remittances. This engagement was a central source of the now highly articulated global Somali diaspora networks.[1]

This book represents the first attempt to map the social and cultural contours of the Somali diaspora in a global context. Using case studies from Somali communities in Africa, Europe, and North America, the contributors to this volume construct a global comparative framework for studying the Somali diaspora. The framework simultaneously compares dispersed Somalis in different social contexts, and captures the fluid, transnational context of the Somali diaspora. The central questions that guide the volume are: how do the different cultural, economic, political, social, and racial contexts inform identity formations and opportunity structures that diasporic Somalis face? Consequently, how do the making and remaking of diasporic identities affect their respective host communities as well as the homeland communities they left behind?

We pursue answers to these questions by constructing an empirically grounded global framework that holds the source country, Somalia, constant and compares the effects of the different processes, conditions, and spaces under which the Somalis diaspora is constituted. By holding the source country constant, we can specifically interrogate social transformations and opportunity structures under different contexts. Such a methodology provides empirical support for Edward Alpers' recent implicit and perceptive question for African diaspora scholarship. Why, despite the presence of large African populations in the western Indian Ocean littoral, did any meaningful diasporic African identity recollections or political struggles not occur in this area as compared to the Atlantic world? What is clear from Alpers' comparison of the Indian Ocean with the black Atlantic is the importance of the source (East Africa versus West Africa) and the destination (the Indian Ocean versus the Atlantic) contexts.

A conceptual framework that holds the source constant allows us to articulate the impact of technology on the relationship between homeland and diaspora and the social networks between different diaspora Somali communities. There is ample evidence that recent advances in transportation and communication systems have compressed time and space, thereby rendering traditional sociological distinctions between home and host societies empirically unsustainable. Unlike the descendants of the transatlantic diaspora, members of the contemporary African diaspora maintain institutionalized ties to ancestral homelands, host societies, and other diaspora communities by simultaneously participating in the economic, social and political processes of various locations. The vivid image of Iraqi Americans casting their ballots in polling stations throughout the United States for an essentially Iraqi political process is powerful testimony to the sociological reality that the nation-state and society no longer converge and the boundary between "the here and there" is unfixed.

A focus on a single contemporary case also reveals the effects of the changing racial demography of international migration and its impact on identity formation in the Somali diaspora. For example, due to increased political and economic instability in much of Africa, along with changes in immigration laws, the black Atlantic is presently in the midst of significant demographic transformation. That is, from predominately descendants of the transatlantic slave trade to a more diverse black community that includes significant African and Caribbean immigrants who speak different languages and do not operate from a collectively shared understanding of everyday realties and cultural and social values. The Somali diaspora not only brings their homeland identities with them, but they also transform and redefine the meaning of racial identity categories within North American black communities. Thus, once we understand that the contemporary African diaspora, as Johnson-Odim put it, "has created 'much of the old country in the new' and in ways not available to those that preceded them primarily via the Atlantic slave trade," a whole new approach to understanding mediated diasporic identities, or who is African or diasporic African becomes possible.[2]

This approach, global diaspora formation, captures how the proliferation of Somali political, social, economic activities, and cultural identities across boundaries, as informed by globalization and by recent advances in technology, turned Somali communities around the world into a truly global diaspora. The global diaspora formation concept borrows from and expands on the work of several scholars including Michael Omi and Howard Winant's *racial formation*, Earl Lewis' *overlapping diasporas*, Stuart Hall's *articulation* of diasporic identities, David Scott's *embodied disputes*, Tiffany Patterson and Robin Kelley's *global diaspora* concept, and Peggy Levitt and Nina Glick Schiller's *simultaneity*. The idea of diaspora formation is meant to capture the level of sociological articulation necessary to reveal the *virtual* processes, conditions, and the spaces that inform dynamics of diasporic overlap or simultaneity that occur, and the degree of embodied disputes among and across the Somali diaspora.[3]

The volume is organized into the following spatial contours: Africa; Europe; and North America. The spatial contours are not, however, intended to convey mutually exclusive diasporas, but rather, are seen as overlapping, embodied disputes. Overlapping in that each spatial contour is comprised of members with various migration histories and future migration ambitions. For example, the Somali diaspora in Egypt consists of persons who migrated from Somalia to Egypt before the civil war in 1991, émigrés who moved from Somali diaspora communities in the West for cultural and religious reasons, and individuals from the Somali diaspora in Kenya, Yemen, or Ethiopia. Moreover, Somalis in Egypt may join the Somali diaspora in Finland as a result of family reunification policies. Yet, after they establish themselves in Finland, they may decide to settle and raise their family in Egypt--and again the process continues. By embodied disputes, we mean to point to the construction and negotiation of disputed diasporic clan identities as indicated by both Al-Sharmani and Bjork's chapters.

In *Part I, Africa,* Omar Eno and Mohamed Eno, Gudrun-Katharina Kroner, and Mulki Al-Sharmani examine slavery, migration dreams and pitfalls, and diasporic identity among Somalis in Africa. Eno and Eno's chapter investigates slavery within Africa--a hitherto unrecognized aspect of African diaspora scholarship. Moreover, Eno and Eno explore the similarities and differences between the experiences of Somali Bantus enslaved within the Continent and those across the Atlantic. Kroner's chapter is a sociological examination of the uncertainty that comes with diasporic exile in Cairo. Although many Somali refugees dream of joining a desirable diaspora community in the West, they often find themselves stuck in Cairo. Al-Sharmani examines how two groups of Somalis in Egypt (refugees and émigrés, naturalized citizens of Western countries) engage in collective efforts to secure livelihood and resist marginalization. In this context, Somalis construct a collective Somali identity, which they call *soomaalinimo*.

In *Part II, Europe,* Francesca Decimo, Petri Hautaniemi, Stephanie Bjork, Nauja Kleist, Anu Isotalo, and Marja Tiilikainen focus on migration policies, transnational networks, clan, gender, and religious identities among Somalis in Europe. Decimo, for example, describes how the Italian social and economic context selected Somali women to work in the flourishing domestic labor market as live-in domestics who care for the growing aging Italian population. The wages these women earn support scattered parents and relatives in Somalia and finance the migration of relatives in Africa to choice destinations in Europe and North America. Here, again, we see the overlap between the Somali diaspora in Italy and those in other diaspora communities and in the homeland. Hautaniemi critically examines the use of DNA-testing in family reunification cases in Finland and the procedure's impact on Somali families. Using an anthropological lens, Bjork investigates how and why Somalis in Finland tell and read clan in everyday life. Kleist analyses the experiences and discourses of discrimination and belonging among Somalis in Denmark. Isotalo examines social meanings of appropriate and inappropriate socio-spatial behavior for Somali girls in Turku, Finland. Tiilikainen explores how Somali women in Finland negotiate and create religious and cultural identities in their transnational lives.

In *Part III, North America,* Rima Berns-McGown, Franklin Goza, Cindy Horst, and Jessica Schaid and Zoltán Grossman examine cultural and gender identity formation, socio-economic assimilation, and transnational linkages among Somalis in North America. Berns-McGown investigates how Somali women in Toronto, Canada negotiate Somali cultural traditions with the realities of urban public housing. Goza provides a detailed socio-economic portrait of Somalis in the United States. Horst explores the complex relationship between Somalis in Minneapolis and their relatives in refugee camps in Africa. Horst articulates the theoretical gap between the economic expectations that Somali refugees in Africa have of their relative in Minneapolis and the economic condition of the Somali diaspora in North America. Schaid and Grossman examine the experiences of Somalis in Barron, Wisconsin, a small factory town in the American Midwest.

The studies presented in this volume can hardly do justice to the entire spectrum of the Somali diaspora. It is a first step, though, and like all first steps, we achieved important things, but missed, we are sure, even more important issues. One such issue is the need for a comprehensive examination of the socio-economic assimilation of Somalis in their respective host societies. How are Somali children faring in education? This is significant simply because education is vital for economic well-being in the West. Another understudied area is the Somali diaspora's political and economic role in the making and maintenance of the Somali civil war. Perhaps, more importantly, the Somali diaspora represents one of the first significant black, African, non-Christian, and non-English speaking community in the West. In some contexts, such as in Barron, Wisconsin, and Helsinki, Finland, Somalis constitute the only sizably significant African population. These qualities, as Kusow has shown in his research, have implications for the ways in which racial identities are articulated in the West. In this regard, research that illuminates whether or not Somali immigrants and African-Americans have a collectively shared understanding of blackness and black identities would add to the literature on the social construction of racial identities.[4]

Notes

1. For a good description of the Somali community in Dixon and Toronto in the mid-1990s, see Stoffman, D. (1995, August). Dispatch from Dixon. *Toronto Life*, 29, 11, 40-47.
2. See Johnson-Odim, C. (2000). Unfinished migrations: Commentary and response. *African Studies Review*, 43, 51-53. p. 52.
3. For discussion of diaspora and transnational concepts see Akyeampong, E. (2000). Africans in the diaspora: The diaspora and Africa. *African Affairs,* 99, 183-215; Alpers, E. (2000). Recollecting Africa: Diasporic memory in the Indian Ocean world. *African Studies Review,* 43 (1), 83-99; Butler, K. (2000). From black history to diasporan history: Brazilian abolition in Afro-Atlantic context. *African Studies Review,* 43 (1), 125-139; Byfield, J. (2000). Introduction: Rethinking the African diaspora. *African Studies Review,* 43, 1-10; Clifford, J. (1994). Diasporas. *Cultural Anthropology,* 9, 302-338; Cohen, R. (1996). Diaspora and the nation-state: From victims to challengers. *International Affairs,* 72 (3), 507-520; Hall, S. (2003). Cultural identity and diaspora. In J. E. Braziel and A. Mannur (Eds.), *Theorizing diaspora: A Reader* (233-246). Malden, MA & Oxford, UK: Blackwell Publishing; Hanchard, M. (1990). Identity, meaning, and the African-American. *Social Text,* 24, 31-42; Hanchard, M. (1999). Afro-Modernity: Temporality, politics, and the African diaspora. *Public Culture,* 11, 245-68; Hine, D. C. (2001). Frontiers in black diaspora studies and comparative black history: Enhanced knowledge of our complex past. *Negro Educational Review,* 52, 101-108; Lewis, E. (1995). To Turn as on a pivot: Writing African Americans into a history of overlapping diasporas. *The American Historical Review,* 100 (3), 765-787; Mintz, S. W., & Price, R. (1992). *The birth of African-American culture: An anthropological perspective*. Boston: Beacon Press. Johnson-Odim, C. (2000). Unfinished migrations: Commentary and response. *African Studies Review,* 43, 51-53; Omi, M., & Winant, H. A. (1986). *Racial formation in the United States: From the 1960s to the 1980s*. New York: Routledge and Kegan Paul. Palmer, C. (1998). Defining and studying the modern African diaspora. *Perspectives: American Historical Association Newsletter,* 36 (6), 21-25; Patterson, T. R., & Kelley, R. D. G. (2000). Unfinished Migrations: Reflections on the African diaspora and the making of the modern world. *African Studies Review,* 43 (1), 11-45; Safran, W. (1991). Diasporas in modern societies: Myths of homeland and return. *Diaspora,* 1 (1), 83-99; Tölölyan, K. (1996). Rethinking diaspora(s): Stateless power in transnational

moment. *Diaspora,* 5 (1), 3-36; Zeleza, P. T. (2005). Rewriting the African diaspora: Beyond the black Atlantic. *African Affairs,* 104 (414), 35-68; Kearney, M. (1995). The local and the global: The anthropology of globalization and transnationalism. *Annual Review of Anthropology*, 24, 547-565; Levitt, P., & Glick Schiller, N. (2004). Conceptualizing simultaneity: A transnational social field perspective on society. *International Migration Review*, 38 (145):1002-1039.

4. Kusow's most recent work on Somali immigrants and racial identities in North America include: Ajrouch, K., & Kusow A. M. (2007). Racial and religious contexts: Situational identities among Lebanese and Somali Muslim immigrants in North America. *Ethnic and Racial Studies,* 30, 72-94; Kusow, A. M. (2007). Africa: East. In M. Waters & R. Ueda with H. Marrow (Eds.), *The new Americans*: *A guide to immigration since 1965*, (295-306). Cambridge: Harvard University Press; Kusow, A. M. (2006). Migration and racial formations among Somali immigrants in North America. *Journal of Ethnic and Migration Studies,* 32, 533-551; Kusow, A. M. (2004). Contesting stigma: On Goffman's assumptions of normative order. *Symbolic Interaction* 27, 179-19.

Part I

Africa

Chapter 1

THE JOURNEY BACK TO THE ANCESTRAL HOMELAND: THE RETURN OF THE SOMALI BANTU (WAZIGWA) TO MODERN TANZANIA

Omar A. Eno and Mohamed A. Eno

INTRODUCTION

By using a case study from the historical and social experiences of the Wazigwa (Bantu, Shambara, and Wazigwa will be used interchangeably) Somali Bantu community in Southern Somalia, this chapter contributes to the contemporary African diaspora scholarship by elaborating an aspect of the inter-African diaspora. The chapter specifically examines three issues. First, we provide a historical background of how the Wazigwa Bantu Somali community came into Somalia as victims of inter-Africa slavery. In other words, we will examine the nature and dynamics of the Wazigwa slavery from East Africa to the Somali Banadir Coast. Second; we will discuss a comparative analysis of how the return migration of the Wazigwa Somali Bantu, as led by Wana-Kucha, was in many ways similar to the American "Underground Railroad" system, led by the now famous Harriet Tubman; and third, we will highlight the factors that led to the Somali Wazigwa's return migration to their original homeland in modern Tanzania.

HISTORICAL BACKGROUND

Among the distinguished communities living in Southern Somalia are two clusters of Bantu people who are predominantly sedentary farmers. One group consists of the residents along the Shabelle River and its environs; they are the indigenous natives to their current settlement, and are beyond the purpose of this chapter. The second group, which is the main focus of this study, comprises those along the Juba River, also known as Gosha (forest) people. The latter group includes people who originated from southeast Africa such as Mozambique, Malawi, Tanganyika, and Zanzibar (modern Tanzania). For the purpose of this chapter, our concern is on the Bantu sub-group, the Wazigwa, who originated from modern Tanzania.

The contemporary Wazigwa population of southern Somalia originally resulted from slaves imported from Southeast Africa by Arab/Swahili commercial planters and slave traders around the turn of the 19th century. They were specifically brought from Tanganyika by boats and dhows, and later exported from the Zanzibar Island and from other Tanzanian cities like Bagamoyo and brought to the coastal cities of southern Somalia such as Brava, Kismayo, Marka, and Mogadishu. They were initially used as slave laborers in the commercial plantations exploited by a combination of Arab/Swahili and Somali merchants for the exportation of grain and other food commodities to the then expanding population of the Omani Empire in the East African Coast and to markets in Southern Arabia and the Middle East.[a] They were also used as porters in the movement of goods to and from the southern Somali interior to the coast as well as potential human resource for the flourishing textile industry in the Banadir area, particularly in the city of Marka. Some of the Wazigwa people still remember their origin and accounts of how they were brought to Somalia. According to Cassanelli, in about 1903, Salemi, a runaway slave in Somalia who sought refuge or protection of the Italian abolitionists, said he was captured on the Mrima coast of Tanganyika and transported into Somalia through the port of Marka some 20 years ago with about 40 companions by Arab traders of Sur.[2]

In their own oral traditions, the Wazigwa left their country of origin (modern Tanzania) because of a severe famine and a possibility to work on a fertile land in southern Somalia.[3] However, in the process, the Arab traders who had promised to take them to work in a fertile land where famine and drought had never been experienced tricked them into slavery.[4] Other scholars suspect that some of these slaves might have sold themselves off because of several consecutive years of drought that hit Tanganyika early in the 19th century. The Arab-Omanis brought them to Somalia and later vended them to Somalis along the coastal cities as slaves to meet the increasing demand for labor to grow grains; particularly sorghum, maize, and sesame seeds.[5] By the 1840s, European travelers were astonished by the huge amount of grain supplies and agricultural riches produced along the Shabelle River. The major agricultural change that was achieved in the Shebelle valley economy was facilitated by the tapping of a large reservoir of slave labor (unwillingly) supplied by the resident Bantu population.[6] Part of the profits generated by the exploitation of the slave workforce was ventured to purchase more slaves which in turn led to further expansion of the cultivated lands and the encouragement of slave trade.[7]

Beyond using slaves for labor, though, the slave owners treated the Wazigwa viciously and sadistically. The reason for this mistreatment was partly to capitalize on the slave labor. Antonio Del Bocca indicates that the well-being of the warlike Bimal, settled in the area between the Webi-Shebelli River and the Indian Ocean and in the hinterland of Marka and its environs, was mainly dependent on grain and other agricultural products grown by Bantu slaves, a portion of which the Bimal used to trade for imported cloths and hardware in the markets of Marka. The Bimal, who possessed the nomadic Somali's traditional disdain for agriculture, would not have survived without Bantu slave labor.[8] Colonial officers like Christopher also reported that slaves families were inhumanly mistreated by slave-owners in the Banadir Coasts.[9] Unlike in West Africa, where slave treatment was more passive, in the sense that slaves somehow resigned themselves to their servile status but silently struggled to resist and create more room for themselves,[10] in East Africa slaves were harshly treated because they were kinless in that area. This mistreatment finally caused them to rebel against their masters. A combination of all these insensitive treatments and poor living conditions might have been responsible for the slave revolt in southern Somalia, masterminded by Wana-kucha, a female leader of the Wazigwa.

Literally, according to lexical morphology, Wana-Kucha's name should have been Mwana-Kucha, considering that the Kiswahili semantic "Mwana" (child of) is normally used to refer to a single person, while (Wana) refers to multiple persons and hence the plural of the former. According to our informants, she (Wana-Kucha) is probably referred to as 'Wana' because of the respect she had among her community as a leader who could foresee and foretell future events.[11] Among the major accomplishments of Wana-Kucha's leadership is the escape of to lead her community from slavery to freedom. From this perspective, an approach to the history of diaspora slavery gives us the desire to believe that the nature of Wana-Kucha's escape plan for the Wazigwa draws a resemblance to that of Harriet Tubman's Underground Railroad, a subject of relevant discussion in a later segment of this study.

IMPACT OF SLAVERY ON THE WAZIGWA

Upon realizing that the Arab Omani merchants had duped them into slavery and sold them to local Somali coastal people, who in turn resold them to the interior Somalis, the Wazigwa instigated a plan for their escape out of the bondage of slavery, but it was not easy. By the 1840s, especially as European abolitionist impetus gained momentum and European traders also increased along the Nile Valley and the coast of East Africa, the Wazigwa began to question the morality of their enslavement. In their own interest, the Somalis (coastal and interior people) were not willing to liberate their slaves, hence the Wazigwa's escape into the forests where they formed fugitive communities maintaining their East African ethnic identities. Given their social condition and their common opposition to enslavement, ethnic differences among the fugitives and runaways had to be harmonized, paving way for the formation of multi-ethnic alliances for the purpose of survival and communal defense.

Wana-Kucha, who was a well respected female within her community as a leader invested with mystical powers, had risen as their savior from slavery. She did in fact rise with a vision. She predicted to her people that they would enjoy the fresh air of freedom in the near future. In those days, slave-owners did not allow slaves to visit each other's villages because of the fear that the slaves would flee.

The strictness had to a certain extent impeded the slaves from easy communication. However, Wana-Kucha devised an interesting technique by utilizing folklore dance as an opportunity for communication across villages so that they could plan for their escape undetected.

According to our informants, slave villages at the time were geographically vicinal; when slaves of one village were singing and dancing, they could be heard from the surrounding villages.[12] Accordingly, Wana-Kucha advised her people to adapt the habit of dancing and singing after the completion of their daily work as a vehicle of communication. Within the lyrics of the songs, a medium incomprehensible to the Somali slave-herders, and the rhythm of the drums that accompanied them, the singers were actually sending a message to escape to freedom. The villages soon adapted the same style of dance and exchanged messages to one another through the lore of their culture. This huge operation of Underground Railroad-like proportions was coordinated by Wana-Kucha, as an architect of the master plan. It was so well coordinated that slave owners woke up to their shock one morning to find the entirety of the able-bodied slaves had run away simultaneously from several villages without the slightest detection by either the slave overseers or masters themselves.

The objective of this escape was the attainment of freedom and the desire of the enslaved Wazigwa ethnic community to return to Tanganyika (modern Tanzania), their country of origin. Although they succeeded in their escape from slavery, they failed to reach Tanganyika by foot. Various oral traditions suggest that the failure to return to the homeland confirmed the predictions of their leader, Wana-kucha, who had prophesized this obstacle.

The Wazigwa escapees decided to settle in the Gosha area, a location along the banks of the Juba River within the environs of the city of Kismayu. Wana-Kucha had a vision that her people would not easily succeed in returning to their homeland in Tanganyika.[13] In most cases, what has contributed to the survival of these fugitive slaves was their farming expertise, which inspired them to subsist without the support of their masters. As a self-regulating runaway community, they cleared the forestland in Gosha for farming and erected their residences independently. According to oral accounts, these runaways found other Bantu/Jareer groups already residing in the vicinity of Gosha such as the Gawawiin, the Eyle and so on. Quoting one of his informants, Mohamed Eno writes, "When the Mushunguli (Wazigwa) reached the Juba valley, they were received and absorbed into other existing Bantu aborigine/Negroid communities who were scattered in small and large villages on both banks of the river."[14] Later, they established their own polity by the Juba River around the 1840s, providing a safe asylum for other runaway slaves.[15]

Besides Gosha, another remarkable sanctuary for runaway slaves was also established at Avai,[16] situated a considerable distance to the west of the coastal city of Brava.[17] The founder of the latter fugitive community is believed to be a man by the name of Makarane, reportedly a Bantu runaway slave. According to Barile, ex-Somali slave masters from different sub-clans including the Tuni, Beghed[i], Giddu, and Bimal had tried several times to destroy [Avai], the new run-away slave settlement, but failed.[18] During colonial days, several countries, such as Italy, Egypt, and Zanzibar, recognized Avai as an independent entity. As a result, the Italian colonial authority sent fugitive slaves to this new haven in order to save them from recapture by their pursuing Somali masters.[19]

Meanwhile, the renegade slaves in Gosha spread out along the banks of the Juba River and into the surrounding villages of the coastal city of Kisimayo,[20] where they erected strong defenses to protect themselves from outside invaders (most likely their ex-masters).[21] As more slaves took refuge in Gosha, the population multiplied dramatically, eventually leading to the emergence of the settlement as an independent state recognized by the colonial authorities. According to Grottanelli, many Wazigwa escaped from their Somali masters after serving only for a few years as farmers and domestic laborers because they realized that they had been entrapped and sold as slaves by the Arabs.[22] As we stated earlier, the purpose of the Wazigwa escape was not just the achievement of freedom or the establishment of residence in the Gosha area, but in fact a strong longing to return to their original homeland in modern Tanzania.[23]

Estimates by Besteman and Menkhaus show that between 1865 and 1895, over 20,000 slaves made their way into the safe havens.[24] Although the largest number of the runaways escaped from the plantations,[25] there is ample evidence suggesting that other slaves released on shore by British anti-slavery naval patrols increased the number, later developing Gosh into a small but autonomous state under independent Bantu leadership. In the ensuing years the new state of Gosha[26] became prosperous under several leaders such as: Shungor Mafula, Wana-kucha, Mkomo Maliku, Nassib Bunde (a Yao hero who fought against the Somali ex-slave masters and later the Italian colonialists), and Sheykh Murjan (a prominent religious leader).[27] Bricchetti, an Italian anti-slavery activist, reported that the Wazigwa had sworn in the name of God and equality that they would fight to maintain their freedom to the last person and that they would never submit themselves to their Somali ex-masters. Oral traditions of elderly Wazigwa interviewed in various locations also coincide with this remark, as Mohamed Eno elaborates, "that there would be no looking back once the journey to freedom had started; also, anyone who abandoned his people would be dealt with by the ancestors' wrath and curse."[28]

To date, the Wazigwa still maintain the languages and dialects of their country of origin (modern Tanzania); their customs, traditions and cultural heritage are very identical to those of their brethren in the coastal parts of Tanzania.[29] Another important characteristic of the Wazigwa is that, after living in Somalia for almost two centuries, they are not entirely "Somalized." They retain their distinct language, Kizigwa, a Bantu dialect related to Tanzania; the fact that they lived in Gosha, a territory so isolated from the penetration of the nomadic Somalis, might have contributed to the retention. Even though communication in Gosha is conducted in diverse media, Maay and Swahili (Kiswahili) languages surface as the lingua franca, notwithstanding the recent changes in language policy which frustrated the dominant socio-linguistic infrastructure after Siyad Barre's major linguistic revolutionization campaign.[30]

Furthermore, most of these groups still maintain their cultural and genealogical links to their Southeast African ethnic groups such as: the Yao, the Nyasa, the Mushunguli (or Wazigwa), the Makua, and the Ngindu.[31] In Gosha, some communities remain significantly matrilineal compared to the Somali nomad's patrilineal kinship system. Moreover, village settlements were exclusively based along the lines of their Southeast African tribal origin. For instance, citing Kersten, Besteman writes that the Wazigwa did not allow a fugitive to settle in their village if he/she did not belong to their ethnic group. However, they (the Wazigwa) would only accept an outsider fugitive to join them if he/she came along with a gun and gun-powder.[32] Late in the 19th century, although the social rules for village settlements were changing, it was never easy to join a village. In fact, there were new runaways arriving in Gosha who had largely been enslaved as children who did not have any affinity to their respective ethnic groups; they too had difficulties being accepted.[33]

Upon its formation, the citizens of Gosha were forced to pay tribute to the Sultan of Zanzibar, who in turn provided them with guns, a strategy which allowed the Gosha community to defeat the surrounding enemy, the Somali nomads. A political alliance was forged between Gosha and the Sultan of Zanzibar, a very significant factor that boosted the popularity and legitimacy of Gosha as a viable state.

Under the leadership of Nassib Bunde, the Yao ex-slave, the state of Gosha had achieved several victories against their rival Somali nomads. In the narratives of our informants, the most important victory was the encounter in which they mercilessly crushed the mighty Ogaaden nomadic group of the Darod clan family. This event, known as Ooji-yoow abuur reeb,[34] closely translates to, "you Gosha fellows, don't eradicate us, spare some of (our) off-spring for future reproduction." Many feared Nassib Bunde due to his reputation as a strong leader with magical power and the ability to perform miracles. He eventually declared himself a Sultan, and succeeded in the unification of the Gosha area into a formidable confederacy. He was recognized as a leader locally and internationally, particularly by the colonial administrations of both Britain and Italy.[35] Since most of the runaways in Gosha, specifically those from modern Tanzania (Wazigwa) were already Muslims, Nassib Bunde converted to Islam; thereafter his subjects gradually embraced Islam. Muslim brotherhoods were established in the state of Gosha and its environs where many runaways kept seeking refuge.

Enemies surrounding the state of Gosha, above all the Somali nomads, were a serious concern and a constant fear of each other prevailed for a long time. Due to this hostile environment, trade between neighbors was very difficult. Since both sides (Gosha and nomads) needed bilateral trade interaction but feared one another, a solution had to be found to alleviate that neighborhood tension. Both groups agreed to carry their trade transactions at a place called Regatta, a plain with wide visibility, and little opportunity for subterfuge.[36]

By the late 19th century, the state of Gosha was dismantled by the European colonial authorities, particularly the Italians, who took over Somalia Banadir as part of their domain. Immediately after taking over Somalia Banadir from the Sultan of Zanzibar, Italy tried to abolish slavery for those who could not escape with Wana-Kucha but failed in the attempt. It was only in the early 20th century when colonial Italy seriously implemented and re-enforced the abolition act against slavery in Somalia Banadir. Even though slavery was abolished in Somalia Banadir, the status of the Somali Bantu, including the Wazigwa continues to remain undesirable. The stigma and legacy of slavery still haunts them.

After abolition and upon the grant of independence, the Italian colonial authorities did not make any effort in changing the social status of the indigenous and imported Bantu populations as equal to that of the Somali nomads. Instead, they upheld the nomadic claim of mythical "nobility" and contaminated the ethno-history of the distinct Bantu groups, indigenous Bantus and those affect by diaspora, by lumping them together and stratifying all of them as descendants from slaves. This misconception created class stratification based on nomadic "superordinates" and Bantu "subordinates," effecting a deeply-rooted implementation of stiff marginalization by the former against the latter.

Consequently, the above-mentioned colonial fallacy played as an instrument for the unilateral tribal manipulation of political power of an ethnically diverse population but mythically portrayed as homogeneous, a shortsighted incident that has bedeviled Somalia since the peninsula became independent in 1960. The value label attached to this festering quandary has been key in the deliberate ostracization of the Bantu people, which in the Wazigwa case could be partially attributed to the unaccomplishment of their return journey home. This is to suggest that although Wana-Kucha succeeded in the quest of leading her people to freedom, the unanticipated length of the strenuous trip on foot affected their objective to return to Tanganyika. In the following section of the chapter we will demonstrate comparative similarities between these two outstanding women (Harriet Tubman and Wana-Kucha) who led their people from slavery to freedom under different environments but with similar objectives.

HARRIET TUBMAN AND THE UNDERGOUND RAILROAD

African and African-American women are rarely deemed the tribute and recognition they deserve for the intrepid work they contributed to the freedom of their communities and to society in general. However, the exhausting endeavors of Harriet Tubman from Virginia and Wana-kucha from Southern Somalia, and their sacrifices to free their people from slavery, cannot be easily ignored. Although Harriet Tubman has received some acknowledgement and appreciation for her astounding effort to free the slaves (thanks to African-American Studies), Wana-Kucha's recognition and accolade for her success of freeing the slaves remains unmentioned in any of the educational curricula of Somali history, despite certain figures like Sayid Mohamed Abdulle Hassan, Ahmed Gurey, and Hawa Osman Tako being worshipped as heroes and heroines. Wana-Kucha's role and place in the social history of the Wazigwa was disappointingly denied a mention by all the independent Somali administrations which fed the world with the wrong impression of a "homogeneous" Somali society.

These two amazing heroines, who lived in two different continents of the world, yet shared a common status as bondage slaves, had some significant similarities in their ambitions for liberty and personal characteristics as described in the following paragraphs. Nevertheless, before we proceed, we must briefly mention the motivating factors to the culmination of their bondage to slavery.

After witnessing the dismal treatments of slaves by their soulless slave owners, these heroic woman decided to risk their lives for the freedom of their people, African-Americans and the Wazigwa/Shambara.[37] From this background, we can argue that both women were leading the kind of slave revolts and resistances which scholars of slavery would term as an extensive regime of unprecedented human exploitation with the sole interest of gainful results in favor of the oppressors.[38] Because, according to Morris, revolts and conspiracies are "tactics employed by slaves in their struggle to topple the slave regime."[39]

Similarly, both women belonged to a diaspora household. For example, Harriet Tubman was ethnically and originally a woman of Bantu descent, probably an Ashanti from Ghana, as suggested by Clinton.[40] She was an African-American in the Americas. Wana-kucha was also ethnically a Bantu woman from Tanganyika who was affected by the intra-African diaspora to Somalia, meaning a Tanganyika diaspora within Africa. Both women, Tubman and Wana-kucha, became known for their gallantry, outstandingly engineering their respective successful escapes in difficult situations as diaspora. It was due to their influence that the art of escape reached its highest level as a form of resistance against slavery in the US and in the Banadir coast of Somalia respectively.

Harriet Tubman, a runaway slave from Virginia, a soldier, and abolitionist, led her people into freedom through what has become known as the Underground Railroad.[41] Though she did not have any biological children, she adopted a daughter at a time when social and economic life was tough for the Black diaspora in the Americas. In the antebellum period; "If a master had slaves [and] he just could not rule...he would ask him if he wanted to go to another plantation and if he said he did, then he would give him a pass that would read: 'Give this nigger hell.' Of course, when the patrollers or other plantation boos would read the pass, he would beat him nearly to death and send him back."[42] Further, in the southern United States, slaves were treated with extreme inhumanity; women were molested, raped, and the men were often whipped naked in front of friends and family members.[43] In one merciless incident, Robert Newsom of Missouri purchased Celia, a 14 year old Negro girl. He did not purchase her to serve him as a domestic slave, but as his sexual slave. After enduring sexual abuse for many years, Celia struck one night and killed Newsom with a log. Unfortunately, in court, the law in Missouri at the time said, the sexual assault of a slave woman by white males was considered merely trespass, not rape. An owner could not be charged with trespassing upon his own property, so Celia was found guilty of killing her abuser.[44]

Tubman had witnessed and lived among the unbearable sufferings and the human degradation of her people by slave owners in Virginia. Thus, she became determined to free her people from slavery. That deep sentiment and the longing for liberty can be detected in her tone, when she narrated, "I had seen their tears and sighs and I had heard their groans, and I would give every drop of blood in my veins to free them."[45] Before implementing her plan to escape into freedom, Tubman listened and gathered information and stories about successful escapes and rumors about wonderful events in the North. She was amazed to learn that, unlike in the South, black men in the North could actually talk in public and white men would listen to them.

According to Rev. Henry Highland Garnet in New York, "a vision came to her [Harriet] in the night of emancipation of her people. Whether a dream or one of those glimpses into the future, which sometimes seem to have been granted to her, no one can say, but the effect upon her was very remarkable."[46] In addition, Tubman was known by her people as the "Moses," which is referred to the biblical epoch when Moses led his people (the Israelites) in their migration from Egypt to the Promised Land in Israel.[47] Tubman was also known by her people as someone who possessed a mystical charm of power; as a consequence, slave masters could not catch her. Of all the fugitives that she piloted from slavery to liberty, not one of them was ever recaptured.[48]

It has been agreed amongst the majority of historians that Tubman had led to freedom about 500 of her people and the impact of her actions has freed thousands of slaves over the years. For example, in the midst of the escape journey some of Harriet's escapee members were frightened and desired to return to their respective masters. Amazingly, she dealt with a situation like that decisively: by holding her gun to the slave's head and saying, "Brother, you go on or you die." And they always went on to their own freedom.[49] Although Harriet Tubman led some slaves to their freedom, many were left behind to live in the calamity of slavery and lived as destitute in squalid ghetto neighborhoods. They lived a very difficult and miserable life without the prospect of a decent mode of subsistence, a brutal life that promised little for the future.

After the Second World War, the emancipated slaves in the South had enough living a despondent life that seemed eternal and imbued with poverty, without access to education and prominent jobs. Alternatively, they migrated to the North. This has resulted in the mass movement of people from South to the North known as "the great migration." In essence, the Underground Railroad symbolizes the escape of slaves from the deep-seated institutionalized slave-owning Southerners to the abolitionist Northerners in the United Sates where people were tolerant and receptive to blacks as humans.

WANA-KUCHA'S ODYSSEY TO THE FREEDOM OF THE WAZIGWA

Like Harriet Tubman, Wana-kucha, an Mzigwa fugitive slave from the Banadir coast of southern Somalia led her enslaved people into freedom and settled them in a safe haven in Gosha.[50] Wana-kucha herself settled in a village known as Mikwa/Migwa where she later died at the age of about 70. Her grave is still in Mikwa/Migwa where people go to visit and commemorate her as a heroine and leader who saved her people from the vicious exploitations of slavery. Just like Harriet Tubman, Wana-kucha did not have any children of her own. It is even unclear whether or not Wana-kucha got married in a certain period of her life. Similar to Tubman, Wana-Kucha was forced to take the tough task of freeing her people after she witnessed their mistreatments by their masters. An instance of this is reflected in the accounts of Lt. Christopher who wrote: "slaves were harshly treated, often kept in manacles and fetters, overworked, and underfed."[51] Earlier Lt. Christopher, a British naval officer who visited the Banadir in 1842 also noted that: "slaves and their wives, being laborers, were housed miserably in small, half-roofed huts, with their usual food [of] parched Indian corn and fish from the river."[52]

Wana-kucha, a Tanganyika born woman who was considered intelligent in her time, had experienced the torture and toil of slavery exacted on her people by the Somali and Arab slave masters as she witnessed the pain and anguish of her people. Subsequently, she secretly planned a massive escape from various plantation villages where slaves were confined to provide labor for the growing industry to produce grain. She led her people through the forest and opted to fight with wild animals for passage rather than remain enslaved. Although she did not go back again and again to rescue more of her people as did Tubman, Wana-kucha often organized and secretly sent back a brigade of active and resourceful young men to rescue more and more slaves to freedom. One of the most incredible similarities between these two African diaspora heroines was the foresight of their vision. In the case of Wana-kucha, Mzee Shariffu Mayanga says: "she had a vision in her dream, detailing the chart of the blueprint of her escape plan and its organization. In that vision she saw the propitious time to start the escape and to which direction. In some mysterious way, she knew when to stop for rest and when to continue the journey. She could also feel and sense from far, with her mystic powers, when the slave owners, who never succeeded to recapture them, were in pursuit of them."[53]

For instance, after Wana-kucha's successful escape with her people to a secure sanctuary, namely Gosha along the Juba River, the news encouraged many slaves in other villages who rebelliously ran away to their freedom. Afterwards, other runaway slaves created another safe haven at Avai. Like Tubman, Wana-kucha was known by her people as a seer with mystical powers who could predict the future by foreseeing events. Indeed, none of her fugitives was ever recaptured even though the pursuing Somali slave owners had attacked them on several occasions, during which she always defeated them.

Despite her people's acknowledgement as a heroine and a leader who risked her life for their freedom, the exact number of people Wana-Kucha led into freedom is hard to substantiate, but what has endured beyond uncertainty is that the impact of her escape has encouraged to freedom thousands of her kinship. Relying both on oral accounts and Italian archives, Wana-kucha told the frightened among the slaves who wanted to go back to their masters, "you will either continue escaping with me or I will abandon you in the middle of the forest for easy prey to wild animals." One of the mottos she used was: "Vivere liberi e liberi morire,"[54] which in English means "We live free and die free." Indeed, she ultimately led them to their freedom. Reminiscent of that excruciating journey is a village in Gosha known as "Funga Moyo" which means, "Keep your heart strong." The attribute is usually devoted to Wana-Kucha who often used that jargon to encourage her people in times of difficulty.

Wana-Kucha's people from various villages in Tanganyika (modern Tanzania), particularly in the district of Handeni, have undergone a cultural hybridization prior to their arrival to the Banadir coastal cities of Somalia as slaves. Early in the 19th century, the coastal cities of modern Tanzania were already under the realm of the Arab Omani Sultanate with its head office in Zanzibar Island. As a result, the culture of the indigenous Africans including the Wazigwa was already heavily influenced by the presence and domination of an Omani-Arab interaction. Most of the coastal cities were prevalently exposed to Islamic proselytization. Furthermore, the local Swahili language became somehow Arabicized because of its borrowing of a substantial corpus from Arabic. The original African way of dressing was also influenced by the incoming Arab Omani Islamic culture. Another significant cultural influence by the Arabs affected the food and the daily dishes consumed by the indigenous Africans.

After arriving on Somalia's shores, the Wazigwa have once again undergone another cultural fusion by adapting some of the local Somali mores. For instance, they largely adapted the Maay Maay language; they became accustomed to a new way of dressing like the local Somalis; and they predominantly continued the practice of Islam although they also maintained, throughout their life in the diaspora, most of their ancestral culture from their country of origin, Tanzania.

During the 1991 Somali tribal clashes, the Wazigwa were affected appallingly; they were looted, raped and gang-raped, maimed, and killed by militia from the dominant Somali clans. Since the Wazigwa are unarmed, they were and still are vulnerable. In a bid to avoid further heinous acts from the savage nomadic militia, they opted to escape into neighboring Kenya. After crossing the Kenyan border, they were housed in various refugee camps established by the United Nations High Commission for Refugees. As they fled from slavery early in the 19th century, the Wazigwa fled once again from the devastation and atrocities of the warring Somali clans, but this time without a leader like Wana-Kucha to whom they owe the current free air they breathe.

Like the aforementioned African Americans, The Great Migration for the Wazigwa to reach their ancestral homeland of modern Tanzania came late and under a different circumstance. Unlike the African American Southerners, the Bantu did not leave Gosha voluntarily. The negative impact of the war compelled them to flee from further genocide.

ILLS, ATROCITIES AND A MASS EXODUS FROM SOMALIA

On gaining independence in 1960, the northern and the southern regions had conflated and formed the "Republic of Somalia." During the first decade of independence, Somalia's political and social systems were smoldering. In 1969, the fire became fully flamed and the military took over under Siyad Barre's leadership. General Mohamed Siyad Barre's rise to power in October 1969 gained him swift popularity, mainly by deceitful nationalist rhetoric and vowing to restore equality, justice, and economic development to all Somalis. Barre exploited tantalizing themes such as: unifying the disintegrated five Somali territories into one that would realize the nomadic dream of unprecedented Greater Somalia ideology, reconciling inter-tribal differences, enforcing the rights of women and minorities, bringing self-sufficiency, and egalitarianism that would satisfy the wishes of the general public.[55] In due course, his frail strategy to please the public did not last long as the government indulged in suppressing opposing ideologies. Amid that situation, Barre's clan and their loyalists became the most prominent citizens who enjoyed extensive privileges and impunity.

In early 1991 Barre's military regime collapsed, giving birth to prolonged clan conflicts, which in the process devastated the country, particularly the southern regions, creating a shell-shocked society. From 1969 to 1991, Barre's military putsch turned into the reality of a dictatorship, especially in view of the marginalized groups such as the Wazigwa. This is to say, Somalia's social discontent under Barre led not only to his removal by militia groups in 1991, but even more significantly, to the vengeance of years of endless inter-clan and intra-clan conflicts, a war in which Somalia became reduced to ruins and submissive to the total anarchy that persists to date.

In the early wake of the war, the general Somali populace sounded very enthusiastic about the militia takeover from the late dictator. Soon, however, mutual frustration developed within their ranks and clans. Very similar to the Sri-Lankan situation,[56] Somalia has failed to construct a concrete foundation for a constitution that safeguards the rights, justice and equality of the poly-ethnic cultures that foster the social fabric, in order to promote an equitable but also genuine power-sharing mechanism. In reality, it is the absence of the implementation of these essential components that initially plunged the country into chaotic atrocities and instability; the genocide continues with the development of newly emerging dynamics of the conflict such as: the proxy wars on Somali territory between Ethiopia and Eritrea; the emergence of clan-affiliated religious groups in the name of Islamic Courts; and, Ethiopia's invasion of Somalia under the cover of fighting Islamic extremism and global terrorism but with the aim of empowering the administration of which it was the brainchild. Since the emergence of Somalia's inter-clan and intra-clan regional war in late 1990, "homogeneous" Somalia has fragmented into the indisputable heterogeneity the society constitutes, particularly considering that: northern Somalia has seceded and declared its own independent state, the Republic of Somaliland; and the central regions have declared self-autonomy and called themselves The Administration of Puntland, with all eyes set on the southern regions, which mostly belong to the marginalized and unarmed groups. Instead of liberating the people from Siyad Barre's tyranny, the militias became the new colonial powers by legalizing the looting and plundering of almost all the arable land in the south.

As we argued elsewhere regarding the reasons behind the Somali war, we reiterate that one of the main ingredients precipitating Somalia's tribal war and the current political turmoil is entrenched in the control of Bantu land and human resources, particularly the agriculturally fertile territory between rivers Juba and Shabelle in Southern Somalia, in other words, Banadir and its environs.[57] It is noteworthy emphasizing that the land, which has become the bone of contention among the armed nomadic militias, belongs to Somalia's underprivileged, such as Bantu/Jareer, Banadiri, Digil-Mirifle, Bajunis, and so on. In addition to the aforementioned assertion of resource control are discrimination and class differentiation between the dominant nomadic Somali "tribes" and the disadvantaged sedentary peoples including the Wazigwa. Even though everybody's color is black in Somalia, there is no intermarriage between the dominant clan, Somalis, and those considered the undesirables--the Wazigwa, sometimes locally called "Mushunguli."

According to Mamdani, one of the greatest mistakes that the European colonialists made in Africa was to adapt a single tribal/ethnic culture and impose it upon every other group in a country.[58] This episode is exactly what had happened in Somalia. Unfortunately, the Wazigwa, as well as the autochthonous Jareer people, had been coerced into assimilation of the pastoral traditions that were created under the auspices of nationalist ideals and the Somali tradition of selfsameness. Yet in the same breath, the very assimilators are expropriating the Wazigwa farms and other properties by forcing them to flee from their homes in Somalia at gunpoint. Accordingly, nomadic Somalia had deprived this section of the social thread (the Wazigwa) not only of their properties, but also of their cultural practices and human liberty, realities that could flourish only in a nation where human dignity plays the primary assumption on which all other social relationships are based--qualities absent in nomadic social behavior.

Hypothetically, assuming that some of the Wazigwa were slaves imported into Somalia many centuries ago, and are, to date, without the same rights as other Somali citizens, we wonder how much longer they would still need to wait before they could qualify to become (at least) respected human beings, if at all not respected Somali citizens! This pitiful scenario renders doubt on whether this is the kind of nationalistic attitude that Somalis, including the Wazigwa and the whole Bantu community, fought for against the colonialists! The whole purpose of stirring up a nationalistic movement or ideology was to create a national democratic system that observes the tenets of justice and equality for all Somalis. If, practically, egalitarianism and human dignity were to function in Somalia, as Mamdani noted with respect to Africa in general, two paradigms should have occurred: "the deracialization of civil power and the detribalization of customary power, as starting points of an overall democratization that would transcend the legacy of a bifurcated power."[59] Regrettably for the Wazigwa people, and for the entire Somali Bantu community, being born in Somalia alone is not sufficient to qualify them for national prosperity and the enjoyment of the fruits and full respect of Somaliness, which came with independence. According to Mohamed Eno, they need the magic code of a "major tribe" status, with its affiliation to nomadic values affecting physiologically, genealogically as well as geographically. With the presence of these core parameters for gauging Somaliness vis-à-vis Somali "nobility," they could not fit into the framework of "Somaliness." As a result of such aberrant ideologies, African societies will be destined to an everlasting pandemonium and instability, the same as we witness in the case of Somalia and other African nations, which overflow in refugee camps around the world as destitute. The unrealistic notion of Somaliness and the unexpected attitude of a selfsame nation have utterly failed the Wazigwa and others who ultimately sought refuge and a safe haven in the neighboring countries of Kenya, Ethiopia, Djibouti, and Yemen.

THE JOURNEY BACK HOME

In the Kenyan refugee camps, where some dominant clan Somalis and the Somali Bantu refugees were housed, UN officials and individual Bantu dignitaries embarked on seeking a possible resettlement in a third country. Almost all the Somali refugees craved a resettlement to developed nations save the Wazigwa who requested the United Nations High Commission for Refugees to specifically resettle them in their country of origin, modern Tanzania. Other Somali Bantu tribes also requested to be resettled in their respective countries of origin such as Mozambique and Malawi.

Upon arriving in the refugee camps in Kenya, Bantu elders began holding secret meetings to discuss the possibility of returning to the district of Handeni in modern Tanzania, their ancestral land. After a few years, a mission of able-bodied young men was selected and sent to Tanzania as exploring emissaries. The objective of this mission included a negotiation with the Wazigwa elders in Tanzania to bless the remigration and resettlement of their kinsmen from Somalia among them. Subsequently, Wana-Kucha's journey, which began almost two centuries ago, was about to be completed by young Wazigwa descendents of the participants in the earlier failed migration. They endeavored to lead their people from the refugee camps in Kenya across the border into Tanzanian territory by circumventing all official border posts and regulations of immigration.

After several trips back and forth between Wazigwa elders in Tanzania and their counterparts in refugee camps in Kenya, the Tanzanian government intervened by sending a fact-finding mission to the Kenyan camps. The Tanzanian delegation has verified that the Wazigwa refugees were indeed connected genealogically, culturally, linguistically and traditionally to the Wazigwa people of Tanzania. The Wazigwa elders of Handeni district were consulted by the Tanzanian authorities and requested if they would give their blessing to a resettlement scheme of the Somali Wazigwa refugees in their neighborhood. The Handeni elders welcomed the proposal "with open hearts."[60] The elders' acceptance to accommodate thousands of Wazigwa refugees back into their ancestral land was facilitating the conclusion of the journey initiated by Wana-Kucha, which was indeed accomplished.

Commenting on the plight of the Somali Bantu refugees, Portland State University faculty member, Dan Van Lehman, who in the early 1990s as a UNHCR official worked with various groups of refugees in the Kenyan camps, stated:

> The Somali Bantu are considered as a "minority" group in Somalia whose members are ethnically and culturally distinct. They are openly discriminated, oppressed, and abused as inferior people by the dominant Somali clans…There are over 5000 Somali Bantu refugees from Kenyan camps that were accepted for resettlement by the Tanzanian government in the 1990s. These refugees are those who lived along the Juba River and maintained the cultures and traditions of their country of origin, Tanzania. They were resettled in one of their ancestral towns, namely Chogo. Each refugee was given a piece of land to build a house and another parcel to farm.

Lehman further emphasized a concern over the Tanzania resettlement program as he noted:

> Although the Tanzanian government was very receptive and generous to accept and accommodate these needy people, it does not really have the financial capability to build a social support system and a proper survival mechanism for them such as farming equipments, schools, hospitals, markets etc. Up until now the refugees are supported by the United Nations. However, the UNHCR announced recently that it is closing its Chogo operations, without leaving behind an infrastructure to support the refugees. The Bantus are hard working people but, without a "jump start" economic device from donor organizations, a disastrous and very distressing future can be easily foreseen. The Chogo project could be a very good example for future prospects for African refugees needing resettlement in another African nation, a sort of intra-Africa resettlement. However, the sad aspect of the Chogo project is that, its failure may lead to a huge negative impact on any future intra-Africa resettlement possibilities.[61]

RECLAIMING TANZANIAN CITIZENSHIP

Chogo is a safe haven and secure town for the Somali Wazigwa in comparison to war torn Somalia or to the sad experience they have undergone in the various refugee camps in the Dadaab area in Kenya, a region in which sections of the kinship of the war-mongering Somali communities are dominant. Despite security, though, there is no infrastructure in place that would facilitate the minimization of the socio-economic hardship of the newly arrived Somali Wazigwa. But after living many years in this camp in Handeni district, the Tanzanian government finally decided to grant citizenship to the Somali Wazigwa refugees.

The Tanzanian authority's announcement of the award of citizenship to the returnee Wazigwa was received with mixed reactions. While some accepted and moved forward to undergo the necessary procedures for re-naturalization, other immigrants have not welcomed the idea. According to elders like Mberwa Muya Mberwa, the award or acquisition of citizenship alone does not provide an adequate avenue for reintegration, since the Tanzanian government has not put in place an appropriate mechanism for that purpose. Among other factors, the absence of an economic infrastructure and the establishment of an effective organization at the national level to oversee the process undermine the achievement of an efficacious reintegration.[62]

As Hamadi Kumula reiterated, "Reintegration needs a better development focus than mere allocation of a small parcel of land,"[63] hence the allusion that without tangible economic support from the government to boost their ability to make a living, the community may not realize the desirable fruits of citizenship or reintegration. The evidence of this sentiment becomes obvious when one encounters community members in certain urban areas who acquired citizenship, but who spend a large part of the day wandering in search of a job. Moreover, when an offer is made to the lucky few, they may not be in possession of the necessary certificates to demonstrate prior training or skills, as the majority of them had been denied educational advancement in Somalia. Elaborating on the dilemma, school headmaster Omar Muya remarks that the community needs appropriate reintegration more than the acquisition or grant of citizenship, because the possession of the latter is yet to activate the necessary facilitation for the former. Muya believes that had effective reintegration been realized, the community would have probably not seen much of the former, which might have in effect come in the end as a complementary component of the reintegration/re-naturalization process.[64]

Indeed, as we have observed during our field study, at the social level, there is no reliable evidence demonstrating reacceptance and re-absorption of the new returnees, whether into their Wazigwa ethnic-thread or into the wider multi-tribal society of Tanzania. Nevertheless, it is in the competition for survival and livelihood in an economically unsound nation that the returnees lag much farther behind than the host society.

Mzee Salim Hamisi states that the idea of regaining Tanzanian nationality might have fascinated a sector of the community for the purpose of identity recognition, as a kind of reconfirmation of their ethnic sense of belonging; but it does very little, if anything, in the enhancement of the economic situation of the newly reconfirmed community. The elder attempts to prove his point by noting, "Most of the Wazigwa returnees still live in isolation in Chogo.... A meaningful reintegration would have led us right into the center of the various sectors of social development, but the fact that we have abandoned Chogo in favor of Kakuma [a refugee camp in Kenya] is a clear interpretation of the Tanzanian government's lack of commitment in finding a viable solution to the problem."[65]

Others like the late Eheda Mkomwa, who also left Chogo and lived in Kakuma until her death in 2006 hold the view that upon its announcement considering citizenship for the returnee Wazigwa, the Tanzanian government might have been only fulfilling a political agenda before the international community. "Otherwise, we did not see any benefit we have achieved in that."[66] In our point of view, the consequence of the mixed reaction held by the community, coupled with lack of a coordinating body responsible for the facilitation of a strategically designed framework for reintegration, had led to the disappointment of a large number of people who opted to return to and live in other camps in Kenya with the aspiration of qualifying one day for a resettlement in the United States, as has been the case with others from the community.

Life in Chogo has less desirability, from sanitation to food rations. Unlike the refugee camps in Kenya where administration comes under the direct responsibility of the United Nations High Commission for Refugees [UNHCR], the administration and management of Chogo has been entrusted with a private company. The amount of food ration delivered is insufficient and at random times. Lack of health facilities continues to be another problem which hampers the living condition in the camp. Under this situation of inadequate health care, it is mainly women and children, and often the elderly, who bear the brunt.[67]

Recently though, some of these returnees have been accessing minimal support from relatives resettled in the United States. However, it is not enough to help them adjust in to the socio-economic infrastructure of their new country, which is so challenging and has left them off-board the economic radius of the Tanzanian social life. Whether one lives in the camp or in the urban areas, only one meal a day is a common nutritional routine for most of the Wazigwa households. The prevailing situation, as is apparent, does not encourage the achievement of the aspirations held in view of the acquisition of citizenship upon its announcement. Furthermore, the economic disparity is far from mitigating smooth absorption for the Somali-Wazigwa in comparison with the socially more stable Tanzanian-Wazigwa.

However, it is worthwhile noting that very few among the community have succeeded in their venture of what we can term "independent self-reintegration" into the socio-economic structure and do very small-scale businesses in the urban marketplaces to meet the basic requirements for their respective families. Because polygamy is a common practice among the Wazigwa, a man may care for a wife or two in the camp while he lives with another or two in the urban area, another fact which hampers economic growth of the family.

In conclusion, although the journey to the ancestral homeland of modern Tanzania has been completed, however, a new struggle to integrate has begun for the Wazigwa returnees in Chogo, Tanzania.

Notes

1. See Eno, O. (2004). Landless landlords and landed tenants: Plantation slavery in southern Somalia (1840-1940). In A. M. Kusow (Ed.), *Putting the cart before the horse: Contested nationalism and the crisis of the nation-state in Somalia* (pp. 135-154). Trenton, NJ: Red Sea Press.

2. Cassanelli, L. V. (1998). The ending of slavery in Italian Somalia: Liberty and the control of labor, 1890-1935. In S. Miers & R. Roberts (Eds.), *The end of slavery in Africa* (pp. 308-331). Madison: University of Wisconsin Press. pp. 316-317.
3. Menkhaus, K. J. (1989). *Rural transformation and the roots of underdevelopment in Somalia's lower Jubba valley.* Doctoral dissertation, University of South Carolina, Columbia. p. 99.
4. Grottanelli, V. L. (1953). I Bantu del Giuba nelle tradizioni dei Wazigwa. *Geographica Helvetica*, 8, 249-260.

   See also Cassanelli, L. V. (1987). Social construction on the Somali frontier: Bantu former slave communities in the nineteenth century. In I. Kopytoff (Ed.), *The African frontier: The reproduction of traditional African societies* (pp.216-238). Bloomington: Indiana University Press. p. 221.
5. Cassanelli, L. V. (1982). *The shaping of Somali society: Reconstructing the history of a pastoral people, 1600 -1900.* Philadelphia: University of Pennsylvania Press. p. 166.

   See also Menkhaus, K. J. (1989). *Rural transformation and the roots of underdevelopment in Somalia's lower Jubba valley.* Doctoral dissertation, University of South Carolina, Columbia. p. 102-105.
6. Menkhaus, K. J. (1989). *Rural transformation and the roots of underdevelopment in Somalia's lower Jubba valley.* Doctoral dissertation, University of South Carolina, Columbia. p. 103-104.

   Please note that in this study, the names Bantu and Wazigwa are used interchangeably because it's referring to the same people.
7. Robecchi-Brichetti, L. (1904). *Dal Benadir. Lettere illustrate alla società antischiavista d'Italia.* Milano: Società Editrice "La Poligrafica." pp. 63 & 107.
8. Del Boca, A. (1992). *Gli italiani in Africa orientale.* 1st edition. Roma & Bari: Arnoldo Mondadori. pp. 786-789.
9. Lt. C. (1844). On the East Coast of Africa. *Journal of the Royal Geographical Society*, 14, 80.

   For more comments of brutality against the Bantu slaves in southern Somalia:

   Robecchi-Brichetti, L. (1904). *Dal Benadir. Lettere illustrate alla società antischiavista d'Italia.* Milano: Società Editrice "La Poligrafica." pp. 30-31.

10. Kolapo, F. J. (2002). "Documentary "Silences" and Slave Resistance in West Africa during the Era of the Atlantic Slave Trade," (Unpublished manuscript). p. 1.
11. M. M. Mberwa (personal communication, Dar es Salaam, November 2003).
12. E. Mkomwa (personal communication, Dar es Salaam, November 2003).
13. Cassanelli, L. V. (1987). Social construction on the Somali frontier: Bantu former slave communities in the nineteenth century. In I. Kopytoff (Ed.), *The African frontier: The reproduction of traditional African Societies* (pp.216-238). Bloomington: Indiana University Press.
14. Eno, M. A. (2005). *The homogeneity of the Somali people: A study of the Somali Bantu ethnic community*. Unpublished doctoral dissertation, St. Clements University, Turks and Caicos Islands. p. 116.
15. Robecchi-Brichetti, L. (1889). *Somalia e Benadir. Viaggio di esplorazione nell'Africa orientale.* Milano: Società Editrice "La Poligrafica." pp. 209-210.
16. The word Avai can also be written sometimes by some scholars as Hawai; they all refer to the same location.
17. Barile, P. (1935). *Colonizzazione fascista nella Somalia meridionale.* Roma: Società Italiana Arti Grafiche. p.13.
18. Ibid., 125.
19. Robecchi-Brichetti, L. (1904). *Dal Benadir. Lettere illustrate alla società antischiavista d'Italia.* Milano: Società Editrice "La Poligrafica." pp. 142-145.

    See also Cassanelli, L. V. (1987). Social construction on the Somali frontier: Bantu former slave communities in the nineteenth century. In I. Kopytoff (Ed.), *The African frontier: The reproduction of traditional African Societies* (pp.216-238). Bloomington: Indiana University Press. p. 192.
20. Kisimayu is the third largest city in Somalia. The word Kisimayu, which derives from Kisima (Water Well), is derived from the Swahili/Bantu language. Although Kisimayu is one of the coastal cities in southern Somalia--on the Indian Ocean along the Kenyan border--it is known for its copious supply of well water.
21. Besteman, C. L. (1991). *Land tenure, social power, and legacy of slavery in southern Somalia.* Doctoral dissertation, University of Arizona, Tucson. p. 101.

See also Menkhaus, K. J. (1989). *Rural transformation and the roots of underdevelopment in Somalia's lower Jubba valley*. Doctoral dissertation, University of South Carolina, Columbia. p. 127.

See also Declich, F. (1992). *Il processo di formazione della identita' culturale dei gruppi Bantu della Somalia meridionale*. Doctoral dissertation, University of Naples, Italy.

22. Grotanelli, V. L. (1953). I Bantu del Giuba.... *Geografia Helvetica*, 8, 249-260, p. 254.
23. Ibid., 254-255.
24. Besteman, C. L (1991). *Land tenure, social power, and legacy of slavery in southern Somalia.* Doctoral dissertation, University of Arizona, Tucson. p. 96.
25. Menkhaus, K. J. (1989). *Rural transformation and the roots of underdevelopment in Somalia's lower Jubba valley*. Doctoral dissertation, University of South Carolina, Columbia.
26. The word Gosha in Somali means forest. This word insinuates that the inhabitants of Gosha-land are the runaway slaves who hid in the forest. The terms Wazigwa and Gosha are used interchangeably since they refer to the same group of people.

    For more information about the Gosha people see also the comment of the editor: Kopytoff, I. (1987). *The African frontier: The reproduction of traditional African societies*. Bloomington: Indiana University Press. p. 214.
27. Menkhaus, K. J. (1989). *Rural transformation and the roots of underdevelopment in Somalia's lower Jubba valley*. Doctoral dissertation, University of South Carolina, Columbia. p. 128.
28. Eno, M. A. (2005). *The homogeneity of the Somali people: A study of the Somali Bantu ethnic community*. Unpublished doctoral dissertation, St. Clements University, Turks and Caicos Islands. p. 115.
29. Declich, F. (1995). Identity, dance and Islam among people with Bantu origin. In A. J. Ahmed (Ed.), *The invention of Somalia* (pp. 191-222). Trenton, NJ: Red Sea Press.
30. Eno, M. A. (in press). Understanding Somalia through the prism of Bantu Jareer literature. In A. J. Ahmed and T. Adera (Eds.), *The road less traveled: Reflections on the literatures of the Horn of Africa.* Trenton, NJ: Red Sea Press.
31. Besteman, C. L. (1991). *Land tenure, social power, and legacy of slavery in southern Somalia.* Doctoral dissertation, University of Arizona, Tucson. p.129.

32. Ibid., 99.
33. Ibid., 106.

    See also Eno, M. A. Understanding Somalia through the prism of Bantu/Jareer literature. In A. J. Ahmed and T. Adera (Eds.), *The road less traveled: Reflections on the literatures of the Horn of Africa.* Trenton, NJ: Red Sea Press.

34. Eno, M. A. (2005). *The homogeneity of the Somali people: A study of the Somali Bantu ethnic community*, Unpublished doctoral dissertation, St. Clements University, Turks and Caicos Islands.

    Ooji or Oji is a derogatory term referring to the Juba valley people. Despite its use, the exact meaning of the word is obscure. Some sources suggest that it is derived from the Italian word "oggi," the equivalent of "today" in English because of Gosha people's thinking that is limited only to what is today and not beyond or in the future. But obviously, the word must have been used earlier than the arrival of the arrival of the Italian colonialists. In the Shabelle valley, the reference is attributed to someone who has been enslaved and it is used, not to their faces, about people who are known to have been enslaved; the Jareer also use that term for a known descendent of slaves).

35. Besteman, C. L. (1991). *Land tenure, social power, and the legacy of slavery in southern Somalia.* Doctoral dissertation, University of Arizona, Tucson. pp.103-105.
36. Ibid., 102.
37. The Wazigwa people are one of the subgroups of Shambara population in Somalia which was rescued from slavery by Wana-Kucha into freedom.

    Christopher, Lt, W. (1844). On the east coast of Africa. *Journal of the Royal Geographical Society*, 14, 80.

38. Apotheker, H. (1974). American negro slave revolts. New York: International Publishers.

    See also Harding, V. (1983). *There is a river: The black struggle for freedom in America.* New York: Vintage Books.

    Owens, L. (1976). *This species of property: Slave life and culture in the old south.* Oxford: Oxford University Press.

39. Morris, A. (1993). Centuries of black protest: Its significance for America and the world. In H. Hill and J. E. Jones, Jr. (Eds.), *Race in America: The struggle for equality.* Madison: The University of Wisconsin Press.

40. Clinton, C. (2004). *Harriet Tubman: The road to freedom*. New York and Boston: Little Brown and Company. p. 5.
41. Conrad, E. (1973). *Harriet Tubman, Negro soldier and abolitionist.* New York: International Publishers Co. p. 10.

    According to Conrad, the Underground Railroad was a network of secret routes, by land and by sea, over which Negroes traveled in order to reach the Free states and Canada where they were allowed to live and work in relative freedom.

    See also Blight, D. W. (2004). *Passages to freedom: The Underground Railroad in history and memory,* Washington, D.C.: Smithsonian Books in association with the National Underground Railroad Freedom Center. p. 175.

    Blight elaborated that, "despite many specific definitions, the term Underground Railroad is generally used to describe the movement, most widespread during the three decades before the Civil War that sought to assist slaves as they attempted to escape from bondage. In reality, of course, the movement was not a railroad and generally did not run underground, but it did endeavor to move fugitives from one safe place to another, and it was largely secretive in its activities. Since any effort to assist a slave to escape might technically be included under this general description, it could be argued that the Underground Railroad actually started before the nineteenth century. Hamisi, M. S. (personal communication, 2004).

    Wana-Kucha's account was obtained from Mzee Salim Hamisi, an elderly man who returned to the Kakuma refugee camp in Kenya after several years in Tanzanian refugee camps.
42. Blight, D. (2004). *Passages to Freedom: The Underground Railroad in History and Memory,* Washington, DC: p. 41.
43. Ibid., 42.
44. Ibid., 43.
45. Conrad, E. (1973). *Harriet Tubman, Negro soldier and abolitionist.* New York: International Publishers Co. p.8.
46. Bradford, S. (1980). *Harriet Tubman: The Moses of Her People.* Secaucus, New Jersey: The Citadel Press. p. 92.
47. Ibid., 47.
48. Ibid., 46.
49. Conrad E. (1973). *Harriet Tubman, Negro soldier and abolitionist.* New York: International Publishers Co. p.14.

50. Literally, Wazigwa is plural form referred to a group of Zigwa more than one person, while the name mZigwa is singular.
51. Hess, R. (1966). *Italian Colonialism in Somalia.* Chicago: Chicago University Press. pp. 87-99.

    See also Eno, O. A. (2004). Landless landlords, and landed tenants: Plantation slavery in southern Somalia (1840-1940). In A. M. Kusow (Ed.), *Putting the cart before the horse: Contested nationalism and the crisis of the nation-state in Somalia* (pp. 135-154). Trenton, NJ: The Red Sea Press. p. 140.
52. Lt. C. (1884). On the East Coast of Africa. *Journal of the Royal Geographical Society*, 14, 80.

    See also Eno, O. A. 2004. "Landless landlords, and landed tenants: Plantation slavery in southern Somalia (1840-1940)," in A. M. Kusow (Ed.), *Putting the cart before the horse: Contested nationalism and the crisis of the nation-state in* Somalia (pp. 135-154). Trenton, NJ: The Red Sea Press. p. 141.
53. This information was obtained through interviews with Mzee Shariffu Mayanga in Tanzania in 2003 and again in Kakuma 2004.
54. Robecchi-Brichetti, L. (1904). *Dal Benadir. Lettere illustrate alla società antischiavista d'Italia.* Milano: Società Editrice "La Poligrafica." p. 146.
55. The Greater Somalia philosophy is based on the unification of five territories inhabited by Somali-speaking people who were separated by the European colonialists. They are comprised of Italian Somaliland, British Somaliland, Djibouti (The land of the Afars and Issa), Ogaden which is part of modern Ethiopia, and the NFD (North Frontier Districts) which is now the Northeastern Province of Kenya.
56. Tiruchelvan, N. (1999). Devolution and the elusive quest for peace in Sri Lanka. In R. I. Rotberg (Ed.), *Creating peace in Sri Lanka: civil war and reconciliation* (pp. 189-201). Washington, D.C.: Brookings Institution Press. p. 189.
57. The word Banadir is the plural of Bandar, originally derived from Arabic language and later became "Somalized". However, in the Somali language it means ''Port'' or "Ports"; it also refers to the coastal cities or villages in the vicinity of a port. Banadir comprises the coastal cities with ports of Mogadishu, Merca, Brava, Kisimayu, the inter-riverine areas and Uarsheik.
58. Mamdani, M. (1996). *Citizens and subjects: Contemporary Africa and the legacy of late colonialism.* New Jersey: Princeton University Press. pp. 3-34.

59. Ibid, 3-34.
60. A. Mdigo (personal communication, Dar es Salaam, November 2003).
61. Van Lehman. D.: This information was extracted from various discussions, which took place in Nairobi (Kenya) and in the Portland (USA) between the authors and Mr. Dan Van Lehman, 2003 & 2005.
62. M. M. Mberwa (personal communication, Nairobi, February 2002).
63. H. Kumula (personal communication, Kakuma, April 2004).
64. O. Muya (personal communication, Kakuma, August 2003).
65. M. S. Hamisi (personal communication, Chogo, January 2004).
66. E. Mkomwa (personal communication, Kakuma, January 2003).
67. E. Mkomwa (personal communication, Chogo, November 2003).

Chapter 2

TRANSIT OR DEAD END? THE SOMALI DIASPORA IN EGYPT

Gudrun-Katharina Kroner

INTRODUCTION

Broadly speaking, a significant aspect of the scholarship on international migration starts from the assumption that neighboring and second countries primarily service as a transit to a better destination for refugees and immigrants. What is not commonly acknowledged in this scholarship, however, is that, more often, a large number of refugees and immigrants end up not realizing their dream of resettlement in a western country, but instead, they face a "diasporic Dead End." The purpose of this article is to conceptualize the nature and the dynamics of this diasporic Dead End as experienced by the Somalis in Cairo, Egypt; and the social, economic, and identity consequence that such a condition creates. By a diasporic Dead End, I mean a situation in which immigrants and refugees confront a Cul-de-sac, one that does not allow a through exit, but a sure return to the same entrance over and over again. The nature of these experiences is informed by the socio-economic status of the immigrants on the one hand, and structural issues resulting from refugee policy or the activities of the Egyptian government on the other.

The following situations of four Somalis should illustrate the differences of living conditions, attitudes and chances within the Somali community: Ubax is stuck with her husband and her three children in Cairo and because she is recognized according to the Organization of the African Unity (OAU) Convention she does not have big hopes of coming out of this situation.[1] She and her family are completely depending on the small amount of money they get from Caritas.[2] So she says, "We are told that we are recognized by the 1969 OAU Convention, that we only get protection in Egypt . . . there is no hope now, doors are closed." Ali stayed for years with his family in Libya and moved to Egypt after a failed attempt to migrate to Italy; his wife is working for a rich Somali family. Although he is not recognized he still has hope. Ali points out, "Cairo is better than Libya . . . also even though we are not accepted yet, we still have hope to be settled because of the changes at the UNCHR, *fi amal*."[3] Abdi made his way, after staying for some years in Cairo, to the United States: He states happily, "I am in my apartment in NYC, in Manhattan, I was lucky, I got resettled . . . but my case was different than many other refugees; I was somehow lucky because I understood the process." Ubax, Ali and Abdi were applying for refugee status in Egypt and all hope(d) to leave to the west. The fourth person, Suad, has a different case; she came to Cairo after she was granted refugee status and later on British citizenship years ago. She belongs to the "Somali émigrés."[4] She moved with her children, who were born in London, for their education in Egypt. The émigrés are very different from the others in that they have citizenship and the resources that make them part of the middle class, if not the elite, in the Egyptian society. They generally share Suad's feeling as she puts it, "I feel very happy here in Cairo, in Rehab, I feel like I am in Europe . . . and Egypt is a good country . . . because between the culture [of] Egyptians and the culture of Somalis there [is] no big difference." For the purpose of this chapter, different perceptions of "Dead Ends" will be explored as well as the conditions and the policies of the host country and of the United Nations High Commissioner for Refugees (UNHCR) towards the refugees and their impact on identity construction.

METHODOLOGY

The data was gathered in the course of an ethnographic fieldwork project carried out in Egypt from November 2000 until March 2002 and from October to December 2004 and February/March 2005.[5] The main research tools were participant observation (including accompanying refugees to help organizations and hospitals, taking part in social events such as weddings and meetings, and visiting refugees at home and taking part in their daily life) narratives and biographic interviews. I principally relied on the method of narrative interviews or life-stories, as suggested by Hopkins. According to Hopkins, in order to understand the specific situation of refugees it is not only necessary to observe their present situation, but also to have an understanding of their life before the flight, the circumstances which led to their flight, as well as circumstances and times during and after the flight.[6]

The use of life histories makes it possible to explain important biographic changes and details of interpersonal actions and reactions taken against the background of such contextual materials. This will be done out of the refugee's own perspective, including rapid changes in his or her social identity and role transformations.[7] Through this research procedure a specifically concrete access to social reality is opened up, based on the refugee's individuality and on how "this individuality is thought of as socially caused and structured."[8]

It was crucial for me to counteract the tendency to assume that refugees are unreliable sources: Malkki states that refugees are said to be exaggerating or even lying. She critiques that often within refugee agencies "wounds speak louder than words."[9] With this kind of policy the refugees are pressed into a kind of speechlessness; stories are told about, but not by them. Therefore, I tried to use many quotations of refugees in this chapter; statistics play a supporting role.

PROFILE OF SOMALIS IN EGYPT

According to the UNHCR, there were 1,639 Somali refugees in Egypt in 2002. In 2003, the number increased to 3,068.[10] According to the UNHCR Assistant Regional Representative,[11] their number increased until the end of December 2004 to 3,800, and by the end of February 2005, the number of recognized Somali refugees in Egypt was around 4,000.[12] These figures do not include those who were resettled nor does it include those whose files were closed. Almost the entire Somali refugee population in Egypt is living in

Cairo, mainly in Ard il Lewa, Nasr City, Masr el Gadida, and Dokki, while the Somali émigrés are living in more privileged housing in new satellite suburbs around Cairo such as Rehab.

In a study conducted in Cairo by Mulki Al-Sharmani, who in 2003, interviewed 300 Somali refugees (a number that might be adequately representative of the Somali refugee population) the majority of the interviewees were young: 67% of the interviewees were between 20 and 34 years of age. In addition, 54% of them were women; 39% were singles whereas 40% were married but living separately; and only 3% of the 300 interviewees were university graduates, however 30% were high school graduates.[13]

WHY EGYPT?

Egypt does not seem to be the easiest option for Somali refugees. However, fleeing to Egypt is definitely easier than trying to flee to a Western country. Refugee camps in Yemen, Ethiopia, or Kenya seem to be much easier to reach. For example, the Yemeni coast is a 20 hour boat ride from Bossaso, a trip that would only cost 30 to 50 USD.[14] Nevertheless, almost no Somali wants to stay in one of the camps in Yemen as the life circumstances are really bad. As Ali describes: "Many people who were living in that camp [in Yemen] came back to Somalia; they said, 'we ran out of hell and we went to another hell.'"

In the beginning of the civil war the neighbouring countries (Kenya, Ethiopia and Djibouti) and also Yemen were the main countries where Somalis fled to as they were easy to reach and they often had to flee in an abrupt and unorganized way. Now, almost 15 years after the outbreak of the civil war, people are better prepared when leaving their country, as the example of Osman shows:

> I wanted to go to Cairo because in Cairo most of the people will be resettled. Mariam . . . said that it is better for me to go to Cairo. She said that she has asked many people. . . . There were only two possibilities for me to go: Nairobi or Cairo . . . I rejected to go to Kenya myself because I knew about the conditions there."

Like Osman almost all Somalis are well informed about the living conditions and the refugee policies in the countries to which they intend to go. The targeted countries have changed during the years due to state policies, visa requirements and transportation. Mostly, information is passed on through other Somalis who are either in these host countries or have relatives there. Especially, in the last year the exchange became easier through the "new medias" like for example Internet which is used intensely. Afterwards they are balancing the socio-economic factors and refugee policies such as the possibility for resettlement before they decide where to go.[15]

Obtaining a passport with a visa to Egypt is claimed to be a difficult and expensive task. Since January 2003, the Egyptian government no longer issues entry visas for Somali applicants.[16] Before this, one refugee claimed, it was quite easy to claim that the applicant was a family member and be issued a tourist visa as cheaply as 30 USD. Farhia, who came in 2000, stated at the time of her arrival that obtaining a visa and the flight ticket was already more expensive, but still just a matter of money. She says: "We came here for a lot of money with 1,200 USD for one person. If you want to go to Egypt you can go, but you have to pay before you go."

Since the changes in 2003, it became harder and sometimes there are even third parties like Sudanese mediators involved. Ali explains the procedures:

> The visa for Somalis coming to Egypt is actually closed. Sometimes it may take us up to few thousand dollars to find a visa. This visa is arranged through mediators, some Somalis but mainly Sudanese who have contact with the immigration authorities.

Bach (2003) claims in her study that visas have been issued only to members of the Transitional National Government (TNG) since the beginning of 2003 (which implies that only influential members of a majority clan can obtain a visa). This is contradictory to information provided by the UNHCR which claims that mostly, only members of minority clans arrive in Egypt.[17]

The near impossibility of obtaining a visa to Egypt the number of recognized Somali refugees in Egypt is on the rise. The UNHCR report for the year 2000 stated the number of Somali refugees was approximately 2,600, and at the present time this number is about to double. And contrary to Bach's findings, the UNHCR claims that "unlike in previous years, where a sizable number of Somalis were coming to Egypt after having lived for some time in other countries (in particular, Libya, Saudi-Arabia and Yemen), recent arrivals are directly from Somalia."[18]

One of the possible explanations for this rise in number of Somali refugees is that Egypt is the closest country to Somalia with a UNHCR office that will grant resettlement.[19] And even if resettlement to a western country is not granted, there are backdoors to Europe allowing different forms of illegal trafficking for Somali refugees. It would also seem reasonable to assume that Somalis would be encouraged to view the whole situation in Egypt including the chance to get resettled in a very optimistic way, by those running the trade of passports and visas. This may be sometimes compounded by other instances where Somalis are being innocently misinformed by other Somalis about the services they could expect and the ease with which the resettlement process would proceed in Cairo. One of these "victims" is Abdulkadir who sold a piece of land to raise the money for a ticket to Cairo, mainly to get medical treatment. He explains his reason as follows:

> A friend of mine from London was visiting Mogadishu . . . he was telling me to go to Egypt because of the active UNHCR office in Cairo. He said I would get medical treatment and resettlement easily.

Abdulkadir was not getting any medical treatment and he is so disappointed about his situation in Cairo; he says that he does not have even enough money for food and that he is considering returning to Somalia. So, for a Somali wanting to escape to the West, this dream seems "only" a few thousand dollars away, as many Somalis seem to think. In the following section, Somalis' unawareness about the regulations of the UNHCR and the attitude of the Egyptian government will be explored.

BETWEEN THE UNHCR AND THE EGYPTIAN GOVERNMENT

> If it was the Egyptian government that would decide about refugee status or not, if they would have been the ones to take care of us, we would have never come here. It's because of UN. If the UN would open an office in Israel we would go there; they would treat us better because they are not Arabs.

Omar's statement shows that the Egyptian government is neither involved with, nor seems to be interested in the survival and the well being of, the refugees. It also expresses the bitter feeling and the boundaries between Omar and his host society. Contrary to the system in most western countries, the determination of refugee status is undertaken by the UNHCR in Egypt. For all asylum seekers who have applied for refugee status at the UNHCR and are waiting to be interviewed, a UNHCR yellow card is issued. The yellow card means temporary protection and entitles one to fewer services than the blue card, which is provided to those who are recognized as refugees. This blue card is also stamped by the Egyptian Ministry of Interior and the Ministry of Foreign Affairs. Along with the blue card, recognized refugees are also granted a renewable six month residence permit. Not all Somalis are using this possibility to get a residence as it is said that the UNHCR refers only those whose visa is stamped in their passport for resettlement.[20] Faisal is only one of the Somalis who are afraid that if they get the residence permit on their blue card they will be deprived of a possible resettlement. He says:

> I can get a residence through the UNHCR because I have a blue card, but I never did it. . . . and if I take the residence from the blue card they are going to transfer my entry visa to the blue card and my passport is going to be canceled; I don't want that.

Asylum seekers who are denied refugee status by the UNHCR have the right to appeal within a month's time. If their appeal is rejected, they are labeled "file closed." Such a label implies that they do not hold any chance to obtain legal refugee status or resettlement.

They are left in a very difficult situation under a constant threat of detention and deportation.[21] According to the UNHCR Regional Office (RO) Cairo in 2003, the time period between refugee registration and refugee status determination interview was six months. Results of the refugee status determination interview are usually issued two weeks after the interview.[22] An important issue is whether they are recognized as refugees according to 1951 Convention or OAU. As already mentioned, the recognition rate for Somalis prior to 2003 was very low; for example, in 2000 only 52% of all Somali applicants were accepted.[23] Since 2003 the percentage of acceptance increased and reached almost 100% by the beginning of 2005.[24] This is mainly due to the fact that UNHCR started to recognize Somalis according to the OAU Convention. This is on the one hand good because less people are illegally in Egypt; on the other hand Somalis fear the OAU recognition because it implies that they are not eligible for resettlement in a Western country. Another important point is that resettlement is not an internationally recognized right in all cases, which implies that many refugees in Egypt will never obtain resettlement. The countries that provide resettlement opportunities do so voluntarily out of humanitarian concern. While some years ago there were still three countries granting resettlement to refugees from Egypt, Australia and Canada have abandoned this policy and only the United States continues to offer it.

With the current increase in the number of asylum seekers in Egypt, along with the declining budget of the UNHCR office, the resources of the UNHCR are strained to a point that might jeopardize the effectiveness and fairness with which refugee matters are handled.[25] Besides granting refugee status and a potential for resettlement, the UNHCR can offer limited assistance to recognized refugees through a number of implementing partners and NGOs.

Where is the Egyptian government in all this? When signing the 1951 Convention, Egypt voiced reservations concerning the five articles. These articles included some basic human/humanitarian rights, like access to primary education, public assistance, labor legislation, and social security.[26] So the Egyptian government cooperates with the UNHCR, however they will not provide any concrete assistance for refugees. It becomes obvious that although the

Egyptian government is not denying recognized refugees renewable residency permits, it is aborting any potential for their integration into the Egyptian community, thus accepting their presence only as a temporary solution until they are resettled to a third country.[27]

DIFFERENT FORMS OF "DEAD END"

Because of the previously mentioned regulations of the UNHCR, the attitude of the Egyptian government and Egyptian society, refugees encounter different forms of the diasporic dead end. The first dead end relates to those Somalis who have their "files closed." This was mainly feared in the first stage of my research. At that time many refugee applications were denied and people ended up without any protection or any social services. They were completely dependent on their relatives and the Somali community. Although there are still some people who have their files closed, the term is not as horrifying as it once seemed as more and more cases get reviewed by the UNHCR. One of the legal officers from the Africa and Middle East Refugee Assistance (AMERA) stated that most of her cases which were file closed were--after they submitted new information--granted refugee status.[28]

So the main burden of the case resides in another type of dead end which is the case of those Somalis who only came to Egypt on the hope of being resettled and ended up being recognized as refugees but not offered resettlement. This includes those who are considered irregular movers,[29] the ones who are recognized under the OAU Convention since 2003 and those who are recognized according to the 1951 Convention, but not given resettlement until now. While the first two groups are labeled as NER (not eligible for resettlement), the third group is cautiously optimistic. Now, I want to draw a picture of Somali living conditions, worries, hopes and sometimes even successful escapes from Egypt to the West.

BEING STUCK IN CAIRO

Not all refugees get financial assistance from the UNHCR, and if they are supported the money is barely enough to survive and most have to seek other sources of income. 82% of Somalis receive remittances on a monthly basis;[30] nevertheless this money is often not sufficient, and so they have to search for other sources of income. As mentioned before, it is nearly impossible for refugees and other foreigners living in Egypt to obtain a work permit. An Egyptian lawyer explains:

> They are treated like a foreigner, so if a foreigner wants to work here, he needs the endorsement of the employer. He needs to be really needed in their job and needs to demonstrate that an Egyptian cannot do the same job. They also have to pay for their work permit, and there are other rules and regulation, which discourages people from going through the troubles of getting a work permit for a refugee.[ae]

This forces the refugees to work in the informal sector which leads often to exploitation. Many of the Somali men don't work at all; a few are employed by Somali émigrés to teach their children Somali or Koranic Arabic. Most of the women are employed in housekeeping or childcare. While some of my interviewees were working for Egyptians most were employed by Somali émigrés. They prefer working for émigrés as they are paid in dollars and it is culturally more convenient, as Asha confirms:

> Egyptians!? They are foreigners; they are not respecting me that much. When I work for Somalis and I have some problems like my children are sick, I call and I tell them that I cannot come today. Egyptians tell me that I have to come although there are problems.

Another big problem is education. Although Egypt signed the 1989 UN Convention on the Rights of the Child which stipulates among other things that children have the right to free access of education, primary and secondary schools cannot be attended by refugee children.[32] Through a Presidential decree Sudanese children of recognized refugees should be allowed to public schools, nevertheless its implementation has hardly been realized until now.[33] Al-Sharmani's survey shows that 66.7% of Somali school age children don't receive any kind of schooling.[34] A representative of RO UNHCR Cairo says:

> in public schools capacity is limited, very few are enrolled in public schools, and the rest goes to refugee schools. Again refugee schools have also limited capacity and secondly because they are church-run schools they are predominately [attended by] Sudanese.

Consequently, most of the Somali children stay at home and only a few attend church schools. During my research, I met only two Somalis who were able to attend an Egyptian university.

Besides the difficult living conditions created by the reservations of the Egyptian government, many refugees are encountering some hostility by their host country's population. Almost none of the Somalis have close contact with members of their host society. As Muna describes:

> I have neighbors for about 10 months, we are seeing each other, we never say hello to each other. Most of the Somalis are not happy, not only in here, in the Arab countries; they don't like us, they don't treat us well and therefore we also don't like them.

The language barrier might be the major problem which builds boundaries between Somalis and Egyptians.

A constant source of concern and threat is caused by the Egyptian police. Many Africans get harassed by policemen who threaten to arrest them unless they render a small bribe. Not knowing their rights and the local language most of the Somalis are "easily victimized". Hassan described a similar incident:

> They don't know their rights, they don't speak Arabic and they don't know the law and the role of the UNHCR. This it what makes them live in a horrible way. Even the civilians can tell them that they are police. A friend of mine "lost" his mobile and 200 Pounds when he was drunk. He was not completely drunk, but he thought that if they smell the alcohol they will take him to the police station, he was afraid despite the fact that he has a blue card. They searched him and took everything from his pockets. . . . They found the mobile and 200 pounds and a packet of

> cigarettes and a lighter, they took it and said now you can go, if you don't want come with us to the police. He was afraid and quietly left.

In January 2003, hundreds of Africans, mainly asylum seekers and refugees were targeted by the police, rounded up and arrested.[35] Although most of them were released later on, this incident created fear among the Somalis. Africans face racism in the streets where they are called "Samara," "Soda" or "Bunga Bunga"[36]; or children might throw stones on them. One refugee said: "What I always do is just try to avoid them, when you see that there is crowd of people, a gathering, I just take another road, try to find a road which is more empty. Because if you get close to them, you could be endangered."

The media leads the public to believe that many Africans are involved in prostitution and therefore carry venereal diseases. This is illustrated in a conversation I overheard at a mechanic shop where two Egyptians were talking about a group of Africans that passed by:

> H: It seems that the number of these Africans is increasing. What do they do for a living?
> M: They bring us AIDS.

The negative attitude of their host country's population leads the Somalis to form a new group identity versus the Egyptian/Arabs.[37] While in other countries I heard quite often that at least some Somalis have Arab ancestors and they differentiate themselves from other Africans, in Egypt many claim, in opposition to their host country's society, to be Africans. So, said Omar: "The Somali people, who say that they have Arab ancestors don't know what they are talking about. We are Africans!" He goes on to state that "the Arabs are the biggest racists, they are worse than Apartheid. They despise us because we are black." So, in the case of Somalis in Egypt the process which is described by Krulfeld and Camino that "exile forced a group to see itself, sometimes for the first time as unique" takes place.[38] In the case of Somalis in Egypt due to multiple forms of discrimination they embrace an African identity, which seems particular in Egypt and could be perhaps found in other Arab countries, but is contrary to most of the Somalis in the west.[39]

As Malkki states refugees are often considered as a burden or even a threat for the nation state.[40] The latter is not the case in Egypt. Nevertheless, the attitude of the Egyptians towards African refugees has changed; at the beginning of my research most of the Egyptians were quite surprised when I told them that I was working with refugees, and they often questioned "We have refugees in Egypt?" Now it appears that Egyptians are more aware of their existence. The number of Sudanese refugees is often exaggerated and the refugees in general have a negative image. Host societies typically refuse to see that very often refugees are "making a very positive contribution to the local economy".[41] In the case of Somalis they are not given any assistance from the Egyptian government (not even land which is the only contribution from countries such as Kenya and Ethiopia which provide the land for refugee camps), but on the contrary bring in money through the assistance of donor countries and the remittances from relatives who are living in Western countries.

"ESCAPING" TO THE WEST

Because of the circumstances surrounding them and the attitude of the host country's population almost no Somali wants to stay in Egypt. If they don't have any chance for resettlement, they try other ways to reach their goals and as Barbara Harrell-Bond states, "one never knows how many Somalis are managing to get out of Egypt on their own. But . . . it has been known that Somalis are incredibly innovative in their methods."[ap]

In recent years many Somalis, even recognized ones, tried to escape by boat from Libya to Italy. These trips often had disastrous endings. Almost all Somalis who are in Cairo had friends who died during such trips. Hassan recalls:

> One time there was a boat with about 80 people; some of them I knew. Three or four people who were accepted and had the blue card died. The problem is that the boat they used was without a captain, they sailed on their own, because it was cheaper. Only one or two people survived. There is no government asking the Libyan government what was happening there because these people are not registered with immigration. No authority will ask the

> Italians for the bodies to identify them as most of the people don't have any identification. It was even hard to recognize the people, in the Internet, there are pictures of people and some got recognized from the website.

So what leads people who are recognized refugees to take that risk? Of course the living conditions in Egypt and losing any hope of resettlement. Another reason, Hassan said, is that sometimes relatives in western countries get tired of sending remittances for years to their relatives. They prefer to send a one time large fee to bring their relatives to Europe rather than continue paying monthly for many years. Typically, it is expected from those people who make their way to Europe to support those that are left behind as soon as they establish themselves in their new host countries.

In the last year, the number of Somalis who died in the attempt to cross the Mediterranean Sea to Italy decreased. On the one hand, this might be the result of Libya's new policies and the agreement between Italy and Libya, which dictates that Italy sends the refugees back to Libya to be housed in newly built detention centres.[43] On the other hand, new UNHCR policies created some hope among the Somalis in Egypt to get resettled.

BUUFIS

The word *buufis* (a Somali phrase which describes the incessant urge to flee to the West) is always mentioned in context with risky flight attempts. For example, Ali answered my question of why people were still trying to leave after these terrible accidents by boat by declaring that, "they don't like it here because of the situation here. Because of buufis, they see life here as very difficult, and realize that they cannot live here forever." Horst argues that one of the reasons Somali refugees are suffering from buufis is the poor living conditions in the camps.[44] The same applies to the Somalis in Cairo, although they live in an urban area. Bile explains buufis as:

> a new word, which came up with the civil war and when the UNHCR was established in Yemen, Egypt and Kenya . . . it is a kind of psychological disorder. The people who

> have buufis just want to hear stories about the UN and cannot judge anymore if the rumors are right or wrong.

Aisha explains buufis in a different way: buufis is "being obsessed of leaving the country and going to Western countries . . . you are obsessed about travelling." All Somali refugees in Egypt said that they suffer from buufis. In some cases this feeling becomes so overwhelming that women leave their own children. Hassan said:

> Muna wanted to leave her children with me and go to Libya; she was manipulated by a neighbor. This woman left with four children. Three of them died; one survived. She went to Europe with one child. They don't count the losses, they only count the one who survived and made it to Europe.

Nevertheless, I agree with Cindy Horst who does not see only the negative aspect of buufis. She says that buufis is a risk, but also a potential.[45] She elaborates that buufis is a form of stimulation of the collective imagination providing hope in quite a hopeless situation. Buufis is always intertwined with hope, or as they call it in Arabic *amal*. Amal is often mentioned in the context of new policies of the UNHCR.

UNHCR-NEW POLICIES-BETWEEN HOPE AND DESPAIR

"Accepted according to the OAU Convention" became a feared expression like it was before with the expression "file closed." As resettlement countries generally take only those refugees who are accepted according to the 1951 Geneva Convention, this means that "OAU granted people" will be locally integrated. In the section above it was described that there is no such thing as local integration. So, people are greatly affected by this. Bile says:

> In short, they have a very dark future. The OAU has become a kind of neurosis; the person who has OAU is losing hope. Some even tried to go back to Somalia because instead of dying here gradually, they better die there instantly there in crossfire of those militia.

Ubax, whom I quoted in the beginning of the article, said:

> We were told that we were recognized by the 1969 Convention, OAU, that we only get protection in Egypt. Even if they would have told me that there is any chance in the future, I would have felt better, but there is no hope now, doors are closed.

Nevertheless, some actions create hope as the story of one woman who planned to leave for Libya. She was called from the UNHCR and was given resettlement the day before she wanted to leave. Rumors spread fast among Somali refugees, especially the new rumor that there will be a group resettlement of many Somalis regardless of their status according to the OAU or the Geneva Convention. The Assistant Regional Representative of UNHCR RO Cairo confirmed that now they are in the process of "trying to resettle to the United States about 400 cases, which means about 1000 individuals consisting of Somali women at risk" who are typically single heads of households.[46]

Also, while it seems that just a certain group of the Somalis might benefit from the changes, the new policies also created hope among those who do not belong to them, like Ali, who came with his family from Libya. Or Faisal who is a single man and said:

> I was accepted to OAU; first I was sad because they say when you have OAU that you don't have the right to be given resettlement or financial support, only protection, but there is always hope.

This rising hope, or amal, has as buufis a negative and a positive aspect; on the one hand, it keeps people going when the circumstances are quite bad and also keeps them away from risky travels like the one to Italy. On the other hand, people have, as with buufis, the fixed idea that they are leaving. Some Somalis therefore refuse to learn Arabic which would render their lives easier, because they think that they will be resettled soon and there will be no need for Arabic in the United States.

TWO CASES WHO MADE IT

One is Abdi, who was quoted in the beginning of this article. Certainly, he does not fit in one of the groups mentioned by the UNHCR, but rather belongs to that group who is according to a lawyer from the AMERA not going to be resettled:

> I can say this with confidence: single men are not resettled and being a man for sure lessens your chances of being resettled because they will never really know if you are from a minority or a majority clan.
> He is a single, young man from a majority clan, so how did he make it?

Abdi's case was as he stated "different than many other refugees." He came to Egypt, applied for refugee status, earned money by teaching children of émigrés. Then, he started to work for different refugee oriented organizations as a volunteer. There he made contacts as he says with "different people who are working with refugees, from Europe, from America, from American University in Cairo." During this work Abdi learned to understand, as he says:

> the procedures which UNHCR was using. I understood other embassies and agencies involved in the process. I had also the chance to take courses, short courses, seminars, workshops at AUC especially at the forced migration department, where I got educated about international refugee law, basic human rights law, so I knew what my rights were and the definition.

But he did not only learn how to assist refugees and therefore himself, he was also building up social contacts with people who are working, for example, at the UNHCR. He describes the day of his resettlement interview as follows:

> There were four people working in the resettlement department at the morning when I went for my interview and I knew them. They are all four ladies; they are almost friends. That is why I feel that I was really lucky than many other Somali refugees who live in Cairo.

He continues that it was not only the fact that he knew the people to get resettled:

> It doesn't mean that they helped me or they gave me the resettlement because I know how to communicate with them in their language without interpreter or I knew them, or maybe I met them out of the office, but you know, when you know this person and you have been talked to that person for a while and you met this person in different occasions, you know, you just feel kind of comfortable, you don't get frustrated, you don't get afraid.

Abdi went to New York and found a job immediately. A short time after we met there, he moved to Minneapolis where he is again working with a refugee organization dealing with Somalis. Of course his main goal is as he says to help his people with his experience, but beside this there is the nice side effect of getting to know the United States refugee system and assistance from inside, which can be useful also for him.

The other person is a young girl, Mariam, who was born in Somalia, and attended an Egyptian school there. At the time of the civil war she moved with her grandmother and her sisters and brothers to Cairo. She was one of the two Somalis I know who finished their university education in Egypt. She received a BA in Biochemistry. Later, she also started to work with the Somali community and refugee aid organizations. Her grandmother wanted to stay in Egypt because it was a Muslim country and she wanted her grandchildren to finish their education. Mariam's brother left by himself to the United States. When Mariam tried to leave after her university degree her grandmother, on whose file she was written, was denied resettlement due to different reasons. Mariam was torn between two societies. Somalis did not fully accept her in the beginning because her Somali language competence was not high and in Cairo Egyptians sometimes called her *Samara* or chocolate. She was given a scholarship for her university education, but after graduating she was not allowed to work. She said:

> The Egyptians are not bad, they are good to us. . . . Egypt is good for education, but as a foreigner to get work here in Egypt it is very difficult. . . . This is the situation I learnt from living here and if you get someone who can send you money, you can live in Egypt, but to earn money in Egypt it is too difficult.

Her ambiguity about her identity shows in the next statement:

> The only thing we are sharing is the religion. But in the culture we share nothing. As Mariam, if I was educated in Somalia and got their traditions and culture and then came to Egypt it will be too hard for me to understand Egyptians, as the Somalis who are currently arriving, it is difficult for them, but at this time I was a young girl and I was just happy that I am talking like them in Arabic, not talking as Somali. I am already inside them, I already used to be with them, and so I think I have already lost my culture.

Although the majority of her friends were Egyptians or Sudanese, although her Arabic was better than her Somali and despite the fact that she received her education in Egypt, Mariam realized that Egypt had no future for her; it was a dead end. She would never be allowed to work in her field and would never be accepted by the majority of the society just because of her appearance. She tried hard to leave in the legal way, tried to get separated from the file of her grandmother, asked many times for resettlement, but her case was always denied. At a certain time she got desperate and even considered marrying somebody just to leave. Also she got buufis, and instead of continuing legally through resettlement, she went via a tourist visa supplied by some of her relatives to England. She applied there for refugee status and finally got accepted. She is now working part-time while attending college. These two stories are some of the few with a happy end. But it also demonstrates that even when Somalis really try hard to integrate in the Egyptian society due to obstructionist governmental regulations it is not possible, it is a dead-end and to continue their education or work in the formal sector both had to leave.

DEAD END OR EN VOGUE DESTINATION

Ironically, almost weekly, Somali émigrés move to Cairo, which is seen by the refugees as a dead end.[47] The main reasons why Somalis consistently arrive in Egypt are for economic reasons and to educate their children in a country with an Islamic culture. Typically, the husband stays in the West to work, and visits his wife and children during the holidays in Cairo. They come on tourist visas and through their children's enrollment in schools they can obtain residence permits.

Lately, there are a lot of new arrivals. Information about Cairo is usually transmitted orally, as Suad says: "Yes, I told them, because everybody is thinking because there are so many problems there. . . . There are so many people who are coming now." Information is also communicated via the Internet or as Al-Sharmani (2004) describes on videotape. In this case, some Somalis come and videotape Cairo's daily life, the different residential areas, and so forth. These tapes are passed on from one person to another. Suad claims that she has come for the education of her children. She thinks that the schools in Egypt are similar to those in Somalia where the teachers force the children to study hard, while in England the children are only studying if they want to. In Rihab there are private international language schools (e.g. an American, British and French school). Besides the Somalis, middle class/middle upper-class Egyptian children also attend these schools. Aside from educational issues culture is also important: "I brought them here just to know some culture, Muslim culture" (Suad). Possible economic reasons for immigration and their particular economic status were not openly addressed in interviews. In England, the United States or other Western countries they don't belong to the middle class, cannot afford expensive private schools and often have to work in labor intensive jobs. Life in Egypt is completely different. While Suad was working long shifts in England at Sainsbury supermarket and doing all her housework, she now has two maids staying with her and she is doing some "charity work" at the school her children attend. Differences do exist between the émigrés, who live in newly built gated residential compounds at the outskirts of Cairo and the refugees living in densely populated areas like Ard il Lewa. The differences are not only economical ones although they might derive from them. The attitude towards their host country's society is diverse between the Somali groups. The refugees in crowded areas don't have a lot of interaction with the Egyptians and if they do they quite often face racism. While Suad told me that she had Egyptian friends and being segregated in their compound it is much less likely that they would be offended by Egyptians. The refugees build, as already mentioned, an opposition to their host country's society, and claim that they are Africans and have a different culture, while the émigrés come exactly because of this culture and find that "between the culture of Egyptians and the culture of Somalis there is no big difference."[48]

One controversial subject between the two groups is their perception about the West and the Islamic/Arabic countries. Many émigrés think that the refugees don't know about the life in the West. As Suad says, "they think when they go there the government gives them money, everybody lives happy, but nobody knows exactly what is going on." Others go even further and preach in coffeehouses against the western countries, as Ali angrily stated:

He tells us that it is not good to mix up with Western society. He advices the people not to go to the US or Europe that they have to stay in the Arabic world. . . . So, we understand that after he filled his wallet and he got the credit card, now he wants to live in the Arab world, which is cheaper than US or Canada, and make also business. We will go as he did before twenty years and we will see what he saw, so he should keep his advices for himself.

CONCLUSION

As Gilad states: "In some . . . countries, there are special sanctuary plans and living arrangements, while in others there are none, and refugees are left to make do however they can, even illegally."[49] As I tried to show, Egypt belongs to the second group with the ongoing obstacles and difficulties of daily life including among other things the inability to obtain a work permit, medical care, or education. Adding to the frustrations of this bureaucratic stalemate is the subtle discrimination directed at Somalis by the Egyptian population, which transforms Egypt into a literal dead-end for Somalis. The main goal, to reach a western country through resettlement, is only obtained by a few, leaving the rest stranded. Somalis in Egypt try to survive by remittances and working for Somali émigrés mainly because they don't feel like integrating into a society whose government does not make any effort to ameliorate their everyday life conditions. In a more mobile and globalized world "fantasies of wanting to move" as described by Appadurai are emerging.[50] In the case of the Somalis in Egypt, their living conditions increase these "fantasies" (buufis); some Somalis revolve their lives around this often unrealistic notion.

As an act of resistance against their host society, they build a modified group identity which in opposition to Arabs, strongly identifies with African culture. I agree to a large extent with Stuart Hall who says, "Diaspora identities are those which are constantly producing and reproducing themselves anew, through transformation and difference."[51] But such a statement disregards the impact that differing economic circumstances have on identity formation. Somali refugees in Cairo who are living in unprivileged economic conditions are forming a group identity against their unwelcoming host society as this statement illustrates: "The only thing we are sharing is the religion. But in the culture we share nothing" (Mariam). At the same time, well to do émigrés claim that "between the culture of Egyptians and the culture of Somalis there is no big difference" (Suad). In other words, one has to inspect more closely the effects of economic factors when evaluating group identities.

Notes

1. All of the names in this chapter have been changed to preserve the anonymity of the interviewees.
2. Caritas is a worldwide operating Catholic relief, development and social service organization. In Cairo Caritas is functioning as one implementing partner of the UNHCR.
3. *fi amal* is an Arabic term for there is hope.
4. Somali émigrés are those people who were living for years in western countries, got citizenship there and then moved in the last years to Cairo. For more in-depth information about émigrés see Al-Sharmani, M. (2004). Refugees and citizens: The Somali diaspora in Cairo. Doctoral dissertation, Johns Hopkins University, Baltimore, MD.

5. This dissertation research was funded by the Austrian Academy of Science. The re-studies were funded by the Fritz-Thyssen Stiftung.
6. Hopkins, M. (1998). Whose live, whose work? Struggeling along the subject-colleague continuum. In R. M. Krulfeld & J. L. MacDonald (Eds.), *Power, ethics, and human rights: Anthropological studies of refugee research and action* (pp. 57-72). New York & Oxford: Rowman & Littlefield Publishers.
7. Omidian, P. A. (1994). Life out of context: Recording Afghan refugees' stories. In L. A. Camino & R. M. Krulfeld (Eds.), *Reconstructing lives, recapturing meaning: Refugee identity, gender, and cultural change* (pp. 151-178). Amsterdam: Gordon and Breach Publishers.
8. Lamnek, S. (1993). Qualitative Sozialforschung, Bd.2: Methoden und Techniken, Weinheim, Beltz, Psychologie-Verlag-Union. p. 329.
9. Malkki, L. H. (1997a). National geographic: The rooting of peoples and the territorialization of national identity among scholars and refugees. In A. Gupta & J. Ferguson (Eds.), *Culture, power, place: Explorations in critical anthropology* (pp. 52-74). Durham, NC & London: Duke University Press. p. 232.
10. UNHCR. (2003). Statistical Yearbook 2003. Retrieved from http://www.unhcr.org/cgi-bin/texis/vtx/statistics/opendoc.htm?tbl=STATISTICS&id=42aff7e84. p. 139.
11. D. Dessalegno (personal communication, March 2005).
12. Quite often not only the person, who is leaving, but relatives and friends are involved in the decision making as one refugee in Cairo, who wanted to leave to Italy, states: "I consulted my parents and my cousin's brother and they told me not to go, because it is dangerous."
13. Al-Sharmani, M. (2003). Livelihood and identity constructions of Somali refugees in Cairo. Forced Migration & Refugee Studies working paper no. 2. Cairo: American University in Cairo.
14. BBC News. (2004, April 28). Retrieved from http://news.bbc.co.uk/go/pr/fr/-/2/hi/africa/3664633.stm.
15. Kenya also has a resettlement program but the number of people who get resettled compared to the number of refugees is rather low.
16. Al-Sharmani, M. (2003). Livelihood and identity constructions of Somali refugees in Cairo. Forced Migration & Refugee Studies working paper no. 2. Cairo: American University in Cairo.
17. Bach, S. (2003). Information concerning travel routes and visa acquisition of Somali asylum seekers in Egypt. Cairo: EOHR Refugee Legal Aid Project. Unpublished manuscript, American University in Cairo.

18. UNHCR. (2005). UNHCR Country Operations Plan: Egypt.
19. UNCHR. (2005). UNHCR Country Operations Plan: Egypt. pp. 2-3.
20. At the moment, the UNHCR is advising not to deport Somali refugees who are coming from the Southern part of Somalia. I never heard about Somalis being deported to Somalia by the Egyptian government.
21. Bach, S. (2003). Information concerning travel routes and visa acquisition of Somali asylum seekers in Egypt. Cairo: EOHR Refugee Legal Aid Project. Unpublished manuscript, American University in Cairo.
22. This includes 1st instance (first interview) as well as 2nd instance (appeal) cases.
23. UNHCR. (2003). Statistical Yearbook 2003. Retrieved from http://www.unhcr.org/cgi-bin/texis/vtx/statistics/opendoc.htm?tbl=STATISTICS&id=42aff7e84.
24. D. Dessalegno (personal communication, March 2005).
25. R. Ibrahimin (personal communication, February 2005).
26. Kagan, M. (2002). Assessment of refugee status determination procedure at UNHCR's Cairo office, 2001- 2002. Cairo: FMRS Working Papers 1. Retrieved from http://www.aucegypt.edu/fmrs/documents/RSDReport.pdf.
27. Needs and Responses: FMO Research Guide Egypt. (undated). Retrieved from http://www.forcedmigration.org/guides/fmo029/fmo029.pdf.
28. Sperl, S. (2001). Evaluation of UNHCR's policy on refugees in urban areas: A case study review of Cairo. Geneva, Switzerland: United Nations High Commissioner for Refugees Evaluation and Policy Unit, 2001.
29. It seems that the number of the first group is decreasing. As UNHCR is stating that most of the "new" Somali asylum seekers are directly coming from Somalia and the term of irregular mover does not have the same definition at RO UNHCR Cairo as for example in European countries. Dessalegno states that ". . . in the case of Somalis, at least the ones who come from the Gulf, from Yemen, they are not irregular movers. . . ." Also the people who come from Libya he does not consider as irregular movers, so he continues: "in Libya the Somalis are just working, they are not even applying for asylum." D. Dessalegno (personal communication, March 2005).
30. Al-sharmani, M. (2003). Livelihood and identity constructions of Somali refugees in Cairo. Forced Migration & Refugee Studies working paper no. 2. Cairo: American University in Cairo.

31. R. Ibrahimin (personal communication, February 2005).
32. Zohry, A, & Harrell-Bond, B. (2003). Contemporary Egyptian migration: An overview of voluntary and forced migration, Working Paper C3. Development Research Centre on Migration, Globalisation and Poverty. Retrieved from http://www.migrationdrc.org/publications/working_papers/WP-C3.pdf.
33. Afifi, W. (2003). Research report on education for refugees in Cairo. Unpublished manuscript, American University in Cairo.

    Dingemans, E. (2002). Educational needs and priorities for south Sudanese refugees in Cairo. Field Report. Cairo: American University in Cairo, Forced Migration & Refugee Studies Department.
34. Al-Sharmani, M. (2003). Livelihood and identity constructions of Somali refugees in Cairo. Forced Migration & Refugee Studies working paper no. 2. Cairo: American University in Cairo.
35. Human Rights Watch. (2003). Retrieved from http://www.hrw.org/press/2003/02/egypt0206.htm.
36. Samara is not necessarily an insult, it means tanned or dark person, and "soda" is more derogative and can be translated as "Blacky." "Bunga Bunga" is a derogatory sound mimicking African languages.
37. I use the term Egyptian/Arabs because Somalis refer to Egyptians as Arabs, contrary to that a large number of Egyptians would reject being called an Arab.
38. Camino, L. A & R. M. Krulfeld. (1994). Introduction. In L. A. Camino & R. M. Krulfeld (Eds.), *Reconstructing lives, recapturing meaning: Refugee identity, gender, and cultural change* (IX-XVIII). Amsterdam: Gordon and Breach Publishers. p. xi.
39. See Bjork, Stephanie R. (2007). Modernity meets clan: Cultural intimacy in the Somali diaspora. In A. M. Kusow and S. R. Bjork (Eds.), *From Mogadishu to Dixon: The Somali diaspora in a global context.* Trenton, NJ: Red Sea Press.

    Kroner, G. (2000). Stationen einer Vertreibung: Somalische Flüchtlinserfahrungen in Ostafrika und im Westen Master's thesis, University of Vienna.
40. Malkki, L. H. (1997a). National geographic: The rooting of peoples and the territorialization of national identity among scholars and refugees. In A. Gupta & J. Ferguson (Eds.), *Culture, power, place: Explorations in critical anthropology* (52-74). Durham, NC & London: Duke University Press. p. 232.

    Malkki, L. H. (1997b). Speechless emissaries: Refugees, humanitarianism, and dehistoricization. In K. Fog Olwig, & K. Hastrup (Eds.),

Siting culture: The shifting anthropological object (223-254). London & New York: Routledge.

41. Harrell-Bond, B. E. (1986). *Imposing aid: Emergency assistance to refugees*. Oxford: Oxford Press. p. 331.
42. B. Harrell-Bond (personal communication, March 2005).
43. Since this agreement, the border controls between Libya and Egypt were intensified.
44. Horst. C. (2003). Transnational nomads: How Somalis cope with refugee life in the Dadaab camps in Kenya. Amsterdam: Amsterdam Research Institute for Global Issues and Development Studies and Center for Resource Studies for Development.
45. Horst. C. (2003). Transnational nomads: How Somalis cope with refugee life in the Dadaab camps in Kenya. Amsterdam: Amsterdam Research Institute for Global Issues and Development Studies and Center for Resource Studies for Development. p. 173.
46. D. Dessalegno (personal communication, March 2005).
47. According to Al-Sharmani (2004) there are about 200 Somali-émigré families living in Cairo.

    Al-Sharmani, M. (2004). Refugees and citizens: The Somali diaspora in Cairo. Doctoral dissertation, Johns Hopkins University, Baltimore, MD.
48. Al-Sharmani, M. (2004). Refugees and citizens: The Somali diaspora in Cairo. Doctoral dissertation, Johns Hopkins University, Baltimore, MD.
49. Gilad, L. (1990). *The northern route: An ethnography of refugee experiences*. St. John's, Canada: Institute of Social and Economic Research, Memorial University of Newfoundland. p 110.
50. Appadurai, A. (1991). Global ethnoscapes. In: R. G. Fox (Ed.), *Recapturing anthropology. Working in the present* (191-210). Santa Fe, NM: School of American Research Press: Distributed by the University of Washington Press. p. 192.
51. Hall, S. (1996). Cultural identity and diaspora. In P. Williams & L. Chrisman (Eds.), *Colonial discourse & postcolonial theory: A reader* (392-403). Harvester Whaeatsheaf. p. 402.

Chapter 3

DIASPORIC SOMALIS IN CAIRO: THE POETICS AND PRACTICES OF SOOMAALINIMO

Mulki Al-Sharmani

INTRODUCTION

In the summer of 2001, I attended a series of meetings held by groups of Somali refugees and expatriates in Cairo. The main goal of these meetings was to organize community work to address refugee needs. These meetings resulted in the establishment of the Somali Refugee Committee of Egypt (SRCOE), an informal association that worked towards addressing the grievances Somali refugees had towards the UNHCR. In the subsequent three and a half years, SRCOE participated in a series of discussions with the UNHCR to advocate on behalf of Somali refugees and established a home schooling project for refugee children. SRCOE, however, had many conflicts and divisions among its members, and in the fall of 2003 the association was dismantled. Since then there have been several efforts to establish new organizations, which resulted in the establishment of the Somali Development Organization (SODO).[a]

An issue repeatedly brought up in the SRCOE meetings as well as in discussions among other groups involved in community work was the importance of reclaiming what informants often referred to as *soomaalinimo*. The word soomaalinimo means *Somaliness* or being a Somali. However, informants often talked about it in very distinct terms. It was described as a positive identity rooted in the moral values associated with being Somali. Moreover, informants often described soomaalinimo in terms of its main antitheses: the culture of violence and anarchy that pervaded the homeland in the aftermath of the civil war and values of self-interest, dishonesty, and lack of commitment to one's family and diasporic community. Reclaiming 'soomaalinimo' was thought to be vital not only to end the war and reconstruct the nation in the homeland, but also to be able to meet the immediate needs of diasporic Somalis, i.e., securing livelihood, and living a secure and dignified life.

In this chapter, I examine how diasporic soomaalinimo is articulated and lived by Somali refugees in Cairo and émigrés who have relocated to the Egyptian capital from Western countries. For these refugees and émigrés, soomaalinimo is a collective diasporic identity that is rooted in "an imagined moral community".[2] It is based on granting a higher moral ground to the Somali diaspora than to the homeland since the latter is associated with atrocities and chaos. This collective diasporic identity has its distinct narrative language (poetics) and daily enactments (practices). Diasporic soomaalinimo, however, is not only grounded in a national past but also in a diasporic present in which refugees and émigrés have different experiences and uneven resources and legal rights. For example, because of their harsh living conditions and limited legal rights, Somali refugees need community support for daily survival, and thus become invested in creation of a collective identity that they can appeal to in their efforts to seek support from one another. Somali émigrés, on the other hand, have relocated to Cairo to escape economic and cultural marginalization in their countries of citizenship. In Cairo, the émigrés enjoy a middle class life because of their status as Western nationals, which grants them more legal rights than refugees and opportunities to generate income through transnational trading activities. Most of all, the émigrés become powerful members of the Somali community in Cairo because of their financial support for community-building and developmental efforts. Nevertheless, both the refugees and émigrés have to grapple with the tensions entailed in the process of constructing a community and a diasporic collective identity. Who in diaspora participates in the construction of this moral community and how? Should it be those who have been away from the homeland for a long time or recent arrivals? Those who want to have a central place for clan identities in this larger identity that is being constructed? Or those who find diasporic ties of friendship and cooperation a stronger basis for a unified community? In other words the construction of soomaalinimo, is contested by these diasporic groups of Somalis not only because of their differentiated past histories and affiliations but also due to their varied diasporic experiences and identities.

The analysis presented in this article is based on data collected from in-depth interviews, case studies, questionnaires, and participant observations conducted during dissertation fieldwork in Cairo, Egypt between 2001 and 2003. The article is divided into six sections. In the first section, I will present a profile of the refugees and the émigrés. In the second section, I will analyze the role of soomaalinimo as a discourse of survival and support in the lives of different groups of Somali refugees. I will highlight, in particular, the distinct living conditions and diasporic histories that impact the refugees' understanding and experiences of soomaalinimo. In the third section, I will examine soomaalinimo as a discourse of resistance and empowerment from the perspective of the émigrés. In the fourth section, I will analyze the meaning and significance of soomaalinimo as a narrative language that is collectively constructed by refugees and émigrés. In the fifth section, I will examine community building efforts as distinct practices through which both refugees and émigrés enact soomaalinimo. Then in the final and concluding section, I will link my analysis of soomaalinimo to current debates in the field of Somali Studies about the foundation of Somali national identity and the causes of the downfall of the nation.

PROFILE OF SOMALIS IN CAIRO

With the collapse of the Somali state and the civil war in 1991, a large number of refugees fled to Cairo from the homeland as well as from neighboring Gulf countries. Most of these refugees and their families had resettled in North America, Europe, and Australia by the mid-nineties. Since the late nineties, Cairo has attracted again a diverse group of Somalis refugees from neighboring countries such as Libya, Saudi Arabia, and Yemen as well as refugees from Kenya and Somalia. Refugees who arrived from other host societies fled the homeland either in the late eighties (with the advent of the civil war) or in the early nineties with the collapse of the state. The number of these refugees is currently 3,609, including recognized refugees and asylum seekers.[3] The main reasons refugees gave for leaving other Middle Eastern countries to come to Cairo were: lack of a legal residence status, fears of deportation, and experiences of harassment and racism in daily encounters with government officials, employers, and other members of host societies. Moreover, many of these refugees were attracted to Cairo because of a shared perception that the UNHCR office in the city resettled many Somalis in Western countries.

The reasons that many Somali refugees pursue resettlement in the West can be partially explained by their pursuit of a safer and better life through the acquisition of legal citizenship, employment, and a better standard of living. But seeking resettlement in the West for Somali refugees can be better understood if we also examine how these refugees are an integral part of a network of transnational interlinked families and communities whose members pool resources, debate, and make collective decisions about the future of different members living in different nation-states. Refugees in Cairo depend on their transnational families and communities for livelihood and securing a better future for themselves and their relatives. They invest in this transnational support system by sharing a variety of resources including money, housing, information about different host societies, and family obligations such as taking care of children, elderly relatives, or invalid family members.

The advantages and the limitations of resettlement in the West are ever more real for the refugees in Cairo as they share the city with an increasing number of Somali families who are citizens of Western countries and have moved to Egypt since the late nineties. Although there is no official count of this group of Somali émigrés, my three-year tally of these families indicates that the number is a little over 200 families. Most of these families consist of mothers and their small or teenage children. The husbands and older children usually stay behind in the country of citizenship where they hold jobs and remit money to the family in Cairo. Meanwhile, the mothers start small trading activities in Cairo.[4] Refugees aspire to the higher status of diasporic Somalis who hold Western passports that ensure them mobility and eligibility for residence in different nation-states. On the one hand, refugees desire the advantages of Western citizenship as they observe Somali Americans or Europeans obtain and renew residence in Cairo as Western nationals and rent or buy apartments in new middle-class neighborhoods with the economic assets that they acquired from employment in the West and running small trading businesses in the Middle East. On the other hand, the limitations of Western citizenship, which have not helped Somalis in Western countries escape the lives of racialized and economically marginalized immigrants, are recounted again and again to refugees by their fellow Somalis who moved to Cairo from the West.

DIASPORIC SOOMAALINIMO AND LOCAL IDENTITIES

For daily survival in Cairo, refugees depend on one another as well as on affluent fellow Somali immigrants from the West. Somali émigrés employ female refugees as domestic workers and some of the male refugees as tutors for their children or as personal assistants who run errands for them. Refugees from different clans and regions share housing, food, financial resources, and information for livelihood purposes. This sense of a community that cross-cuts different local identities is, on the one hand, real and necessary for the practical purposes of securing livelihood in a host society where many immigrants and non-national settlers cannot participate in the economy and are not eligible for permanent residence and citizenship rights. On the other hand, juxtaposed to the daily efforts of creating a unified Somali community are conflicts and divisions that take place within clans and among clans as well as among different groups of Somalis who form solidarities based on common diasporic experiences such as residence in former host societies (e.g. Libya or Saudi Arabia) and current residential areas in Cairo.

Soomaalinimo is very much shaped by the rights and living conditions of refugees in the host society. Since the Egyptian government became a signatory to the 1951 United Nation Convention for Refugees, it has delegated to the UNHCR the responsibilities of reviewing and deciding refugees' claims. Therefore, refugees tend to feel that it is the UNHCR rather than the Egyptian state, and its policies, that is discriminating against them. Restrictions on employment and temporary residence permits that do not protect refugees from police harassment, and lack of sufficient and affordable health care and education services are some of these refugees' grievances. They realize that even legal refugee status does not make them eligible for long-term residence and citizenship. Thus the refugees believe that these insurmountable problems make their demands for resettlement in Western countries a moral right. To address these grievances, refugees feel they have to be and act like a community in order to exert pressure on the UNHCR.

In an environment where another larger African refugee group, the Sudanese, is much more organized and visible due to their longer immigrant history, creating a national bloc becomes very important for Somali refugees. In fact, there is a sense among many refugees that acting and speaking as a unified national group will help them change the perception of Somali refugees as divided and dishonest, which, they believe, is held by many UNHCR staff members and other NGOs that work with refugee populations in Cairo. Changing this perception is important because the Somali refugees feel they are competing with Southern Sudanese refugees for recognition, support, and services. Also, since many of the Southern Sudanese refugees in Cairo are Christian and most of the NGOs working with refugees are church-based, the Somalis' articulation of their collective identity vis-à-vis Sudanese refugees and NGOs is both nationalistic and religious.

However, while the refugees' relationship with the UNHCR on one level motivates them to act as a unified collectivity, certain kinds of interactions with the UNHCR create contexts in which refugees have to present themselves in localized terms. Some of this latter kind of interaction takes place in refugee status determination interviews. For example, based on my observations of several of these interviews and discussions with refugees and UNHCR refugee protection officers, I have noted the following: First, the style of questioning that UNHCR staff use in these interviews often encourages refugees to recount their experiences of violence and flight in a way that emphasizes their clan identities. Second, refugees often hold gatherings in which they exchange knowledge about the procedures of the interviews and the expectations of the UNHCR staff.[5] The dual processes of presenting oneself to the UNHCR as an individual refugee in local, often clan-based identity terms and engaging in daily efforts to create a united Somali refugee community are sometimes contradictory and conducive to tensions. On the one hand refugees sometimes witness, suffer from, or engage in individual acts of spying on one another to the UNHCR for purposes of personal or clan revenge. On other hand, they continue to support and engage in daily practices of creating and articulating a collective identity.

Also, the refugees' reflections on events in the homeland often influence and are impacted by their efforts to create a cohesive community among themselves. Refugees avidly follow news of the homeland through communications with family members in Somalia and elsewhere, from on-line discussions with fellow Somalis, and through one another in their evening gatherings in local coffee shops. The causes of the chaos and the violence in the homeland are debated along the lines of clan affiliations and regional identities. While clan-based conflicts between warring factions in the homeland are not replicated in Cairo, sometimes the news of such conflicts exacerbates existing tensions. For example, in spring 2002 Somalis in Cairo were following the news of fierce fighting in Mogadishu that was initiated by a faction controlled by the *Habr Gidir* sub-clan (of the *Hawiya* clan-family) against other sub-clans from within as well as outside the clan-family. This news coincided with a rape crime that was committed against a young divorced Somali woman in Ard il Liwa. The victim belonged to the *Majerteen* sub-clan (of the *Darood* clan-family) and the accused was a young man from the Habr Gidir sub-clan, who had arrived from the homeland few months earlier. Many Somalis in Ard il Liwa and Nasr City were extremely disturbed by this incident, especially since it took place a few months after a Somali Bantu woman in Nasr City was also allegedly raped by a man from the Habr Gidir sub-clan. Community activists from the SRCOE held several meetings in which they argued passionately about the crime and the appropriate measures to be taken. The accused said that it was a consensual sexual relationship, while the victim maintained that it was rape and said that bruises on different parts of her body were evidence that she was assaulted.

The ways in which community leaders dealt with this incident reveal the interplay between their diasporic concerns and homeland politics. Because of the news of recent fighting in the homeland for which Habr Gidir factions were blamed, the rape crime in Cairo was described by some Somalis as part of destructive actions that were being committed by Somalis who belonged to certain clans. Other informants described the crime as an example of aggression between two larger groups: the Hawiya (the clan-family of the accused) and the Darood (the victim's clan-family). This is reflective of another layer of clan politics in the homeland in which the Darood and the Hawiya clan-families are seen in some contexts as arch enemies (the former having dominated the previous regime and the latter forming the initial coalition of opposition movements that overthrew Barre's government). When some of the refugees who belonged to the same sub-clan as the accused attempted to resolve the problem by offering compensation money to the family of the victim, other refugees refused, arguing that the crime was so heinous that the community could not heal without expelling the transgressor.[6] Others saw the rape crime as an example of the destructive ways of recent arrivals from the homeland that were seen as lacking in the values of soomaalinimo and posing a threat to community-building efforts. In fact, some community activists argued that the accused transgressed not only against the victim, but also against the community they were struggling to build.

Thus, the different ways in which informants dealt with this rape crime were shaped by both the development of the war in the homeland and the daily politics of living in diaspora. Tensions that arise from local conflicts between diasporic groups (e.g. recent arrivals and old arrivals) become entangled with politics in the homeland. The articulation of these tensions echoes on one level clan divisions in the homeland and on another level new group affiliations and divisions in diaspora. For community activists and their supporters, the men who were accused of the two rape crimes represented not only clan-based conflict in the homeland but also a threat posed by a group of young refugee men who arrived recently from the homeland. These men are seen as destructive to community building efforts because their ways of life involve spending money and time drinking with other men rather than contributing to community development projects. In short, while clan-based conflicts in the homeland shape some refugees' perceptions of who belong or do not belong to the community, the kinds of lives Somalis lead in diaspora are also a significant factor.

Diasporic identity becomes a new and increasingly important factor that also shapes informants' understanding of the collapse of the country. A large number of the refugees who have been away from the homeland for the past ten years or more privilege the experience of diaspora as a positive condition that protects one from the suspicions of being implicated in the atrocities of the war and also makes one more appreciative of the importance of a national identity as a source of unity and empowerment. In fact, recent arrivals from the homeland, particularly from majority clans, are often made to feel defensive and have to demonstrate that they have not participated in the violence in the homeland. Thus, for some recent arrivals, active involvement in community efforts to create unity among the refugees and advance their collective welfare becomes a way of distancing themselves from the anarchy and violence of the homeland and demonstrating their claims to soomaalinimo.

While the experience of diaspora becomes a basis for a claim to a purer kind of national identity, it also acts as a source of new local identities. Attachments that have been established among different groups of refugees based on shared diasporic trajectories sometimes compete with their efforts to create a larger community of Somali refugees. For example, a large number of refugees who settled in Ard il Liwa were part of a circle of Somali families that shared neighborly and friendly relationships during their residence in Libya in the 1990s. These refugees moved to the same neighborhood in Cairo through a common network of friends and former neighbors. The narrow and enclosed physical setting of their current residential area has also strengthened their unity. Although these refugees have been active in the establishment of the first community association (SRCOE), they also exhibit an awareness of themselves as a distinct local community. This creates tension with groups that make claims to other localized diasporic ties, such as among refugees who lived together in Saudi Arabia. For example, some Somalis from Saudi

Arabia complain that those from Libya often get more student slots in language classes for adults and in the home-schooling project for children. Somalis from Libya counter-argue that these accusations are based on other groups' jealousy of the strong ties that Somalis from Libya share with one another. They point out that their attachment is, in fact, a result of their commitment to a Somali unity in diaspora that cuts across clan affiliations. It is affiliations with Somalis, with whom one had lived or known in Libya, that are the outcome of past efforts of establishing a united diasporic community.

To conclude, Somali refugees in Cairo seek the creation of a diasporic Somali national identity for multiple reasons that are related to their conditions in the diaspora as well as to politics in the homeland. This goal is pursued through community and advocacy work. Yet, the process of articulating and experiencing diasporic soomaalinimo is complicated by competing attachments of the localized identities of refugees, which are again shaped not only by the history of the nation but also by different diasporic experiences. Furthermore, the kind of diasporic soomaalinimo that is being constructed through community work is also shaped by Somali émigrés from the West who play significant roles in this process because of their financial, educational, and legal capital.

DIASPORIC SOOMAALINIMO: A DISCOURSE OF MULTIPLE IDENTITIES

The participation of Somali émigrés in the construction of a diasporic soomaalinimo seems to be intertwined with their redefinitions of different layers of identities that they make claims to. These identities are shaped by their citizenship in Western countries, their membership in particular local groups in the history of the Somali nation, and their Muslim faith.

First, the move to Cairo for many of these families is motivated by a sense of frustration with their experiences as second-class citizens in Western countries. Many feel their legal status as citizens does not translate into equitable economic and cultural membership. This is a humiliating experience for these Somalis, many of whom came to the West with a relatively high level of education. Even after pursuing further educational and professional training in their new home countries, many could still not find jobs in their fields. They explain their economic marginalization and lack of social mobility as the outcome of the cultural and racial marginalization of black and Muslim immigrant groups. To illustrate this, I recount an incident that has happened to one of the émigrés, a forty-one year old mother of two children with undergraduate and graduate degrees in accounting from a reputable university in Ottawa. She said:

> My friend and I found out that the local government was holding this open meeting so that people can come and hand in their resumes to apply for government jobs. We went. We waited in a line for jobs for MA holders. When my turn came to hand in my application, the lady taking the papers asked me, "Do you know these jobs are for MA holders?" I said, "Yes and I have an MA. Degree." This shows you what they think of us. It does not matter if we are citizens or educated. They don't see us like that. We did not get the jobs. My friend works now as a receptionist in a clinic and I work in a school. They hired me to work with new immigrant children and their parents. It has nothing to do with my degree.

According to this informant and others from Canada, discrimination against immigrant groups is prevalent in Canadian society in different ways. These émigrés point out that Canadian employers require job applicants to have "Canadian experience," i.e., previous employment experience in Canadian workplaces. This reduces new immigrants' opportunities of finding jobs, and forces some of them to stay on welfare. The sense of being kept out of a successful professional life, in which immigrants can have good government or private sector jobs, is also shared by educated émigrés from other Western countries. For instance, an engineer who relocated his family and children from Sweden to Cairo was bitter that he could not find a job in his field, and was supporting his family by working in a Somali money transfer office (x*awala*) in the Swedish capital.

Another form of which marginalization that these Somalis complain is the limited educational possibilities available for their children in the lower-class and often racially segregated neighborhoods where these Somalis live. Some children drop out of school. Those who stay in school sometimes have to spend too much time in remedial classes, which parents think are often a waste of time and a way for the school to get funding from local governments. The move to Cairo has enabled many of these families to send their children to affordable private schools, to engage in small income-generating projects, and to lead a middle class life. Moreover, families hope that the fruits of a middle class life in Cairo, such as good education, will increase their children's opportunities to pursue a college education in the West and escape dead-end jobs when they return.

Thus, while their citizenship status does not shield émigrés from economic and cultural marginalization in Western societies, it creates opportunities for a better life with more positive self-identifications in Cairo. Moreover, making claims to a diasporic Somali identity that is grounded in values of honesty, hard work, generosity, and devotion to the family and community offers an alternative to a pathologized culture of poverty and crime with which they are often associated in their countries of citizenship. Giving financial support to refugee community work, for example, makes this new class of Somalis feel like active and valued members of a community.

Furthermore, émigrés who come from marginalized clans use their new roles as valued community leaders to create a new and more powerful role for their clans in the reconstruction of a Somali nation--albeit in diaspora. For example, some of the female émigrés from the *Rahanweyn* clan have led efforts to raise money for community work. Their roles as community activists have enhanced the construction of a collective Somali identity and helped create a positive and more powerful image of the clan of these émigrés among the Somalis in Cairo. In other words, not only are these émigrés viewed as individuals committed to soomaalinimo but also their clans gain honor because of their community activism. At the same time émigrés from marginalized clans often tend to be involved in efforts to preserve their own local cultures. Rahanweyn émigrés, for example, organize efforts to teach the children of their clan *Af-maymay* (their local language). In other words, mixing community activism and acts of assertion of local identities leads to interplay of clan identities and soomaalinimo that works well in the case of marginalized clans.

Lastly, some émigrés from the West commit to the construction of a diasporic Somali identity as a part of their efforts to redefine themselves as 'good' Muslims. A considerable number of the émigrés recount how the experiences of the war and diasporic life in the West have made them realize that their religious identity is of paramount importance. They believe that an integral part of being a good Muslim requires espousing and practicing a core of moral values in addition to observing religious rituals. Among these values are devotion and generosity to one's family and people, helping those in need, and overcoming inner divisions and conflicts. Therefore for these émigrés contributing to the construction of a diasporic soomaalinimo becomes a way of being true to their religious faith. It is interesting that in this case, an appeal to Muslim identity (which in itself supercedes nationalistic ties) reaffirms particular national sentiments and attachments. I think this is because most Somalis who left the country in the past fifteen years and settled in different countries in the West have lived in co-ethnic neighborhoods and maintained close ties to one another. Those who have adopted an overt religious discourse were often mentored in classes offered by Somali religious scholars who kept close ties with Somali religious groups in different countries. This religious discourse was largely motivated by a desire to address specific problems that faced diasporic Somalis (e.g. the shame of the fall of the nation, family tensions in diaspora, the influence of non-Muslim black culture on Somali youth).[7]

THE POETICS OF DIASPORIC SOOMAALINIMO: "SOMALIS DON'T UNDERSTAND SOOMAALINIMO"

Refugees and émigrés are creating a new kind of language in which the nation is imagined as a community grounded in particular moral values that are missing in the homeland, and whose lack has led to the collapse of the nation. One interesting aspect of this new language is the distinction between *Somalis* and *soomaalinimo*. The former is often used to refer to those held responsible for the fall of the nation, those who are violent, dishonest, self-interested, and put their individual goals before the welfare of their families and communities. Refugees and émigrés often use the term *Somalis* to describe the warring factions in the homeland or unspecified Somalis in diaspora who are described as irresponsible and self-interested. These "immoral" collectivities that are referred to as Somalis and are blamed for the downfall of the country are given physical descriptions. They are men wearing *macawiis* (a Somali traditional piece of cloth that men wrap around their body from the waist down) with long dark faces and red eyes from long nights of killing and chewing *qat* (mild narcotic leaves that mostly men chew in the homeland and recently have been heavily consumed by young militia men). It is significant, I believe, that in these descriptions of Somalis who destroyed the nation and who do not know soomaalinimo, their clan affiliations are always left unspecified. Although this does not mean that narrators and audiences do not have specific positions on the conflicts between different clan-based warring factions in Somalia, it reflects the need of Somalis in Cairo to create a collective identity which all can embrace regardless of clan affiliations.

Yet, *Somali* as an adjective is sometimes used in a positive light. For example, in community meetings, SRCOE and SODO members often praise female émigrés for their support of community work by referring to them as "Somali women," and the participants in these meetings often nod in agreement. Individuals who put in a lot of time and effort in community work and, most, of all have a reputation for being impartial in the allocation of community services to different clans, are also referred to by different people as being a "Somali man" or a "Somali woman." In other words, when particular people are described as being Somali, the common understanding among most Somalis in Cairo is that these individuals possess the true values of soomaalinimo. For instance, a SRCOE member described one of the respectable and valued community activists as follows: "He is a Somali man. He thinks of the people and helps them. He doesn't think of himself first. He does not know *musuq maasaq* (dishonesty and corruption)."

Thus, the word *Somali* has multiple, contradictory meanings. As a collective plural noun, it is often used to describe what is antithetical to soomaalinimo, but it has also positive connotations as an adjective that is used to describe specific people and actions. Meanwhile, *soomaalinimo* is always used by Somalis in Cairo to refer to a core of positive values and a behavior that characterizes what they imagine to be a community of Somalis. It seems to be first and foremost a moral rather than a territorial imagination of a particular community.[8] Furthermore; the articulations of this identity are always based on an opposition to destructive values and actions that are associated with current life in the homeland. The opposition of soomaalinimo to the moral malaise in the homeland is reinforced as informants follow the news of the violence and failed efforts of peace negotiations from communications with family members, the mass media, and fellow Somalis in online chat rooms. The need to ground this imagined nation in moral values is also influenced by the living conditions in Cairo, where refugees need to overcome the realities and perceptions of the divisions among them for the purposes of livelihood, empowerment, and the creation of better future for themselves.

This diasporic national identity is articulated in narratives that informants exchange about the unnatural things that are taking place in Somalia because people there *ma yaqaaniin soomaalinimo* (don't know soomaalinimo). These narratives were frequently recounted to me by informants from both refugee and émigré groups. I heard the narratives in different settings such as SRCOE meetings, social visits among neighbors, coffee shops frequented by men, and religious gatherings organized by women to commemorate the anniversary of Prophet Mohamed's birthday or local Sufi saints. In other words, the narratives constituted a body of knowledge that was shared by a large number of Somalis from different clans, diasporic trajectories, class, and gender. For purposes of illustration, I will summarize one of these narratives:

> Two *mooryaan* men (the Somali word for a militia man who loots and kills) killed a farmer and took his land. Then the two men fought among themselves over the land, one of them killed the other. The killer started digging a grave to bury his friend. When he put the body in the ground, he was pulled under by an invisible force. He was buried alive with the dead body.

Several points are noteworthy about these widely circulated stories. First, most of these stories are about incidents of killing, looting, and subsequent unfolding of unnatural events. As I have mentioned, when informants recount these kinds of stories, killers are not identified as belonging to specific clans. Also those who commit acts of killing in these stories are not pictured as collective group of people fighting for a particular cause but as immoral brutal men who only care about themselves. In many of the stories, the killers and looters do not only terrorize other families and communities but also their own. In addition, informants often do not show any interest in establishing the truth and accuracy of these narratives. They exchange these stories in gatherings where the news of the homeland is discussed, and conclude with analyzing what had happened and how the nation could be rebuilt. Thus, it seems that what is important for the narrators and participants in these gatherings is their collective creation of an imagined moral community of Somalis versus a pathologized way of life in the homeland.

Although the language of diasporic soomaalinimo privileges the diaspora to the homeland, the relationship between the two is complex. On the one hand, Somalis in Cairo maintain close ties with their families and their local communities in the homeland. Remittance money is sent regularly to families as well as local communities that need financial support for reconstruction efforts in the homeland. Families in Cairo and the homeland communicate regularly through the Internet and by phone. Some émigrés, who come from relatively safe regions in Somalia such as the northwest and northeast, go back with their children for family visits. Furthermore, the future that is imagined by many refugees and émigrés is one in which living in the homeland is not ruled out; however, it is considered as merely part of a complex way of life. Many Somalis talk about pursuing a transnational life in which they have families, communities, and homes in Somalia, Cairo, and the West. Thus, as one of the main nodes of a chain of interdependent transnational Somali families and communities, the homeland is important for the present and future of refugees and émigrés.

On the other hand, the homeland becomes a discursive narrative that exemplifies the fall of the nation, the disruption of a past life, wide-spread lawlessness, and lack of a secure future. This narrative is used on a daily basis by refugees and émigrés to distinguish between a rejected way of being and living (associated with the civil war in Somalia), and a diasporic way of life in which refugees and émigrés re-define what makes them a community.

THE PRACTICES OF DIASPORIC SOOMAALINIMO

A diasporic national identity is also constructed through daily practices that revolve around community work. These practices involve collecting donations for families in need and for community-run educational projects; planning meetings with UNHCR staff, local NGOs, and research organizations; and gathering and distributing information about laws and policies pertaining to refugees in Cairo. While the organizational work is carried out by individuals who are part of informal refugee associations such as the SRCOE and the SODO, a large number of Somalis in different neighborhoods are drawn into the process. For example donations are collected from refugees and émigrés from the West. These donations have been used in a number of ways that have been indicative of the ongoing process of building a united moral community despite inner divisions. For example, some of the donations have been used among other things to assist refugees who are sick and cannot afford healthcare and those who lost family members and loved ones in a recent fire accident in one of the local neighborhoods in Cairo. Also some of the donations are used to sponsor community-run educational projects for children and adults. While informants sometimes disagree about the extent to which the donations are used to benefit Somalis from different local groups, the majority of my informants affirm that giving donations is an important value of soomaalinimo.

Community meetings are another arena in which a collective identity is constructed among different Somalis. These meetings are held in various venues such as coffee shops, refugee households, and on several occasions the Forced Migration and Refugee Studies Program at the American University in Cairo. In these meetings, the participants address the concerns of Somalis and ways of dealings with those concerns. The organization of these meetings is indicative of how the process of creating a unified community of diasporic Somalis is intertwined with negotiating new and old local identities. Clan affiliations are by no means the main basis of local identity for new attachments to particular diasporic groups, or identifications based on gender and age, also become significant. Thus not only clan elders, but also leaders from diasporic groups, representatives of different residential areas, women, and young people compete for central roles in these meetings.

These practices of creating a community of Somalis are carried out in a language and through rituals that are distinctly drawn from Somali culture--albeit in new and creative ways. For example, the donations collected regularly are called *qaraan*, the Somali word for money collected by clan members for others in their clan who are in need. However, the donations are collected from different clans and the recipients of financial assistance or education services also come from different clans. Thus, qaraan, a clan-oriented Somali practice acquires new nationalistic connotations. Moreover, community meetings are often held in the format of *shir*, which is traditionally a meeting between clan elders and members to resolve inner disputes. But in these community meetings, nationalistic and local identities as well as those who make claims to them are much more diverse and distinct from those who traditionally constituted the Somali society.

There are also spaces where practices of soomaalinimo are differentiated by distinct diasporic trajectories, the particular concerns, and class distinctions between the refugees and émigrés. On the one hand, community meetings with the UNHCR and public demonstrations are venues through which refugees enact their sense of community as they pursue particular goals such as resettlements and better access to resources (e.g. education, employment, and healthcare). On the other hand, émigrés organize religious lectures and social gatherings for other émigrés and a select number of refugees to articulate a particular kind of soomaalinimo that privileges not only diasporic Somalis but also those who, like the émigrés, make claims to a distinct understanding of what defines Somali diaspora and Somali identity because of their diasporic experiences in Western countries, educational and professional background, economic activities, and their community activism.

CONCLUSION

In identifying the causes of the dissolution of Somalia, scholars in the field of Somali Studies refer to failed state, clanism, an economically and racially stratified society, and foreign meddling. While all scholars agree on the detrimental role that the Barre government played in the creation of the circumstances that led to the civil war and the collapse of the country, they disagree about other factors and the significance they attach to them.

Anthropologist I. M. Lewis, who has written extensively about Somali society since the last decade of the colonial era, is the main voice in the literature who firmly argues that the Somali clan system is central to the dissolution of the nation:

> The collapse of the colonially created state represents technically a triumph for the segmentary lineage system and the political power of kinship....Given, then, that like nationalism, clanship is a human invention, is it in the 1990s basically the same phenomenon that it was in 1890s? Linguistically the answer must be "yes," since the same terminology has been employed throughout the recorded history of Somalis. Sociologically, the evidence also supports this view. Indeed, the argument of this book is that clanship is and was essentially a multipurpose, culturally constructed resource of compelling power because of its ostensibly inherent character "bred in the bone" and running "in the blood."[9]

Other scholars take Lewis to task for what they agree to be his essentialist and reductionist depiction of Somali kinship system and its role in the society. For example, Abdurahman Moallin Baadiyow makes a distinction between what he calls social tribalism and political tribalism.[10] Baadiyow explains that the former, which is the basis of Somali kinship, is a social support system that Somali communities used throughout their history for their welfare. As a social system, it is not inherently divisive since it also consists of laws, customs, and codes of behavior that ensure cooperation and establishment of ties among different kin groups. Political tribalism, on the other hand, according to Baadiyow, is an urban phenomenon created by Somali post-independent states that led to urban elites' control of national resources through the use of "tribal networks and loyalties within the national institutions".[11] Baadiyow's conclusion is that while social tribalism is part of Somali culture and is not antithetical to the existence of a Somali nation, political tribalism is an outcome of a particular political environment, and it constitutes part of a larger political malaise that led to the civil war and the dissolution of the country.

Abdi Samatar also rejects Lewis' position. He argues that it is not that Somali kinship system is inherently incompatible with the creation of a nation, but that the state and the urban elite failed to renew the social and cultural capital of the nation through the creation of public institutions that facilitate the participation and membership of different segments of the populations.[12]

Ahmed Samatar also finds Lewis' analysis to be flawed in its rigid and static depiction of Somali kinship system.[13] Samatar adds that the clan-centered explanation, however, is not the only one that tends to essentialize Somali society and its cultural and political history. He also critiques analyses that explain the collapse of the nation and state in binary terms such as a dominating nomadic class versus marginalized sedentary farming class, or a decentralized pastoralist culture versus a centralized modern nation-state.[14] Samatar argues instead for an approach that denaturalizes and historicizes all elements that contributed to the war.

Other scholars adopt a different angle in their analysis of the collapse of the nation. They contend that the above-mentioned explanations do not take into account the stratification of Somali society on the basis of class, race, and regional cultures during most of the post-independence era. They believe these are significant factors contributing to the disintegration of the nation, and inhibiting current efforts to rebuild the nation. This stratification, they argue, has marginalized minority clans, particularly farming communities in the south. For example, the official national history and culture that were constructed by post-independence governments did not reflect the local linguistic and social heritage of these communities.[15] In public discourses such communities were represented as having questionable claims to Somali identity because of their racial and linguistic differences. The land policies of Barre government also usurped many of the communities of their lands, which led to their economic marginalization. In the aftermath of the collapse of the state, the inter-riverine communities represented a disproportionate number of the victims of violence and looting because of their racial marginalization and the competition among warring factions over access to their farming lands. In short, these scholars call for a revisionist reading of the dominant narratives that constituted the nation and which silenced large segments of the population living in its territory.

These different analyses highlight important and valid elements in the history of a Somali nation and its post-independence challenges. I agree with authors who critique Lewis' analysis of clan affiliations and politics as the central lens through which to analyze the failure of the state and nation. In addition to treating clan affiliations and their significance in Somali society as ahistorical entities, the main problem with Lewis' position is that it hides too much under the name of clanism. The other authors, such as Ahmed Samatar, Abdi Samatar, Abdi Kusow and Catherine Besteman, propose more comprehensive explanations because of their deconstruction of entities such as the state and the clan. Besteman's analysis is also helpful in highlighting the roles of class and race in post-independent Somali society, which contributed to the conflict.

However, I would like to propose a new set of questions that might illuminate this debate better. Instead of asking why the nation failed and whether it had valid foundations to start with, we could ask: How do people experience the collapse of their nation after they have fled the homeland? What do they do? How do the old bases of national unity and sources of divisions play out and change in their diasporic lives? The significance of examining how diasporic Somalis construct and experience a Somali national identity is twofold: First, it highlights the fluidity and complexity of identity claims argued in the literature as being either the foundation of the nation (e.g. ethnic nationalism) or the main cause of its downfall (e.g. clan affiliations). Second, it reveals the privileged (but also complicated) role that a diaspora can play in the reconstruction of a nation whose main grounding is moral rather than territorial.

In Cairo, Somali refugees and émigrés engage in distinct daily acts of constructing and articulating a collective Somali identity (soomaalinimo). Yet, their articulations of this identity are neither uniform nor free from tensions. At play in the processes of the contestations and articulation of this diasporic soomaalinimo are both local identities that have been shaped by individual and group histories in the homeland as well as new identities that have been formed by informants' distinct diasporic experiences. The language in which this diasporic Somali identity is imagined, and the daily practices in which it is experienced and contested, are quite distinct. In other words, a new kind of a Somali nation is being imagined and created by diasporic Somalis.

Notes

1. SODO was established in September 2003. Since late 2003, SODO has been a variety of educational services for Somali refugees and communicating with the UNHCR for advocacy work.
2. Malkki, L. (1995). *Purity and exile: Violence, memory, and national cosmology among Hutu refugees in Tanzania*. Chicago, IL: University of Chicago Press. p. 254.
3. See UNHCR 2005. UNHCR Country Operations Plan: Egypt.
4. For more in-depth analysis of the economic activities of émigrés and refugees see Al-Sharmani, M. (2004). Refugees and citizens: The Somali diaspora in Cairo (Unpublished doctoral dissertation, the Johns Hopkins University, Baltimore, MD).
5. I am not suggesting that either the UNHCR staff deliberately solicit false testimonies from refugees or that the latter purposefully give untrue information in these interviews. However, I argue that the understandings that some UNHCR staff have of the dynamics of the civil war and the violence in Somalia sometimes result in the advertent need to place refugees' experiences of violence in neat and clear-cut terminology of clan-based conflicts. It is also my contention that refugees have understood this and incorporated it into their shared knowledge of effective styles of testimonial giving in order to better convey their claims for asylum, which they believe to be true and valid.
6. Those who argued for compensation money as a form of restitution claimed that it was a tradition in the homeland. Those who opposed it argued that conflicts that resulted from crimes such as rape could

not be resolved by compensation money. This latter group argued that while rape has always been a horrible crime in the homeland, it is even worse in diaspora where Somalis need to free their communities from the destructive values of warring factions in the homeland. The accused in both rape cases ended up fleeing Egypt (one to Libya and one to the homeland) after several community activists reported the crimes to Egyptian police and the UNHCR office.

7. See McGown Berns, R. (1999). *Muslims in the diaspora: The Somali communities of London and Toronto*. Toronto: University of Toronto Press.
8. In some aspects, this way of imagining the nation is similar to that of the Hutu refugees in the Mishamo camp in Malkki, L. (1995). *Purity and exile: Violence, memory, and national cosmology among Hutu refugees in Tanzania*. Chicago, IL: University of Chicago Press.
9. Lewis, I. M. (1994). *Blood and bone: The call of kinship in Somali society*. Lawrenceville, NJ: The Red Sea Press. p. 233.
10. Baadiyow, A. M. (2001). Tribalism and Islam: Variations on the basics of Somaliness. In S. M. Lilius (Ed.), *Proceedings of the international congress of Somali studies: Variations on the theme of Somaliness* (pp. 227-240). Turku, Finland: Abo Akademi University.
11. Baadiyow, A. M. (2001). Tribalism and Islam: Variations on the basics of Somaliness. In S. M. Lilius (Ed.), *Proceedings of the international congress of Somali studies: Variations on the theme of Somaliness* (pp. 227-240). Turku, Finland: Abo Akademi University. p. 230.
12. Samatar, A. (2001). The Somali catastrophe: Explanations and implications. In: S. M. Lilius, (Ed.), *Proceedings of international congress of Somali studies: Variations on the theme of Somaliness* (pp. 7-30). Turku, Finland: Abo Akademi University.
13. Samatar, A. (2001). Somali reconstruction and local initiative: Amoud University. World Development, 29(4), 641-656.
14. As examples of such analyses, Ahmed Samatar refers to Mohamed Haji Mukhtar's Between Self-determination and Chaos; Omar Eno's The Untold Apartheid Imposed on the Bantu/Jareer People in Somalia; and Amina Sharif Hassan's Somalis: The Forgotten People. In H. Adam and R. Ford. (Eds.), *Mending rips in the sky: Options for Somali communities in the 21st century*. Lawrenceville, NJ: The Red Sea Press.
15. Besteman, C. (1996). Violent politics and the politics of violence: The dissolution of Somali nation-state. *American Ethnologist*, 23(5), 579-596.

    Kusow, A. M. (1994). The genesis of the Somali civil war: A new perspective. *Northeast African Studies*, 1(1), 31-46.

Kusow, A. M. (1995). The Somali origin: Myth or reality. In A. J. Ahmed (Ed.), *The invention of Somalia* (pp. 81-106). Lawrenceville, NJ: The Red Sea Press.

Mukhtar, M. H. (1997). Somalia: Between self-determination and chaos. In: H. Adam & R. Ford. (Eds.), *Mending rips in the sky: Options for Somali communities in the 21st century* (pp. 49-64). Lawrenceville, NJ: The Red Sea Press.

Part II

Europe

Chapter 4

GLOBALIZING DIASPORIC NETWORKS: SOMALI FEMALE WORKERS IN ITALY

Francesca Decimo

INTRODUCTION

Over the past few decades, and particularly since the civil war in early 1991, Somalis have emigrated in large numbers to Europe, North America, and Australia. Today, small but significant Somali communities have claimed their little corners as far north as Alberta, Canada, to as far south as Durban, South Africa. Italy is one of the European countries that have attracted a significant Somali migration. However, a number of specific features distinguish the Somali community in Italy from the rest of the Somali diaspora. First, the Somali diaspora in Italy consists primarily of single women employed in the lowest bracket of the care labor market, particularly in nursing homes caring for the elderly and the sick.[1] Second, and more important, the Somali community in Italy is less established socially, economically, and politically than other Somali diaspora communities and immigrant communities in Italy.[2] One fundamental irony is that these features are strikingly in contrast to the long history shared by the two countries. In fact, not only did Italy occupy Somalia from 1889 to 1941 as a colonial power, but also until quite recently it had a close relationship with Somalia. Between 1950 and 1960, Italy served as Somali's 'guardian' on behalf of the United Nations, and in subsequent years it was Somalia's main trading partner, principal donor country, and the country most involved in building its infrastructure.

Against this historical background, it is all the more difficult to understand why Somalis in Italy have not consolidated their settlements, when many other immigrant groups have done so without the benefit of sharing a long history of bilateral collaboration.[3] One possible explanation may be related to how the Italian ruling class sponsored the Somali dictatorship in the 1980s. Numerous commentators have denounced the inadequacy of the Italian ruling class of the time, which continued to legitimate Siad Barre as its political interlocutor, even when his government had undermined fundamental civil rights, and when other countries like Great Britain, Germany and the United States had distanced themselves from his regime.[4] Italy's recognition of Siad Barre—not only political and military, but also taking the form of substantial economic support—in fact fuelled corruption and misgovernment in both parts.[5] Siad Barre's downfall coincided with the numerous judicial proceedings brought in those same years against the parties of Italy's governing coalition, provoking the demise of the ruling class that had hitherto maintained stable relations with the Somali government. This murky scenario explains why many of the forms of transnational mobility directly or indirectly connected with the ex-colonial relationships between the two countries ceased in subsequent years. With the demise of the Siad Barre regime and the profound political change that took place in Italy, most of the points of reference used by Somalis to move from one country to the other disappeared.

Yet these events still do not explain why, since the violent onset of civil war in its country of origin, the Somali community in Italy has not increased and diversified through greater family rootedness, as typically results from the action of migratory networks, but has instead diminished and grown increasingly female. I specifically ask why, despite a longer historical relationship between the Italian and Somali societies, the Somali diaspora in Italy primarily consists of single females, and remains the least socially, economically, and politically organized community among immigrants in Italy or among Somali diasporas. In order to answer these questions, I will conduct detailed analysis of the Somali migration from a gender perspective. The analysis is based on two studies on Somali immigration which I conducted in Naples and Bologna between 1993-1994, 1997-1999 and 2005.[6] The research was carried using an ethnographic approach which sought to reconstruct social life in public meeting-places and in private places. I reconstructed the social networks in these different urban settings and then conducted life-history analysis by means of unstructured, in-depth, reiterated and recorded interviews.[7]

I will show in particular that current female migrations are inextricably bound with the diasporic process now taking place on a global scale. And I will conclude by showing the crucial role performed by Somali women in Italy in ensuring the stability and continuity of their distant—yet never dispersed—families.

FEMALE MIGRATORY NETWORKS

Prior to the civil war, the majority of Somali immigrants in Italy came with the intention of returning home once they accumulated enough money to go back and start a better life in Somalia. But after the civil war, they slowly came to realize that it is impossible to predict when they will return home; more importantly, they have become obliged to send cash remittances to family members afflicted by the war.

On inspecting the many paths and projects undertaken by Somalis in Italy, one finds that entry into the humblest positions has proved to be immediately profitable. In other words, it is work in domestic service that provides the women with the monetary resources necessary to send remittances home to family members in difficulty. They have thus set an example which immigrant women—whether students, tourists, business persons, or whatever else—have slowly but surely emulated. They act as links in a complex migratory chain created by the summoning of these early immigrants by family members in Somalia. Now examined, therefore, is the pattern assumed by the migratory process undertaken by these early immigrants, the social networks on which it is based, and the resources that it conveys.[8]

The testimony provided by Fatma evinces the "summoning action" performed by female immigrants. In 1989, when Fatma arrived in Rome, she went to stay with her aunt and cousin, who had already been living in Italy for a number of years. When the war broke out, she sent enough money for her family members to be able to flee to Kenya. In 1992 she was joined by her sister and a cousin, and then by another cousin in 1995. In the summer of 1996, Fatma went to Kenya, got married and returned to Italy, bringing her mother with her. Her household grew even further in the same year, when it was joined by an aunt, who brought her husband's daughter. Finally, in 1972 Fatma's husband—the only man in this long migration chain—would arrive in Italy.

> First there were eleven people in Africa, and little by little we managed to get them here. My sister arrived after me, then one cousin in 1992, and then another one in 1995. One of them I helped the other one came through her. Now there are three left, and my husband, for whom I've done the documents for family reunion. I've got to wait for these documents and then next month he'll come here. (Fatma)

The migration chains thus formed are anchored in embedded solidarity networks created by the female immigrants who have already settled in Italy. Strong solidarity arises because the women must undertake the difficult role of acting as the main income-earners for their family groups. They are women forced to cope on their own with the innumerable difficulties faced by immigrants in a country which, apart from relatively easy entry, offers little social protection, and in which they can find only precarious, physically demanding, and often irregular work.

In order to counter this situation of potential social risk, Somali women immigrants in Italy have created informal networks, the basic units of which are domestic groups. In order to defend themselves against the ever-present risk of long spells of unemployment, and therefore of homelessness, they have joined together in groups and rented flats. Each of these flats is regulated by the pooling of the resources produced by each member. Thus, a permanent economic fund is created which enables the women to cope with even the severest difficulties.

> There's a good collection for those who have to stay at home without work. Each of us takes between 50 and

> 100 thousand lire out of our wages to pay the rent for those who have to stay at home.[9] This is the agreement among us, so the money serves to keep those who stay at home, food, everything they need for the home, shopping. There are ten of us, and at the moment only four of us are working. (Fatima)

Only a few women need to work in order to rent a flat for use by relatives and friends. In reality, the women who provide economically for the domestic expenses are precisely those who benefit least from them, because they live in the households where they work. But each of them, by paying a small sum every month to maintain the flat and the women living in it, implicitly invests in stable reciprocal relations. According to generalized and balanced reciprocity rules, the woman concerned can draw upon these relations if she is dismissed, or if she quits a job which she dislikes, or in any situation of crisis.[10]

These domestic units therefore act as rallying points for all recently-immigrated Somali women requiring accommodation and assistance as they settle into a foreign city and look for work. By following the links of international migration chains, the women arrive in Italian cities where they know that they will find a reception network consisting of close and distant relatives, as well as friends and acquaintances.[11] This network functions in the same way for all new arrivals: whether they have 100 or 2000 dollars—the currency most widely used for migrant journeys—the early period in Italy takes practically the same form for all of them.

> I kept myself among acquaintances and friends. I had $2000 with me. I met friends and my step-brother here; although he didn't help me very much, he was a support, a presence. After three months I went to live with the friends that I'd made. Being short of money wasn't a problem; for example the friend who did the shopping bought stuff for me as well. (Imaan)

> I came with a family who were friends of my uncle and who were leaving for Italy, then I came to Naples. There was a friend of mine living in Naples, so there

> were several reasons that brought me here. I spent some time with them, some with my friend, two months going around friends. (Yasmin)
>
> I had around $2000. I stayed with my cousin. I ate, slept, even school was free. There was a load of people, dozens of people coming and going.... For us giving presents or offering hospitality is nothing, it's something common to all Somalis. (Fahmo)
>
> I only had $100 but I knew that wherever I went there would be a Somali or a friend who certainly wouldn't say "you pay to eat," that's for sure. Even if I see a Somali that I don't know, I say "I've just arrived and I don't know where to go, I want somewhere to stay." Two girls will even sleep together in the same bed to help you until you find your clan, a job; they help you in any way, and then they say you have to look for something.
>
> They put me up until I found a job. For the month I stayed with them I ate, I slept. They told me: "Even this $100 we'll send to your family and you'll eat until you find work"; also the return ticket [i.e. the money reimbursed for the return ticket] they sent back. (Amina)

The migratory network thus formed over time enables an increasingly larger number of women to emigrate. More and more family groups in Somalia and neighboring countries acquire material guarantees for social reproduction by exporting female labor for employment in the niches of Italy's domestic and care work labor market opened up by the early immigrants. Recruitment takes place through the above-mentioned rallying networks, and it grows more intense with the closer the relations among the network's various members. Hence, whilst the first migrants were mainly the strongest and most experienced women, as the flow has increased the "selection" process has broadened, and women who would otherwise be considered unsuitable may be forced to emigrate. This is evidenced by the testimonies of Verdosa and Jima, women of an age inappropriate for work: Verdosa became the main family income-earner at a very young age; Jima is over fifty, and because she is in Italy, she is the "well-off" member of her large family group and therefore duty-bound to "help" it.

> I missed my mother, my brothers and sisters, but I had to stay because when I left my father had died when I was 11 years old. My mother was alone; there were six of us brothers and sisters, four boys and two girls, and I was the oldest. We're like that, at the age of 11 or 12 we begin to use our heads; we begin to keep the family. (Verdosa)

> When I arrived in 1992 I didn't feel good and I thought I would stay for 3 or 4 months and then go back to Somalia. My children in Finland phoned and told me not to go, there's a war on, stay there. So I began looking for work, which I found, and I help my family members who need it. There's my husband, who has another wife, and Halima is his daughter, and he's hungry and I help him; then there's my brother who has many children, they all need me, almost 20 people. For our religion you must always help. For us Somali Muslims, if someone is well-off they must help. (Jima)

It is in this manner, therefore, that the migratory network of the Somali women in Italy expands and strengthens. Each of the women maintains multiple exchange relations with her co-nationals and invests in a network of personal relationships which turns into an efficient mutual aid system in crises. There thus arises a pervasive and latent relational network which keeps those women who have achieved a certain degree of economic stability in contact with the many others on the margins of the productive system and suffering a general lack of means. These cross-linkages enable resources to circulate where a social and economic vacuum would otherwise exist, and they thus lay the material bases for the migratory process to continue.

Moreover, these social networks furnish protection and security for individual immigrant women, and they indirectly operate to the benefit of the extended families which depend on them. We know, in fact, that the demanding work that these women perform enables them to accumulate the resources necessary to remit substantial sums of money to their distant families. From this point of view, therefore, the networks constructed by the Somali women in Italy are the hubs of more complex circuits through which money earned in Italy—as elsewhere in the world—is sent to Somalia. The next section will not examine the numerous uses to which such money is put but will focus more specifically on how it sustains and drives the Somali diaspora on a global scale.[12]

STRONG TIES IN EMIGRATION: HOW DIASPORA IS SUSTAINED

The female migration chain which the Somali women follow is not restricted to movement between Somalia and Italy. Awareness that elsewhere in the world Somalis may be granted refugee status because of the enormous tragedy afflicting their country enlarges the map of possible destinations. This induces the immigrant women in Italy to work so that they can economically support further migrations by their relatives to the countries of North Europe and North America, where they can enjoy the benefits granted by welfare systems more generous than Italy's. Thus, looking beyond Italy on a broader global scale, one grasps the complexity of this migratory system founded on the differentiation of the productive and reproductive roles that the women occupy at different times and in different places:[13] They work in Italy so that their families elsewhere can survive – as shown by the stories of Yemma and Assia, who explain how they have ensured the well-being of their relatives, and supported broader and more complex projects for family mobility and reproduction.

In 1990 this cursed war exploded. Then my sister wrote a letter saying "help me." So with my other sister and the help of some friends, and after a year of sacrifices, we brought my sister to Italy. When I'd got her to Italy, I changed jobs because I couldn't manage on 300,000 lire a month. My parents relied on me because the bank didn't return the money and the shops had everything stolen. They were punished because the president kicked them out. They didn't have any power; indeed, their survival depended on us. So I and my other sister got together to help the family. There was also my brother, who was a shopkeeper, and then my little sister; everyone helped us, and I put everything into it. Treats, luxuries, all these you forget when your loved ones are at stake.... In the end they all came here. My little sister came here through friends. My brother came and he married a Somali girl here. Only one, his wife and four children we took to Cairo. But there were five in my brother's family and they expected us [they expected us to send them money]. We were five brothers and sisters here, two didn't work, only three of us worked. What we earned [went on] the rent for a flat, all for food and sending money there. So maybe you didn't go out so you wouldn't spend 2,000 lire, spending 2,000 lire was to take it away from the others, so we suffered greatly. We're not a family that's used to these things.

> I and my sisters were left, with my brother, who didn't work. I earned 8,000 lire and my sister 800,000 lire. We paid 1 million lire for rent, plus 100,000 for electricity and gas, 100,000 lire we sent back. I and my sister had steady work and we didn't sleep. At home were my little sister, my brother, and my sister-in-law, who was pregnant. Having a baby here was tough, because we couldn't afford clothes, the doctor. So my sister, who'd been working for two years, took her severance bonus in advance and went to Switzerland. Then I took mine, and my brother went with his wife. So we finally got some peace. There was only my little sister left, and then the wife of my brother in Cairo; luckily, life there is a bit less expensive, even if you give $100 they can manage for two months.
>
> Luckily, where my sister worked they took in my little sister, and we left the flat. So at least we could put something by. So when we got to 10 million lire, we sent my sister-in-law and my nephews from Cairo to Canada. My older brother had joined them in the meantime. Only that we had to send clothes because when they arrive there was no one, it was too cold. So we had some peace.... In Canada and Switzerland they fortunately accepted them as immigrants. Because when you arrive there, you go to the police office, immigration, and they sort you out, they give you somewhere to live. We got political

asylum, because we'd left destroyed families behind.... It cost around 5 or 6 thousand lire each, for documents and everything. (Yemma)

My father died in 1986, and then my little sister in 1987; she was 30 and left children.... Then the war broke out in Somalia. My mother telephoned and said: "Assia, there's a war on, don't come, just think about your brothers." One's a vet and he was in England, where the government had sent him to specialize, and he said "I've got to work as well," and he went to Saudi Arabia to look for work. He went there, and he worked there as a doctor. Then he met a girl, they got married and had two male children. Then there was some war in Saudi Arabia, they didn't earn anything, and he, the children and the wife came to Italy in 1992. I kept them, my brother and children, to eat, and family in Somalia. I put half of my wages aside for them, half here, half there, it ended like that. Then my brother said, "Assia, I can't stay here;" because he was rowing with his wife, and he said he wanted to go back to England. So I paid for the ticket and he went back to England. After a year I sent the wife and children as well, and then I took the children and we sent them to Somalia.

Another of my brothers, a younger one, went to Switzerland, got married, and he's got a family as well. I paid for the ticket from Somalia, and he's still in Switzerland. Then I brought out another sister, she's in Padua, on my father's side [step-sister] though, and she has twins. The husband left, and I can't keep them all. So I said it's better to pay his ticket and have him work for himself, and she'll look after the family. She's now in Padua and is doing well; she looks after her family, her mother and her children. I still keep my brothers, my father's children, step-brothers and sisters; we're of the same blood and I still keep them. We were four children of my mother, a female who's dead, two males, my mother's with the two girls and some other step-children; they all live together. So when I'm earning, I send something from my wages, $200 or $300 so they can eat for a month or so. Then I bought a truck, a little one, which they used when they left the city when the war

> broke out, or they also used for work, this little truck with room for so many people. All step-brothers and sisters who knew my mama and don't want their mama, because when they were born, the mother left. When my father divorced that woman, the children were left at home, and they all went to my mama, and my mama brought them up, because my mother is a wonderful woman, and these children stayed with my mother, and they all call her "mama," and my mother is also their mama. They can go to so many places, but they don't want to, they want to be here, where my mother is. (Assia)

The testimonies of Yemma and Assia eloquently demonstrate how the Somali women working in Italy do not simply send cash remittances to distant family members, but actively participate in the construction of a transnational community network which creates, supports, and strengthens further relations and exchanges. The accounts of the two women show that among Somalia, Switzerland and Saudi Arabia, Canada, Egypt, Britain and Italy, entire family groups in danger are moved to safe havens: mothers with small children are protected where the state offers them greater benefits, lone mothers are enabled to work and achieve independence, and young men are given the means with which to start businesses. Operating at the center of these networks are our female protagonists, who dispense money, make travel arrangements, and create the conditions for every member of their family group to occupy the positions most advantageous to them on a global scale.

The immigration of Somali women into Italy can thus be viewed as part of a collective and structured response with which domestic units and broad kinship groups diversify their sources of income and survival strategies. In other words, this is a diaspora organized by the members of kinship groups distinguished on the basis of gender and age in order to attain destinations selected according to the employment opportunities and social protections that they offer. Observing the pattern assumed by this web of transnational movements from Italy, we find that the women come to Italy to work, while their dependent men, women and family members go to the European and American countries whose welfare systems grant minimum protections such as lodging and economic subsistence. The possibilities for such movement depend closely on female tenacity and spirit of sacrifice. It is therefore this affective bond constraining the Somali women to a system of family loyalty and membership which obliges those who have achieved "advantageous" economic positions to support family members in difficulties, as Juma stated in the testimony quoted earlier. The female migration chain of Somali women in Italy replicates that of the family, and thus extends and strengthens through the forceful affirmation of values and goals centered on the obligation to maintain continuity with the group of origin; this is an obligation with which all the women comply by extreme commitment to work so that they can activate a complex system of cash remittances, but which obliges them to put the needs of their families before their own desires and projects.

THE WEIGHT OF CONTINUITY

We are now finally able to understand why the Somali settlements in Italy consist mainly of single women who are separated, widowed or, especially, unmarried.[14] These are women whose primary familial bonds are ascendant with their parents and lateral with their siblings. By emigrating, these young women comply with a strong obligation of familial continuity with their groups of origin. They do so not only because they assume the crucial task of producing income, and therefore enter into a permanent relation of economic dependence with their kin. Above all, given their endeavor to maximize economic utility through work, and given their particular occupational niche, where they are employed "day and night" as domestic workers, they indefinitely postpone marriage and motherhood, as well as any affective relationship not subordinate to their obligations of unity and continuity towards their original family group. It is this system of moral precepts and feelings of belonging, of kinship bonds and economic relations, which keeps so many young female immigrants from Somalia in a state of perpetual spinsterhood, as explained by Shukry, who had unhesitatingly excluded from her life all the men that she had known during seven years spent in Italy.

> I've had fiancés, but at the moment I haven't got one. Here I had a boyfriend in 1990, some months after I arrived, but unfortunately the story finished because our personalities

> were too different, certain things I couldn't stomach. For example, I'm a girl very attached to her family, and he said "Ah, you're so attached to your family, that thing...." So I said to him, "Look, you still haven't become part of my life – my life doesn't concern you." He said, "Do you want to help your family all your life?" So I said "As long as they need me, I'm ready for them here, because without my family I couldn't have grown up, I wouldn't have come into the world without my parents, right?" And he said, "Goodbye, if you think like that we can't go on." (Shukry)

These individual positions are confirmed in the community by a structure of social bonds which displays a split or segregation between male and female relations, as well as forms of social control which sanction female behavior deemed to be deviant. On the one hand, the few Somali men present, especially if they are young and without kinship ties, are systematically excluded from female circuits. This exclusion practice, which is motivated by the generally bad reputation of Somali males, is stable and enduring in the absence of matrimonial agreements among families. Ayaan and Fatma explain that it is the obscure origins of many of the Somali males, and their state of permanent unemployment, which make the women suspicious of them, and dubious that marriages between emigrants can be successful.[15]

> They met here and we didn't know what he did before coming here, what he was like, a vagrant, an idler who didn't want to work, if he was intelligent, the family he came from, we didn't know if he'd studied. So they met here, they fell in love, and they soon set up together, but they didn't get on. And then the Somali boys are like that because the girls keep them and they don't go to work. (Ayan)

> Then the men are real cheats, they're leopards; I was afraid at first, I never trusted men. For example, even if I'm married I always say "Watch out, eh!" I don't trust them, because first they say, "Ah, I love you, you're the only woman for me," then they soon change, especially

> here, because then they find another girl, who gives them money, because here Somali men don't work, so they look for a woman so that they can go to the cinema and the disco; they change like that, eh! immediately! I don't trust them at all! (Fatma)

Acting on the other hand is the pervasive system of social control exercised mainly by the more elderly women over the younger ones. This control is not directly connected with customary norms, even though these are stringent,[16] but pertains more specifically to the functioning of the migration chains, and hence with reproduction of broad kinship groups in the diaspora. Treated as deviant behaviors are reluctance to undertake domestic work, not supporting needy family members and having intimate relations with men, whether Somali or Italian—relations, that is, which may induce the women to relativize the paramount importance of the bonds with their families of origin. The sanction consists of the progressive exclusion of the woman from community networks made necessary by the overriding need to ensure the moral conformism on which the material solidarity among co-nationals is based. This is testified by the experience recounted by Jima, the elder of the group, and as explained by Awua and Fatima when asked about cases when disapproval, severity, and exclusion are necessary.

> There's war and famine in our country, so we have many children and mothers and fathers, and someone's father is dead and her mother's alive, someone's mother is dead and the father's alive, and there are families with eight children, twelve children; so the eldest daughter comes here, and when she's here she works and helps the family. When you see a girl who works and helps, she's a good girl, but there are lots who aren't good! So this girl, 15 or 16 years old, I brought her here; she's the oldest in the family, her mother died when she was young, 10 years old. So when she died I said to my cousin, "Aunt's dead, and the uncle, we've got to do something about this girl, we can bring her [abroad], learn to study, if she doesn't want to study, when she's a grown woman she can work with an elderly lady or in a family." So she went there

> until Saturday or Sunday, two days free, and those two days she stayed at home with us, so there was money to help the children, with seven people, they're all right, good girl! Then she can easily find work because she speaks well and is strong. It should always go like this! But she starts going there [to the square], meets someone who's no good, begins to have feelings, does that sort of thing, and if something comes up, what's to be done? She gets like an Italian and starts saying "fuck off," and she's on the street. And then the mother weeps in Somalia because she sent her here to be helped, and instead she's immediately found someone. Always this problem of meeting an Italian or even a Somali, and saying "I'm not going to work any more." She said "I'll find work with an elderly person and help," then she goes out in the evening, because she's free, and when you feel free who commands now? Nobody! So when it's too much, there's little you can do. (Jima)

> For example, a young Somali girl, who wants to have fun with Italian men, but also with Somali men, because it's the same if she does, right? And she doesn't want to work, and she doesn't want to respect religion, and she doesn't want to respect her upbringing, her education, I see her. Because someone who doesn't respect all this, someone who dresses like that [Western clothes], drinks what we can't drink, for example wine, right? For example if she wants to wear a miniskirt, they see her and watch her with men. (Awua)

> This one's 13 years old and little and she wants to go to the square and see older men, they steal her head away! Because a woman's really sensitive, but when they say, "But I'm in love!," then they lose their heads.... When I see a young girl going to the square or the disco, I feel really bad, but everyone has their freedom, and when a person goes their own way and doesn't return, you understand? Then it's useless. (Fatima)

The protracted spinsterhood of many Somali women, as well as the stringent forms of social control to which they are subject, is explained by the important material and moral responsibilities that they bear towards their distant families. But this is also the factor which, with the tension after continuity, profoundly compromises the sequential nature of family succession. For there is an evident missing link in this chain: the masculine link, and with it the possibility of regenerating the primary generational bond that gives rise to new family units.

The story of Caaliya, collected in 1994 in Milan by Nurrudin Farah, is a harsh indictment of the asymmetry in the gender distribution of the material and moral responsibilities aggravated by the diaspora. Caaliya, at the time just over 30 years old, and therefore the same age as most of our Somali informants, moved her seven brothers and sisters from Somalia to Italy, spending $300 for each of them, and then sent three of the sisters to Canada. Here follow the reflections which Nurrudin Farah based on Caaliya's narrative:

> When the women employed an arsenal of God-given talents, the men stood around, doing nothing, busy tracing their line to the antiquated system of clan values, a system which guaranteed them continued financial and moral support from better-off relations. Such imponderables as self-dignity, one's personal honor, being true to a societal ideal: these give way to the exigencies of the day. And like beggars showing off their amputated arms, the men pointed to the harsh conditions consequent on the civil war. The idea was for the families to hold together at all costs, that those who could must work, and those who could not must be supported.[17]

The experience of the Somali women interviewees relates to that of the many men and women forced by violence into exile and who ramify the founding connections of their continuity across the world. Their diaspora, connoted by nostalgia and the redefinition of time between past, present and future, compels them into repression and denial. It has been stressed that these processes of memory erasure and identity annulment may prepare individual and collective consciousnesses for the reception of new signals, which are then combined into positive identity changes. Hence, notwithstanding the harmful impact of coercion and exclusion, positive kinds of identity resistance emerge from the re-elaboration of life-histories, and from deterritorialized and transnational forms of individual and communitarian recognition. In the case of the Somali women in Italy, the social and symbolic capital with which they materialize and give meaning to their continuity in dispersion prevents them from achieving—creatively yet painfully—their own "iconoclastic" culture of the diaspora.[18] Multiple and systematic constraints act against them: the economic dependence of their families upon them, the morally restraining values of continuity of which they themselves are the bearers, the sentiments of nostalgia and loss with which they are burdened, and the social obligations of solidarity and reciprocal social control to which they are subject.

One may therefore appropriately ask to what extent a paradigm which extols the creative potential of the diaspora can accommodate contemporary experiences of dispersion due to war, violence and deportation. And although continuity is indeed a response to dispersion, it is only possible if group-bonding ties are strengthened in time and space. What, therefore, is the gender division of moral as well as material labor necessary to keep dispersed communities connected? The testimonies of the interviewed women are explicit on the matter: the entire Somali social network could extend from East to West, and it persists as long as the women are able to deploy symbols and social constraints and act as embodiments of their irrenounceable origins, the land from which they sprang, the natural sources of their prime life-resources. Thus, invested with the demanding role of the saviors of their families, they are prevented from translating the network of genealogical connections from the actual dimension to the symbolic one.[19] Committed as they are to the endless labor of re-locating and re-knitting pieces of kinship, they too often postpone a diverse awareness of their roles and their identity. Thus, the vanguard of complex systems of mobility, they weave bonds and create connections with patience and dedication, with only a vague notion of how their life-courses will unfold. This inevitably calls to mind the archetypal figure of Penelope as she waits and weaves at her loom.

Notes

1. Italy is one country that makes the most of foreign labor to make up for shortfalls in the supply of domestic workers. Traditionally characterized by a welfare system based on the social networks of households, Italy now has a rapidly aging population, and in recent years it has been structurally unable to find the native-born human resources with which to cope with the increasing demand for care advanced by families. These very briefly-outlined processes have encouraged the use of foreign women, who are employed mainly as domestic care workers co-domiciled with non self-sufficient persons. However, employment conditions differ greatly according to the provenance of the women concerned. The care labor market is markedly segmented, and placement in jobs which differ by pay, contract and working conditions is regulated at various levels: by national policies (Andall, J. (2000). *Gender, migration and domestic service. The politics of black women in Italy*. Aldershot: Ashgate.), by forms of "covert racism" (Anderson, B. (2000). *Doing the dirty work? The global politics of domestic labor*. London: Zed Books), and also by the direct mediation by the so-called Catholic "private-social sector," which effectively controls and orients the match between labor supply and demand (Scrinzi, F. (2004). Professioniste della tradizione. Le donne migranti nel mercato del lavoro domestico. *Polis,* 1, 107-136). The allocation of work in this hierarchical occupational system is therefore discriminatory, and it favors the "ethnic-based" formation of employment niches, the least advantageous of which are occupied by—black and Muslim—Somali women.
2. In 2004 there were fewer than 5000 Somalis in Italy, and 65% of them were women. They formed one of the smallest immigrant communities in Italy (representing just 0.3% of the total immigrant population).
3. For a reconstruction of the Somali presence in Italy at the time, compared with other immigrant groups, see Picciolini A. (1992). I Somali. In G. Mottura (Ed.), *L'Arcipelago immigrazione: caratteristiche e modelli migratori dei lavoratori stranieri in Italia* (pp. 301-321). Roma: Ediesse. For a long-term survey of immigration into Italy see Colombo A., Sciortino G. (2004). *Gli immigrati in Italia.* Bologna: Il Mulino. For comparative analysis of the Italian migratory system which considers both emigration and immigration see Pugliese, E. (2002). *L'Italia tra migrazioni internazionali e migrazioni interne.* Bologna: Il Mulino.

4. Del Boca, A. (1993). *Una sconfitta dell'intelligenza. Italia Somalia.* Roma: Laterza.
5. Consider the severe criticisms made of "cooperation for development" by Del Boca, A. (1993). *Una sconfitta dell'intelligenza. Italia Somalia.* Roma: Laterza. p. 44. Besides describing the grandiose and costly project for the Mogadishu carbamide factory and its failure, Del Boca recalls "other incredible undertakings, like open-sea fishing projects which swallowed up tens of billions [of lire] and then failed; the creation of the Somali Pharmaceutical Institute which twice had to be refinanced, and which produced high-cost medicines that only Italy purchased and then donated to other developing countries; or the construction of dozens of fiberglass silos which melted in the sun."
6. Decimo, F. (1996). Reti di solidarietà e strategie economiche di donne somale immigrate a Napoli. *Studi Emigrazioni - Etudes Migrations,* 123, 473-495.

   Decimo, F. (1998). Living the city: The urban integration of Somali women in Naples. In V. Ferreira, T. Tavares, & S. Portugal (Eds.), *Shifting bonds, shifting bounds. Women, mobility and citizenship in Europe* (pp. 253-259). Oireas: Celta Editora.

   Decimo, F. (2005a). Quando emigrano le donne. Percorsi e reti femminili della mobilità transnazionale. Bologna: il Mulino.

   Decimo, F. (2005b). Donne di una diaspora. Le migranti somale in Italia tra vincoli di continuità e identità traslate. *Africa e Orienti*, 96-109.
7. Epstein, A. L. (1961). The network and the urban social organization. *The Rhodes-Livingstone Journal,* 29, 29-72.

   Mitchell, J. C. (1973). Networks, norms and institutions. In J. Boissevain and J. C. Mitchell (Eds.), *Network analysis: Studies in human interaction* (pp. 15-35). The Hague, Paris: Mouton.

   Bertaux, D. (1998). *Les récits de vie.* Paris: Nathan.
8. A great deal has been written on the influence of social networks on the evolution of the migratory process: see among others Boyd, M. (1989). Family and personal networks in international migration: Recent development and new agendas. *International Migration Review,* 23, 638-70.

   Massey, D.S. (1990). Social structure, household strategies, and the cumulative causation of migration. *Population Index,* 56, 3-26.

   Tilly, C. (1990). Transplanted networks. In V. Yans-McLaughlin (Ed.), *Immigration reconsidered. History, sociology and politics* (pp. 79-95). New York & Oxford: Oxford University Press.

Faist, T. (1997). The crucial Meso-level. In T. Hammar, G. Brochmann, K. Tamas & T. Faist (Eds.), *International migration, immobility and development. Multidisciplinary perspectives* (pp. 187-218). New York & Oxford: Berg.

9. In the 1990s, the Italian currency was still the lira: at the time 2,000 lire was roughly equal to 1 euro.
10. See Sahlins, M. (1972). *Stone Age Economics*. Chicago: Aldine.
11. The cities of first arrival are usually central-southern ones, mainly Rome and Naples, where the Somali communities are more numerous, longer-established, and where it is easier to find hospitality. Further movements northwards (to Florence, Bologna, and Milan) are frequent owing to better employment opportunities.
12. On the current importance of remittances for the Somali economy, and for Mogadishu in particular, see Marchal, R. (1999). Mogadiscio tra rovine e globalizzazione. *Africa e Orienti,* 2, 20-30.
13. For analysis of migration in light of the reorganization of productive and reproductive roles typically localized within particular households see Kearney M. (1986). From the invisible hand to the visible feet: Anthropological studies of migration and development. *Annual Review of Anthropology*, 15, 331-61. Stark, O. (1991). The migration of labor. Cambridge, MA: Basil Blackwell. Bjerén, G. (1997). Gender and reproduction. In T. Hammar, G. Brochmann, K.Tamas, and T. Faist (Eds.), *International migration, immobility and development. Multidisciplinary perspectives* (pp. 219-246). Oxford & New York: Berg.
14. It should be pointed out at this stage of the analysis that the feminization of the Somali community is a feature peculiar to Italy. Considering OECD (2004) data on some of the European destination countries for the Somali diaspora, one finds that contrary to the case of Italy, the female and male components are exactly the same in Finland, Denmark, Norway, Sweden, Britain and Holland. OECD, Sopemi (2004). *Trends in international migration. Continuous reporting system on migration*. Paris: OECD Publication Service.
15. In effect, even when marriage seems possible, it seems that still operating today are the elements of conjugal instability in traditional Somali society described by Lewis, I. M. (1962). *Marriage and the family in Northern Somaliland*. Uganda, Kampala: East African Institute of Social Research. These elements of instability, however, are no longer framed within traditional "kinship policies" and they assume a decidedly more critical significance. See Griffiths, D. J. (2002). Somali and Kurdish refugees in London. New identities in the Diaspora. Alder-

shot: Ashgate. pp. 108-9, whose research on Somali immigrants in London showed the high incidence of single motherhood and the connected risks of social exclusion.

16. On the force of appeals to tradition as a form of social control over young Somali female immigrants in London. See El-Solh, C. (1993). Be true to your culture: gender tensions among Somali Muslims in Britain. *Immigrants and Minorities,* 4, 539-552. p. 33.
17. Farah, N. (2000). Yesterday, tomorrow. Voices from the Somali diaspora. London & New York: Cassel. p. 72.
18. Cohen, R. (1995). Rethinking 'Babylon': Iconoclastic conceptions of the diasporic experience. *New Community*, 1, 5-18.
19. Clifford, J. (1994). Diasporas. *Cultural Anthropology*, 3, 302-338.

Chapter 5

DIASPORIC AUTHENTICITY: CONNECTING GENES AND BUILDING FAMILIES THROUGH DNA-TESTING IN SOMALI FAMILY REUNIFICATION IN FINLAND

Petri Hautaniemi

INTRODUCTION

According to Finnish Immigration Law, a refugee or a person who has a residence permit in Finland has the legal right, at least officially, to have his/her family reunited. However, in the wake of the recent tightening of asylum policies in Europe, the cultural meaning and authenticity of claimed family relations have become controversial. The core of the controversy is derived from the different ways in which Finnish authorities and Somali immigrants understand who is and who is not a family member.

Within Finnish juridical practices, the idea of family and kinship ties does not mirror the very family practices and the ways in which people relate themselves in their everyday lives. The Finnish traditional agrarian and Lutheran kinship practices are continuously challenged by new family formations, such as single sex unions, divorces and remarriages and liberal practices within new reproductive technologies. There is a continuous tension between public and private law spheres as they tend to legitimate the significance of blood or social relatedness differently. However, despite the recent changes and varying dichotomization of the nature and culture within juridical and cultural kinship practices, there has been relatively uniform cultural understanding of "a household" as a core metaphor for real family. This has not only economical implications, but also tends to contribute to the idea of a physical and mentally constructed setting for a core kinship unit: home. The household also tends to reduce the number of family members to a maximum of two adults or spouses parenting a number of children, descending from (or depending on through increasing adoptions) either or both of them. Three or more generational families have become rare. Polygamous marriages are forbidden regardless of sexual orientations. The family and household within a complex state system with extremely regulated taxation and inheritance system and modern individualized lifestyles are strictly defined arenas for relatedness and reproduction.

What delimits family boundaries within the Somali context, however, is radically different from those employed in Finland or in the West in general. In Somalia, and among Somali immigrants in Finland, family is defined in much more broader terms. Being a part of a wide kinship network, a person's kinship identity does not predominantly exclude multigenerational housing or intimate reciprocal ties between many parents and dependant children. Similarly, the physical and mental idea of home may have a different connotation. There has been an interest within Somali kinship studies to evaluate the impact of nomadic traditions in a strong patrilineal kinship system. This system regulates affiliation not only between individuals but also among larger kin groups called clans. Compared with the strong state centered agricultural traditions in the Lutheran North Europe, the significance of family and complex kinship networks is much more crucial in Somalia. The Somali family provides the frame for a welfare system very different from the state run system in Finland. The functions of these Somali welfare systems were tragically proven in the political upheavals and following mass displacement in the Horn of Africa in the late 20th century. Both near and distant family ties were activated in wide networks of trust and reciprocity, very differently from the practices of the modern Western nuclear households.

The different ways in which the two societies understand the cultural meaning of family membership brings forth issues pertaining to the authenticity of claimed family relations for purposes of reunification, at least, in the eyes of Finnish immigration authorities. As such, the central concern, as far as Finnish immigration officers are concerned, becomes one of determining who is qualified as a true member in terms of the Finnish understanding of family relations. It is within this context that Finnish immigration authorities introduced DNA testing as a way to scientifically determine the boundary of family belonging and membership. Available data indicate, however, the use of this biotechnology has been successful neither in making kinship and family relations technologically apparent, nor in resolving immigration backlogs. However, authorities have gained another significant tool in making sense of cultural family differences, simultaneously making these indifferent.

The Finnish Directorate of Immigration practices DNA testing if documentation of family ties based on biological kinship, is in their view, insufficient. A requirement is that it is possible to provide significant proof of the kinship by means of a DNA test. The Directorate of Immigration can allow a DNA test if there is no documentation to prove identity and/or kinship, or if the available documentation is not reliable and interviews with the family members do not provide certainty of biological kinship. The DNA test is paid for from State funds and is principally voluntary, but rejection of testing from the applicant's side may lead to denial of the right of family reunification. The DNA test can be performed if the person to be tested has, of his/her own free will, provided a written consent based on the information received. The test results are not used for any purpose other than establishing the existence of the family ties required for granting a residence permit in cases where the person tested has requested this.[1]

BACKGROUND: THE SOMALI CASE AND FAMILY REUNIFICATION

My interest in family reunification in general, and DNA testing in particular, lies in my ongoing research among young Somali men in Finland. My ethnographic research began in 1996 when I first met a group of young Somali boys who had come to Finland around 1994 and went to Finnish schools in the suburb of Helsinki. Most of the children came to Finland at an early age and spoke fluent Finnish by the time I met them. Ever since I have hung around with them in schools, youth clubs, streets and cafés, and in the process gotten to know approximately 20 young men who are now in their early 30s.

My general interest in this longitude research is the experiences of coming of age in highly dispersed settings, not only in the vein of a local host country, but also culturally and transnationally. The matter at hand, namely DNA testing, touches upon this specific research question in the most profound way. Growing up, after all, is not only a question of coming of age. It is a social process in which relationships such as kinship ties are constituted, experienced, and contested. They are powerful relations for individual and social identifications.[2] DNA testing may both symbolically and physically violate this social process of intimate identifications and personal integrity.

In the early 1990s when the situation in Somalia escalated to an increasingly violent civil war Finland received its first large number of Somali asylum applications. During this time, approximately 3,000 Somalis arrived in Finland and received residence permits.[3] Many of these refugees came to Finland without family members, and only afterwards, with the help of the family unification process, could they receive their relatives in Finland. A great number of these family applicants in Finland were children who had come with persons other than their own parents, officially called "unaccompanied minors." However, only a few of my young Somali acquaintances were living in Helsinki without any relatives. Most of them had at least someone to live with, usually an aunt or an uncle and their families. Of course, some had their own parents too, however, most often only a mother.

Finnish civil servants were busy solving problems such as missing identity documents.[4] Each asylum seeker was given a Finnish personal code based on interviews. This turned out later to be an issue of contest.[5] Namely, some of the boys provided authorities with names other than their given names, (usually one which fit the relatives with whom they were living), when applying for asylum. Also the time and place of birth was often ambiguous. After a few years in Finland, some of the boys changed their minds and applied for family reunification for their "own" parents. Reasons for this were many. Some of them were not satisfied with their new homes and they wanted to move out to the city run child custody organizations, the so called Home of Children. Some were simply missing their mothers, and felt miserable of the bad news they were hearing about the poor living conditions of their families in the Horn of Africa. At the time the boys were about 10 to 13 years old. I also know of cases in which the "official" parents no longer wanted to be responsible for their children and sent one or two children to the Finnish authorities. In some cases, some Somali children were also sent abroad to live in Africa or other places in Europe.

Authorities in the Directorate of Immigration reacted with tightening policies. It became less likely to receive family members in Finland through reunification, as the decisions of applications were commonly negative. This caused confusion not only among the boys, (and still does), but also among the civil servants and individuals in charge of integration issues of immigrants at the grassroots level. On the one hand, they found the situation of young Somali children alarming, but on the other, they could not do anything for them. This was difficult as they were supposed to conduct and implement practical social policy in the name of "the benefits of children." After rounds of discussions among diverse authorities, a new project was launched: a pilot project of DNA testing. Over 300 applicants of family reunification were asked to voluntarily give a blood sample in order to show whether the information of proposed kinship ties was accurate. This entire sample of 300 applicants had already received negative decisions.

For the majority of applicants who gave the blood sample DNA testing gave them a positive decision. The Directorate of Immigration had to change their decisions, as the blood ties were now confirmed. However, many applicants never took the tests for unknown reasons. Some probably did not take part in DNA testing because they did not have blood ties with the persons they wanted to sponsor while others may have not known where their families were.[6]

THE LAW OF DNA INVESTIGATION

In the beginning of 2000, and after the pilot project, a new law was passed in Finland. This law made it possible for state authorities, on a more regular basis, use DNA testing to discover the authenticity of claimed family relations among immigrants, particularly Somalis. The law stated that in cases in which an asylum seeker cannot in any other way prove the existence of "real" family ties, the authorities may ask her/him to prove it with the help of the DNA test. This biotechnology strictly confined the meaning of family membership to those who are biologically related in the first grade. Two immigrant groups were particularly mentioned in the new law, Somalis and Kurds from Iraq; Somalis were the main target of the law for they often lacked valid documentation to prove "real" family ties.

What the biotechnological definition of family membership did not account for, however, was the fact that kinship relationships were more complicated than a scientifically based simple blood relation in the first grade. The life stories of the boys I worked with are particularly illustrative of this dilemma in that in the cultural context, they are all related in various ways and their blood relatedness is of varying and contextual significance. This is, in fact, common knowledge for anthropologists, albeit historically contested.[7] Consequently, the law raises many questions that are relevant not only for Somali asylum seekers and refugees, but also for the state with specific interests in the wellbeing of its legal members and citizens in a globalized and transnational context. I argue that the very process of making certain kinship ties transparent and legally more valid implies those cultural and political boundaries and categories, in which a welfare state reproduces itself in time, space and ideas cannot be maintained without an understanding of the meaning of family relatedness from multiple and global perspectives. The blood and the family are of a strong symbolic relevance in the social reproduction in which the state also categorizes and arranges groups of people, sexes and age of people in its hierarchical order.[8] For example in the Finnish constitution the family is represented as "a cornerstone" of society. However, what constitutes a real family, or the meaning of family, is continuously debated and defined by lawyers, politicians and various experts of NGOs. Welfare and migration policies very often support these restrictions as family and relatedness understood narrowly make them also more "manageable" or easier objects to be governed. Family as a core unit in society is also a matter of values and sentiments evoking emotions and agency among people.

Moreover, to make kinship and blood related family ties technologically transparent for control purposes, does not only give priority to the state actors to define who is and who is not a legitimate refugee, but it also may reveal biological ties which are not necessarily articulated as kin relation from before. It is relatively common within parental testing that the genetic relation does not correlate with the social and psychological relatedness between the father and child, for example. One important question is whether DNA testing and its implementation actually constitutes such kinship ties, which never would otherwise come into being. Also, people may start reproducing blood ties in the long run in order to manage family mobility transnationally.

Mohamed, one of the boys I have known since 1996, told me about his struggle with authorities. His sister and her daughter were expecting the father and the husband to arrive in Finland from the Horn of Africa. They were all involved in the DNA procedure, but had to wait for another year. Mohamed's sister became depressed and Mohamed was just exhausted, helping her day and night. I was surprised that the father had never visited Finland, but still the sister had been living there longer than the age of her daughter. I realized I was reckoning the time of the conception and comparing it to the length of the separation from the father. Mohamed did not go into the details, but made me understand that his sister had visited her husband in Africa. She got pregnant and returned to Finland. After this she applied once more for family reunification.

Afterwards I also kept thinking about potential new ways to manage global kinship and its modes of reproduction, in which for example sperm can be trafficked over distances in order to help people moving from one place to another. After all conception does not require that two persons are present personally. New reproductive technologies have made it possible to make babies and new human beings without sexual intercourse between a man and a woman. Also looking from the transnational biopolitical point of view reproductive substances are increasingly contested commodities.[9] Watching the newly launched promotion video on DNA testing by the authorities at home, I saw how carefully a civil servant from the Directorate of Immigration packed the blood samples in Nairobi and returned to Finland guarded by a police officer. I wondered whether other bodily substances, such as sperm or eggs were on the same plane without the knowledge of these authorities. Transnational connections may operate in many ways and take counterproductive forms. As the transnational governance of kinship practices develops in one direction, paradoxically the very regulative action may produce new kinship practices.

THE REGIMES OF TRUTH

The DNA investigation consists of three parts: the blood sample, the laboratory test, and the result. I interviewed a forensic expert at one of the local universities who helped me understand the process of DNA testing. He told me that with the help of the DNA paternity test one might come to "the truth" as near as possible, but not one hundred percent. The task of a DNA test is to answer a simple question with a simple answer: How probable is it that this woman is mother of this child? It is then the legal question, whether the probability (normally 99. 99% in a positive case) is enough for the officially acknowledged first grade biological tie.

I also interviewed a civil servant in the Directorate of Immigration who works as an important node in the network of involved authorities. She told me that the DNA testing is the only reliable way to find out the "truth" about family members, because, as sad as it may be, people (asylum seekers) do not always speak the truth. For her the most significant goal in the DNA investigation is that the "real" family can be reunited and that children can live with the "parents of their own." However, she added that children with no biological ties might be united with their parents, if there is evidence that they had lived with them as their children. She did not specify the procedure in these cases. Surprisingly blood relation in itself does not guarantee entrance to Finland. It is only extra evidence on the table when the final decision for family reunification is made. However, the blood relatedness weighs most, as there is no other "way to know the truth."

As an educated anthropologist this civil servant has a good understanding of the nature of Somali kinship systems.[10] On the walls of her office are maps of Somali regions, painted with different colors and labeled with names of clans and sub clans. Every applicant, she showed me, has a file, which includes the family history based on an interview. She also draws a family tree on the basis of this information. This take lots of time and can be very complicated, "not least because it is not always a question of father-mother-child relation, but there might also be living children from other marriages and other relatives in families," she says. She then proved to me how difficult her job is by demonstrating how thick one file can physically be.

The process is as follows: after the civil servant has considered the "case," she may ask for extra evidence for existing family ties by asking the applicant and related persons to go to the police for an extra interview in Finland. Relatives in Africa have to go to the embassy for similar interviews in Africa at a specific time and date. The civil servant first compares this "qualitative" data based on the interviews. If this comparison gives certain results, the applicant is asked to give a blood sample. At a specific time on the date of the test the civil servant travels to Africa accompanied by a police officer. The local doctor in Africa takes the blood sample of the relatives, and the civil servant with the help of the police and the staff at the embassy does all the article work. They travel back to Finland and the local laboratory tests the blood samples. Free consent of the applicants is approved by their signature and also fingerprints. "Just to make it sure," she adds. The Finnish authorities do take fingerprints from every asylum seeker, including children. One reason is that many asylum seekers are analphabetic. It is of course relevant to ask how they can sign with a fingerprint if they do not know what they sign. The other reason is that the police are gathering a Pan-European archive based on fingerprints of asylum seekers who enter the European Union.

FAMILIES AND BIOLOGICAL INFORMATION

Understanding family relations at the intersection of civil war and globalised exile is a complicated matter, one that can create a challenge to an anthropologist both methodologically and conceptually. This conceptual and methodological complication occurs because many Somali families live in diasporas and form a kind of transnational, open-ended network. We do not talk of any static and bounded entity of a family type in this context.[11] Actually, the case is the same in the Finnish cultural context. Half of the marriages in Finland end in divorce. It is not uncommon for families to consist of unmarried couples with common children and children from previous unions. Adoption, often of a transnational character, is also a well-known practice in many Finnish families. Again, in Somalia divorces are common. Polygamy and child fostering are common and in families, there can live many non-biological children as well.[12]

Consequently, I would argue in this very general comparative context, that the preoccupation of the Finnish authorities with making biological ties transparent has less to do with actual family lifestyles, than with specific ideas of significant social units in society, and their wish to control them. However, this is not to say that DNA testing would not have any effects on the families and their members. On the contrary, genetic information constructed through modern biotechnology may have various effects.[13] Firstly, DNA testing may produce or question significant information concerning a person's identity. Secondly, it may also touch upon relational networks and a person's sense of belonging to them. This network may change as a result of biological information. Thirdly, genetic relations or lack of them may take away other relations while constructing new ones. Relations within families and between individuals and families may become contested as new information might in addition to personal belonging deal with property, inheritance and subsistence, or obligations and entitlements to these.

The asylum seeker is not tested without his/her informed consent. This is relative, though, as refusing the test automatically leads a negative family reunification decision by the authorities. In a statement from the Ministry of Justice, the person in case is obligated to make his/her own decision regarding to participate in DNA testing when there is no other way to confirm his/her family relations.[14] However, their "own" decision appears ambiguous if we acknowledge that the produced genetic information affects a wider network of people than solely the asylum seeker.

It appears that the law has come into being in the context of disagreement. It may then be analysed as a process in which disagreement arises, and an examination of how it is controlled and in which forums it is handled.[15] The DNA law at hand may then be looked upon as a disagreement of "who is the real family member." In the law, it is explicitly stated that "it is necessary in the name of the benefits of a child that a child through the family reunification comes to its 'real parents.'"

In the present historical context in which the DNA tests are made there are a number of sensitive groups and persons, whose presence may contest this current constitution of biological information. The disagreement of who is the "real" family member questions the correlation between genetic relatedness and the benefits of a child. This relation is evoked and presented in many occasions, (such as in Finnish debates on the law of new reproductive technology and the human genome project),[16] as "cultural fact."[17] However, we do not really know how those who lack this relation interpret it, but still are kinned.[18] In Finland at least adopted children, the Finnish "war children" during the Second World War, the children of mothers raped in wartime, donor inseminated children and children growing up in other than heterosexual unions, may identify their relatedness in a more complex way. Many other people would probably do so as well. We do not know for sure who would like to reject receiving this kind of genetic information. How many would like not to know? Finally, who can choose?

I have been relating these kinds of questions to my ongoing research among a group of young Somali boys. I would argue that for many of them the knowledge that they are not biologically descended from their father would change their lives. In an anthropological discourse, the Somali communities are still strongly patrilineal. However, the potential effects of produced genetic information have not been major issues for the authorities involved in DNA testing. The effects and social consequences are obscure for them all. The experts and state authorities cannot foresee and control the social future after they have produced the information. They may, and they do, aim to be careful and they also try to control asylum seekers′ right to know the test result. The civil servant in the Directorate of Immigration office said to me during the interview, that asylum seekers who are involved in DNA investigation might not at all receive the results from the testing itself. They only receive the decision of family reunification. Only with the help of a lawyer may an asylum seeker come to know the DNA result. Thus, in many cases, the authorities may know the genetic kinship, whereas the asylum seeker only assumes it.

In addition to the unpredictability of social consequences due to DNA-related information, the implementation of biotechnology in itself and in this context may affect social and cultural life in many ways. DNA testing brings with it the potential of a profound new shift in our conceptualization of family, gender relations, and parenthood.[19] The consequences may well be more far-reaching than we expect. I have already mentioned how the DNA law and related technology may constitute new kinship ties. The example of Mohamed's sister serves as my empirical example for this.

CONTESTED TIES

The new DNA law has made it possible for many Somalis to receive their families in Finland. This has been the only way to prove that their family ties are "true." Their blood speaks louder than their words. I have so far recognised the role of biological information and its authority in the context of Finnish immigration practices. As I implied before, biology does not automatically guarantee entrance into the country. Civil servants also verify ties by interviewing and comparing life histories with the help of family trees to determine whether genetic ties also form a social family tie. This verification is significant in the cases of adoption or fostering. Polygamy also makes the situation complicated for authorities. Finnish law forbids polygamy. In Somali families, however, it is not uncommon to be related to several mothers through a father's other wives. The civil servant I interviewed said to me that in these cases, it is not enough to have a biological link; applicants have to show that they lived "under the same roof" for a significant period of time. She continues that a father, who has four wives and applies to receive his children from all marriages to Finland, has to show that he has lived a "real family life" with all of these children. Nonetheless, only one wife is accepted to enter Finland through family reunification.

The case of DNA is rewarding example that illustrates how the states are far from diminishing their power in this time of globalisation. Refugees are commonly treated as a threat to national borders. Different kinds of policies try to govern the mobility of non-citizens and through these refugees become liminal categories of people who do not fit into the national order of things.[20] The order of kinship and family is of particular interest here, and the acts of governance by the authorities may be interpreted as experts of this order.

This order is part of the global bio-politics, where diverse subjectivities are included or excluded to shifting spaces in the vein of body. Fassin calls this "bio political othering"; the legal categorisation of immigrants in France is increasingly done because of mental or physical health, and the diagnostics of these.[21] In this chapter, however, I would also like to highlight the very complex idea of relatedness and welfare bureaucracies. The relationship between law, kinship and emotions are in a constructive relation. The law is itself a crucial force that shapes "emotional atmosphere." The law does not only complicate kin relations, but indeed structures powers of emotion by evoking "desires and strategies that work to skirt and subvert law, as well as carry out its design."[22] In this chapter, such emotion and strategy is a structuring notion that may be found intertwined in law, and technology, and their implementation.

Notes

1. See http://www.uvi.fi
2. Toren, C. (2002). Comparison and ontogeny. In A. Gingrich & R. G. Fox (Eds.), *Anthropology, by Comparison* (pp. 186-203). London: Routledge.
3. Compared to Sweden, Finland received only 3,170 asylum application to Sweden's 16,300. See UNCHR statistics 31.5.2002: Number of Asylum applications in 30 industrial countries 1992-2001.
4. At least the police, social worker, medical worker and the civil servant in the minister of interior are involved in this. In addition staff in the Finnish consulates in the "sending" region does play a role in the process.
5. The personal identification code is so self evident for the Finnish welfare society and for the citizens' perception of the self, that its existence is only seldom questioned. Indeed, it is not very flexible in any sense, least in the cases of change. All welfare benefits, employment, rights and obligations to the society are governed with the personal code. Normally people carry one and the same code from their birth to death.
6. None of the boys were involved in this pilot testing. Their applications apparently stood in the waiting line. Slowly, but surely, many of

them received positive decisions. I could not follow this very clearly, because the boys were not eager to tell about the family reunification in the presence of others. In more personal occasions they usually told much more, but also asked constantly for my help to speed up whatever processes regarding to various authorities.

7. Stone, L. (Ed.). (2002). *New directions in anthropological kinship: Theoretical implications*. New York: Rowman & Littlefield Publishers.

   Carsten, J. (Ed.). (2000). *Cultures of relatedness: New approaches to the study of kinship*. Cambridge: Cambridge University Press.

   Schneider, D. M. (1987). *A critique of the study of kinship*. Ann Arbor: University of Michigan Press.

8. Herzfeld, M. 1997. Anthropology and the politics of significance. *Social Analysis*, 41(3), 107-137.

9. Radin, J. M. (2001). *Contested commodities: The trouble with trade in sex, children, body parts, and other things.* Cambridge: Harvard University Press.

10. It is interesting how anthropological knowledge on Somali kinship from the 1960s is used mechanically in this context. I suppose she relies, at least indirectly, on the works of I.M. Lewis.

11. Bryceson, D., & Vuorela, U. (Eds.). (2002). *Transnational families in Europe: Global networks and new frontiers*. London: Berg.

12. Helander, B. (1991). The Somali Family. In K. Barcik, & S. Normark (Eds.), *Somalia: A Historical, Cultural and Political Analysis* (pp.17-28). Conference Report 1. Uppsala, Sweden: Life & Peace Institute.

13. Strathern, M. (1999). *Property, substance and effect: Anthropological essays on persons and things*. London: The Athlone Press.

14. OML 6.8.1999.

15. Moore, S. F. (1987). Explaining the present: Theoretical dilemmas in processual ethnography. *American Ethnologist* 14, 727-736.

16. See also Berglund, E. (2003). Finland as Information Society: An anthropological critique. *Suomen Antropologi* 4, 2-16. This is an insightful discussion on modern technology and its contemporary history in and outside of Finland.

17. Franklin, S, & Ragoné, H. (Eds.). (1998). *Reproducing reproduction: Kinship, power, and technological innovation*. Philadelphia: University of Pennsylvania Press.

18. Howell, S. (2002). Self-conscious kinship: Some contested values in Norwegian transnational adoption. In S. Franklin & S. McKinnon

(Eds.), *Relative values: Reconfiguring kinship studies* (pp. 203-223). Durham: Duke University Press.

19. Fonseca, C. (2002). *DNA, choice, and destiny in the contemporary Brazilian family*. Paper presented at the 7th EASA conference, Copenhagen.
20. Malkki, L. (1995). *Purity and exile: Violence, memory, and national cosmology among Hutu refugees in Tanzania*. Chicago: University of Chicago Press. p. 8.
21. Fassin, D. (2001). The Biopolitcs of otherness: Undocumented foreigners and racial discrimination in French public debate. *Anthropology Today* 17(1), 3-7.
22. Yanagasiko, S. (2002). Patriarchal desire: Law and sentiments of succession in Italian capitalist families. In J. de Pina-Cabral & A. P. de Lima (Eds.), *Elites: Choice, leadership and succession* (pp. 53-72). Oxford & New York: Berg.

Chapter 6

MODERNITY MEETS CLAN: CULTURAL INTIMACY IN THE SOMALI DIASPORA

Stephanie R. Bjork

INTRODUCTION

Studies of Somali kinship have predominated ethnographic research in Somalia.[1] Since the 1970s and 1980s, however, kinship studies declined in anthropology and Somali studies. At that time, anthropologists considered kinship theory to be rigid, algebraic, and constrained by structural-functionalism. The segmentary lineage system was challenged widely.[2] Moreover, Somalis and Somali scholars tend to claim that clan is no longer relevant. Although I disagree with traditional approaches to clan, I agree with I. M. Lewis'--the prolific scholar of Somali kinship--contention that Somalis can use clan in modern ways.[3]

In this chapter, I utilize a practice approach to clan. What looks like hard structure is achieved through practices on the ground. By focusing on the everyday social practice of *telling*, we see Somalis' seemingly habitual efforts to cultivate clan networks.[4] Telling opens up the potential for individuals to access clan networks. Once an individual legitimizes her or his clan through telling and is successful at having fellow clan members recognize that claim, the individual is in a position to build clan-based social capital. The usefulness of clan is what makes telling and other seemingly habitual everyday practices become a durable pattern that resembles structure--over time and as the result of constant effort.

The primary data are drawn from ethnographic field research in the Helsinki metropolitan area carried out from 2003-2004.[5] This study is based on 186 surveys and informal interviews, in-depth interviews, and participant-observation.[6] Although I situate my fieldwork in Finland, telling is a practice that spans the global Somali diaspora.[7]

THINGS THAT MAKE UNPROGESS

As Somalis migrate to the West, they do not readily acknowledge to outsiders that clan is ever-present in their daily lives even though Somalis understand this to be the case. Somalis who live abroad are embarrassed by clan. Western media coverage of the Somali conflict, coupled with the prominence of *Black Hawk Down*, a 2001 Hollywood film, led the international community to associate Somalis with warlords, clans, and violence.[8] And Somalis themselves blame clannism as the cause of the war and continued civil unrest in Somalia. Moreover, clans seem antiquated in the lives of diasporic Somalis abroad as the following quote from an in-depth interview reveals:

> Author: If I ask Somalis about tribe (Somalis use clan and tribe interchangeably), they tell me that they are against it; but when I am with them, they talk about it all the time and question the tribal affiliation of others. Why?
>
> Farah: Tribe was a primitive system used by people in the countryside. Tribes fought for land and water. Tribe was not used by educated people living in cities. People from different tribes were friends, lived together in neighborhoods, and had business together. Tribe is one of those things that make unprogress. You have to know other people and who they are. Are they a good person? Tribe is only to recognize each other; but in this world now, if you say I just want to be with my tribe, you cannot go far. You must be with everyone, even whites and other Africans--wider than a small group.

Michael Herzfeld's concept of *cultural intimacy* provides an apt foundation to understand the cultural intricacies that shape Somalis' continued contestation of clan. As defined by Herzfeld, cultural intimacy is, "the recognition of those aspects of a cultural identity that are considered a source of external embarrassment but that nevertheless provide insiders with their assurance of common sociability."[9] Perhaps because clan is associated with the barbarity of the warlords and seems antithetical to modernity, diasporic Somalis deny significance of their clan affiliations even as they point out their own and their associates' clans. Even individuals opposed to clan utilize telling signs in their everyday interactions.

Because Somalis abroad consider clan a sensitive, if not taboo, topic for public discourse, they use an array of tactics within conventional social practice to tell clan. According to fieldwork data, Somalis distinguish clan affiliation through telling signs: gestures, language, names (this includes given names, family names, and nicknames), physical appearance, place of birth, and social networks. Since Somalis base these signs on stereotypes, a mixture of myth and reality, the practice of telling is always open to negotiation.

TELLING AS STRATEGY

If Somalis abroad claim that clan does not influence their daily lives or make sense within the context of diaspora, why is it important for Somalis to tell clan? It may be because the relevance of clan is at risk within the cosmopolitan milieu of diaspora Somalis. Also, it may be because Somalis consider clan to be useful. Pierre Bourdieu argues that kinship and family structures must be continuously maintained. Bourdieu notes, "The structures of kinship and family as *bodies* can be perpetuated only through a continuous creation of family feeling, a cognitive principle of vision and division that is at the same time an effective principle of *cohesion*, that is, the adhesion that is vital to the existence of a family group and its interests."[10]

Telling is an everyday social practice Somalis use to reproduce clan socially in the diaspora. In the midst of everyday interaction, clan identities are shaped and negotiated. The signs Somalis use to tell clan are performed tactically, often exaggeratedly, as in Bourdieu's terms, to mark *distinction*.[11] Although in some cases, these signs are concealed to mask clan ascription. The ideological importance of telling is "that it is a social construction of differences which is used to think with and to act upon."[12] Thus, telling is a necessary social skill that Somalis use abroad to legitimize personal claims to clan membership while avoiding potential faux pas.

Also, telling opens up the potential for individuals to access clan networks or, in Bourdieu's terms, social capital. Bourdieu defines *social capital* as follows:

> the aggregate of the actual or potential resources which are linked to possession of a durable network of more or less institutionalized relationships of mutual acquaintance and recognition-or in other words, to membership in a group - - which provides each of its members with the backing of the collectively-owned capital, a 'credential' which entitles them to credit, in the various senses of the word.[13]

Once an individual legitimizes their clan through telling and is successful at obtaining recognition of that claim by fellow clan members, the individual is in a position to build clan-based social capital. Clan, a form of social capital, is not a latent and accruing value, but rather it is capital actively maintained. Membership in a clan or group does not ensure access to social networks. In fact, social networks must be continuously maintained in order for these networks to be useful. Success in garnering clan-based social capital results from an individual's constant effort at engaging social capital (i.e., access, maintenance, and reciprocity). Accordingly, clan provides connections through social networks as well as economic, cultural, and symbolic effects.

Somalis desire and need to tell clan because clans are stratified. Hence, clan is the basis of social equality and inequality. Abdi M. Kusow argues that, "the lineage-based narrative permanently excludes certain segments of the society from the social boundary of *Somaliness*, while it simultaneously includes and excludes others."[14] Minority groups, such as the Madhibaan, the Benadiri, and the Somali Bantus, fall outside the social boundary of Somaliness.[15] This practice of social stratification is based on the assumption that some clans are nobler than other clans are.

Noble Somalis are believed to be descendants of Arabs, whereas less noble Somalis, such as the Somali Bantus, are recognized as having African ancestry. Marriage between noble Somalis and minorities is rare. According to Virginia Luling, "Nobles traditionally would not marry Jareer, and such marriages are still very uncommon."[16] In Somalia, being labeled as Madhibaan is equated with being a member of the untouchable caste in India.[17] Although I never came across an informant who claimed to be Madhibaan or Somali Bantu, several informants claimed that I had surveyed individuals affiliated with these groups.

Throughout the research period, Somalis pointed out their clan and their associates' clan and debated the clan affiliation of individuals who were believed to be masking their ascribed clan status. For example, physical features that appeared African-like as opposed to Arab-like caused Somalis to question the clan affiliation of others. In fact, several informants asked me to disclose the clan affiliation of other surveyed informants based on physical appearance alone. Fortunately, I could direct individuals to my informed consent form that all persons read and signed before participating in the research. This form ensured confidentiality to all participants. For instance, during a household visit, a female informant asked me to confirm the clan affiliation of a woman I had already surveyed. She asked, "Where is Shukri from? What is her clan? Some people say she is from Afgooye." Taking a copy of the informed consent form from my handbag, I asked, "Do you remember this form you signed? I cannot tell you anything someone else has told me. You are not the first person who has asked me about someone's clan. If I tell, no one will talk to me." The woman apologized for the intrusion but dismissed her actions, saying, "Sorry. Somalis are crazy sometimes." Kroner notes that Somalis in Egypt tend to self-identify as Africans.[18]

Although most Somalis could decipher clan affiliation of others through telling signs, some people, like Shukri, were always held suspect. In fact, Shukri was aware that other Somalis suspected her of masking her clan affiliation. As Shukri and I chatted at her home, she pulled a few pieces of hair loose from her ponytail and said, "People [other Somalis] say I am Jareer because of my hair." Jareer translates as hard-textured hair.

Noble Somalis are believed to have *jileec* (soft hair) as opposed to jareer hair. Thus, Shukri reasoned that her physical appearance, (i.e., hair texture, was the basis for this skepticism). Still, it is important to note that Shukri rarely styled her hair or had it chemically relaxed as most women did. Moreover, persons living in Finland, from the clan Shukri claimed as her own, did not openly accept her. In addition to physical appearance, personal characteristics such as likeability may play a role in clan relatives not accepting an individual. Individuals or families with few relatives in Finland are likely to be considered suspect if a collective does not support their claim to clan membership. In terms of numbers living in Finland or in Somalia, persons affiliated with smaller clans are especially subject to suspicion.

POLITE AND PRACTICAL

In everyday speech and social interactions, Somalis strategically use covert and overt references to distinguish between individuals and groups and construct social boundaries of clan and Somaliness. The following encounter between strangers is riddled with telling signs intended for knowing observers to read. These signs enable not-so-distant strangers to locate one another within the Somali clan system while legitimizing their personal claim to clan membership. Xassan, a male informant in his mid-thirties, revealed his clan affiliation to other Somalis by the strategic use of a telling name rather than by brazenly identifying his clan by name.

Upon encountering an unfamiliar Somali, Xassan knowingly introduced himself with his second name rather than with his given name, which lacked any recognizable clan significance.[19] To other Somalis, Xassan's second name is recognizably Abgaal.[20] Xassan said, "I like to tell my clan. I tell my second name. They know it's Abgaal. If I meet someone on the train, I introduce myself using my second name. Then, they will know who I am. Then, we are free to speak. My clan and his clan are put aside, and we are free to talk about other clans."

Upon hearing Xassan's second name, which is recognizably Abgaal, strangers who are cultural insiders--with the necessary cultural competence--can successfully locate Xassan's clan. In a similar fashion, while visiting an Issaq household with Lul, who is Air, our hostess and mutual friend, Kadijah, introduced Lul to her husband as Lul-Habar Gedir-Air.[21] Kadijah's husband greeted Lul: "*Salaan* (greetings) Air Queen." Directly, yet politely, Kadijah informed her husband that Lul was not a clan relative. Kadijah's assertiveness was socially savvy; her strategic move cued her husband to be cautious of his words in Lul's presence. Kadijah and Xassan knew all too well that without identifying clan to strangers, an unpleasant situation might arise as something ill-mannered might be mentioned about the stranger's clan or clan relative.

Observing social networks is another telling sign that Somalis use to distinguish among clans. Men tend to meet at restaurants, cafés, and the Helsinki railway station to discuss current events. In Helsinki, some public places are known to be meeting places for men of particular clans even though other Somalis frequent the same establishments. One male informant reported, "Now people go to the Internet to check what is going on, and when they meet together, they defend their own tribe, but they do talk to each other."

Xassan told me that if he met a group of Abgaal men from his clan and brought another man with him, his clansmen would assume that his companion was also Abgaal. Explaining the social convention for this type of mixed-clan setting, Xassan said, "I must say before the conversation begins that the man is, for example, Daarood, to set it up. So nothing bad is said about Daarood. It's polite."

Throughout my discussions with Xassan, he adamantly stated his contempt for clan. Still, he acknowledged his adherence to the social convention of revealing his clan when encountering unfamiliar Somalis. As social networks are telling of clan affiliation, they are also open to negotiation, especially in mixed-clan settings, which are more prevalent today than in the 1990s. .

Aroos (wedding), a community-wide event for Somalis, is perhaps the most important occasion for maintaining clan networks.[22] After attending a wedding celebration in Vantaa, a female informant, Shukri (noted earlier for her lack of clan acceptance), told me that she was surprised to discover the rightful clan affiliation of Fatima. Like Shukri, Fatima arrived in Finland seeking asylum in the early 1990s. Over the years, Shukri had falsely assumed Fatima's clan affiliation to be Abgaal. Shukri based her false assumption on a series of telling signs such as Fatima's Somali dialect, birthplace, and social networks.

During the wedding celebration, however, Shukri deciphered Fatima's rightful clan affiliation based upon Fatima's close association with Isaaq women from her paternal clan. After the wedding, Shukri explained why Fatima's clan affiliation was difficult to decipher. Shukri said, "Fatima is Issaq, but raised Abgaal."[23] Fatima's mother and father were from different clans, and Fatima was raised among her mother's clan, Abgaal. Fatima did not grow up in the northern territory traditionally associated with the Issaq, her paternal clan. Therefore, she did not learn to speak like people from her clan. In Somali terms, Fatima did not speak Issaq language.

Misreading Fatima's clan in terms of dialect and social networks exposed the key role of her mother's clan, not her paternal clan, in Fatima's everyday life. Nevertheless, survey and interview data indicated that Fatima was successful in garnering clan-based social capital from her paternal clan and her maternal clan. In Finland, Fatima regularly maintained networks with women from both clans through visiting households, attending wedding celebrations, and as an entrepreneur selling Somali goods in the informal economy. Through her economic activities, Fatima strategically converted clan-based social capital and cultural capital (i.e., objectified state) in terms of goods for herself and related consumers into economic capital.

In addition, Fatima maintained clan networks outside of Finland through her social networks in Finland (i.e., sharing news) and via telephone, travel, and the circulation of videos. Fatima called upon these networks found in Europe, Syria, United Arab Emirates, and East Africa during her travels where she purchased goods for resale in Finland and maintained dispersed networks. The uncertainty of Fatima's clan affiliation is just one of many examples in which an individual's clan affiliation is open to obfuscation; these situations indicate the difficulties in determining clan based solely on observational strategies.

As illustrated throughout this chapter, Somalis use an array of tactics within conventional social practice to tell and read clan. In everyday speech, Somalis use clan names as a practical way to set apart individuals and groups. For example, after conducting a survey with Ahmed, a civil servant, he asked me if I had interviewed his colleague Abdi. "Who, Abdi?" our friend, Hawa, inquired. Ahmed responded, "Abdi, Dir."[24] Ahmed explained, "There are too many Abdi. Then, we know which Abdi." Since Abdi is a common Somali name and the individual in question did not have a well-known nickname, Ahmed utilized Abdi's clan as a reference marker.[25] In addition, when discussing upcoming weddings, informants used clan names to refer to individuals.

While accompanying some friends to a shopping mall, we came across a group of other women. One of the women interjected to the group, "A girl, Raxima, is getting married. Are you going?" Another woman inquired, "Who, Raxima?" The first woman responded, "Raxima-Marehan-Koivukylä."[26] In the foregoing example, a series of three words are strategically strung together to help the other women ascertain the rightful identity of the girl to be married. That is, the girl's first name, Raxima, is strung together with two reference markers: Marehan, her clan, and Koivukylä, the area in the city of Vantaa where she resides.

TELLING AS FIELD STRATEGY

The everyday social practice of telling came to shape my own research methodology. In fact, to access Somalis through their own social networks, I utilized the same signs Somalis use to decipher clan. In Finland, Somalis commonly access other Somalis through people they trust: clan relatives. Therefore, when I encountered a new person in the field, I often used names of their relatives in order to establish trust. On most occasions, I could ascertain clan affiliation utilizing the same telling signs Somalis use to read clan. While interviewing Jama, a male in his early 30s, I used that method to establish rapport. Realizing what I had done, Jama said to me, "You are smart. You meet Somalis through relatives; this is the way Somalis meet each other."

Because telling is not foolproof, I misjudged the clan of several individuals based on telling signs, in particular, social networks and physical appearance. Once, when telling went wrong, I falsely assumed that, based on her physical features, a woman I was about to survey was from a lower status clan. In this case, I thoughtlessly associated physical features (i.e., shape of nose and skin color) with clan affiliation, albeit *the front* is perhaps the least reliable telling cue. After the survey, some acquaintances told me that the woman belonged to their clan, a clan of high prestige. During my survey, however, the woman claimed she belonged to a different clan.

Overall, I noted seven discrepancies between what an informant claimed to be their clan as opposed to what others maintained it to be. Possibly these inconsistencies represent different levels of clan competence (e.g., unfamiliarity with the clan family names listed on the survey or their relationship to clans or sub-clans), or, they may indicate that individuals mask their ascribed clan status. With the exception of the woman noted in the previous example, the other six individuals claimed affiliation with higher status clans than what other informants alleged.

The correlation between outward appearance and clan affiliation is based largely on myth. In addition, performative acts such as chemical hair straightening and skin bleaching, along with intermarriage, further blur the notion of ascribed physical features. It is important to note that these performative acts are largely tactics of women. In fact, women spend much time and effort in performing Somaliness and clan distinction. Moreover, Burton claims, "The various interpretations attached to face, eyes, complexion, demeanour and clothing are by no means evenly distributed throughout the population and do not constitute a generally coherent corpus of meaning."[27] In the event that Somalis acknowledge African-like facial features or dark skin color among noble Somalis backed by a clan collective, these exceptions are dismissed in terms of: "They are not beautiful." Nevertheless, many Somalis claim they could tell clan based on appearance.

Key informants such as Nasra regularly helped me access other Somalis. As Nasra and I rode a bus from Itäkeskus, a shopping center in eastern Helsinki, to pick up her child from school, we encountered two middle-aged women. Nasra greeted them in a customary fashion of hugging and kissing each other on their cheeks. Then, Nasra introduced me to the two women and told them about my project. After we talked on the bus until our destinations separated us, the women agreed to an interview and invited us to their Finnish class the following day. As Nasra and I stepped off the bus, she said to me, "They are my clan. That's why they said yes [to participate in the research]. They will answer. I don't like clan, but Somalis are like that." Informants commonly excused these types of culturally intimate actions to me, a cultural outsider, saying, "I don't like clan, but Somalis are like that."

This strategy of accessing informants while accompanying friends of different clans as they carried out daily activities enabled me to map social networks. Nevertheless, other networks formed in the diaspora--networks with classmates, coworkers, neighbors, friends, and in fewer cases, Finns--facilitated access to informants.

During surveys, I directly asked informants to identify their clan, and their responses varied. Some informants were taken aback my frankness and were surprised that an outsider was familiar with Somali kinship. Others responded to my inquiry by outwardly expressing their contempt for clan. Still, most respondents answered my question without hesitation, and the majority of informants had previously seen or met me when I was with other Somalis. Also, Somalis viewed me as an unbiased observer; that is, void of clan affiliation and ethnic Finnish heritage. Since Somalis were aware that I used the same telling signs they use to read clan and utilized clan as reference markers in everyday speech, my social intimacy in the field balanced my cultural distance. Moreover, many Somalis knew of my interest in and familiarity with the clan system and informants may have been more willing to respond to my inquiry because of this.

Almost all individuals who were surveyed, 94 percent, responded to my inquiry of clan. Nevertheless, the extent of their understanding, that is, where they belonged in the Somali kinship system, was relative to their cultural competence (i.e., clan competence). Later in this chapter, I will explain how individuals who arrived in the early to mid-1990s legitimized their clan to each other by exhibiting a certain degree of clan competence. For example, these individuals were skilled at reciting the names of their clan ancestors and the relationship of their clan to other clans. Persons reared in rural areas tended to exhibit a high degree of clan competence, but they were less familiar with clan families outside their home regions. Conversely, young adults, particularly those born in Finland or who were recent arrivals, tended to be familiar only with the name of their own clan or sub-clan.

In my survey of young adults, those who first learned about their genealogy in Finland tended to identify with their clan or sub-clan. Some of these informants could not name the larger clan-family to which their clan or sub-clan belongs. Nevertheless, this pattern does not apply to the numerous children and young adults who travel (usually during summer months) to Somalia or to other countries in the Horn of Africa where grandparents, aunts, uncles, and other relatives knowingly or unknowingly impart clan competence. Hodan, a female informant, noted the disparity of the clan competence of her Finnish-born children as it related to traveling to Somalia:

> Author: How will you teach your children where they are from?
>
> Hodan: Muse went to Somalia twice. He learned [about his clan] from his grandmother. He know my tribe. He know everything. She [her daughter] doesn't know anything. I asked her once where she was from. I listed the tribes. She took the last one each time. I did this twice.

Only six percent of respondents chose not to report their clan to me. A young male informant refused to report his clan, saying, "All Somalis ask this. I don't want." Most Somalis tend to tell clan in socially appropriate ways to appear not to be into clan; however, some individuals prefer to ask strangers to name their clan or sub-clan. A female informant did not reveal her clan affiliation and said, "Clan does not make sense to me." Another young woman responded in Finnish, "*Ei hyvää kysymys* [not a good question]" before revealing her clan. Furthermore, in response to my question, the initial reaction of one forty-year-old male was to say, "I know where I belong. I do not identify with my clan but my nation." Then, with a clever smile, he casually remarked that since I had already interviewed his cousin, I could easily determine his clan affiliation.

Some informants revealed their clan to me, a cultural outsider, through telling place names. Although the question, "Where were you born?" may seem straightforward, it could also be interpreted as "Where are you from?" or "Where is your clan from?" For example, a male in his early 20s responded to this question with "born in Mogadishu but from Hargeisa," meaning "born in Mogadishu but descended from Hargeisa, the ancestral clan territory of the Issaq clan." Aware that citing Mogadishu as his birthplace left his clan uncertain, the young man tagged a place, symbolic of his clan, to legitimize his claim. The city of Hargeisa is clearly associated with the Issaq, his paternal clan. In case I might mistake this association, the informant singled out a male relative with whom he knew I was closely associated. This tactic would undoubtedly ensure that I knew where he was from.

Despite such displays of cultural competence, most informants claimed they knew little about their clan until after they arrived in Finland. This was especially evident among persons raised in Mogadishu, which is the capital city of Somalia, and the most diverse city in Somalia. In this urban context, interclan social interaction was an everyday experience where individuals forged practical relationships with non-kin prior to the outbreak of the Somali civil war.[28] In addition to Mogadishu, other southern cities such as Baidoa and Kismayo were diverse in terms of clan. During interviews, individuals who lived in these areas noted that interclan interaction was widespread and commonly reported that they lived in mixed-clan neighborhoods. In contrast, informants from less diverse areas, such as the northern region (i.e., Somaliland and Puntland) and rural areas, reported that interclan interaction was rare. Moreover, persons residing outside of Somalia prior to the civil war, particularly in the Middle East and Arabian Peninsula, utilized clan networks to find jobs and housing to counteract the discrimination they faced as immigrants.

LESS EXPLICIT BUT NOT LESS IMPORTANT

According to most informants in Finland, clan is less important today than it was 10 to 15 years ago. Each day, Somalis from all clans greet each other in public spaces, particularly while traveling on public transport, shopping, worshipping at mosques, and visiting with neighbors and friends at their homes. This is in stark contrast to what informants reportedly experienced in the early to mid-1990s when Somalia's civil war brought clan to the forefront. Knowing where a person was from was vital for people who arrived early in Finland and who sought to align themselves with persons they could trust: clan relatives.

Findings from in-depth interviews suggest that the first large groups of Somalis who arrived in Finland in the early 1990s organized themselves according to clan affiliation. In some cases, each floor of refugee reception centers became one clan's domain. In addition, informants reported fighting mirroring a clan conflict in Somalia erupted between two clans at a reception center. It was upon encountering other Somalis in Finland that many informants claimed they were first directly asked of their clan affiliation as the following excerpts from in-depth interviews suggest:

> Author: After you arrived in Finland, do you recall the first time someone asked where you were from?
>
> Nur: "When I come to Finland, I went to a Finnish course. It was October 1994. 'Who am I'? 'Who is my tribe'? They [other Somalis] told me what tribe I belong. I did not know. I had to call my father to ask. It was very stupid.
>
> Author: After you arrived in Finland, do you recall the first time someone asked where you were from?
>
> Hodan: We were all on the same plane. Then, in the camp, everyone who was there was looking for their own tribe--asking everyone because there was this war still going on. They were asking everything, details. There was no trust. 'Who are you and what is your tribe?' And, you had to know all the names. If you make a mistake, they do not trust you. Grandfather, blah blah blah.
>
> Author: After you arrived in Finland, do you recall the first time someone asked where you were from?

> Nuura: I didn't know much about clan when I arrived in Finland at the age of 14. I was asked my clan and I could name my father and grandfather's name but no more. People said that I was a person who hides their clan.[29] When my mother came to Finland, I asked her to teach me about my clan. Now I can name many in my lineage.
>
> Author: After you arrived in Finland, do you recall the first time someone asked where you were from?
>
> Mohamed: At the camp [refugee reception center], one man was asking me almost everyday, every month. He was from the countryside in the North. And also he was living in Saudi Arabia-it tells a lot about his behavior. He told everyone, 'He is Madhibaan'. Somalis asked my clan for three years but I would not tell. It took almost three months to know my clan. I told everyone that I did not know [my clan]. People were calling me Madhibaan and a person who hides their clan. This continued until a guy I went to high school with in Somalia told other people I was Majeerteen.[30]

In refugee reception centers, clan was the focal point of these early encounters. In fact, residents directed newcomers to self-identify by clan, and each claim tested an individual's ability to exhibit cultural competence or clan competence. That is, "knowledge of genealogical relationships and of real connections and skill at using them."[31] This specific cultural competence, a form of cultural capital, in its embodied state, is transmitted through socialization.[32] Today, this practice seems antiquated and uncouth.

It was vital for newcomers to know where they were from to legitimize their claim to others; however, many informants lacked cultural competence of clan relationships. Informants reportedly contacted parents or other relatives to teach clan genealogy. This personal investment in clan competence (i.e., cultural capital) paved the way for individuals to build clan-based social capital.

During the 1990s, Somalis formed over 40 separate associations in Finland; clan affiliation organized most of these groups.[33] Irmeli Tuomarla notes that Finnish authorities anticipated uniformity among Somali asylum seekers and refugees; authorities were perplexed by Somalis' inability to unite to represent their community.[34] As asylum seekers or quota refugees, Finns assumed Somalis to embody little more than the label of refugee: "an almost generic, ideal-typical figure."[35] The number of active associations declined by the time I entered the field. However, men continued to manage and support a number of clan-based associations.[36] Fourteen percent of surveyed individuals reported membership in Somali associations. The other 86 percent of respondents cited clannism and related mistrust as reasons for avoiding associations. A reduction in clan-based associations may not support informants' claims that "clan is less important today" than it was in the 1990s. I argue that such a decline points to the opposite.

Informants working as public servants expressed the importance of maintaining a neutral position within the Somali community. By neutral, I mean maintaining an unaligned position, in terms of clan, within the Somali community. These informants equated membership in clan-based Somali associations, a seemingly overt sign of clan affiliation in Finland, as sufficient evidence for other Somalis to suspect that they favored one clan over another. Abdirahman, who worked with youth at risk, said, "Somali associations take money for themselves, and I need to be neutral in my work." Mahamuud, a city social worker, echoed Abdirahman's sentiment. After expressing his avoidance of Somali associations in an effort to remain neutral, he added, "I have little contact with Somalis. I keep to myself. I have access to all of their information on the city database so I have to be careful." I refused invitations to two Somali associations because I, not unlike the public servants, did not want to favor one clan over another. Despite this, several informants told me that they heard a rumor that I had visited one association that--although controversial--is considered an umbrella for Somali groups by the Finnish government.

Dega, a city social worker, who also distanced herself socially from other Somalis, recalled an incident in which a client accused her of favoring clan relatives. She said, "One young man came in [to my workplace], and he said that I only get money for my relatives. I told him that I do not have relatives in Finland--only my husband

and kids. He meant clan relatives." These three public servants did not respond to my inquiry as to their clan affiliation. They maintain (as many Somalis do), that clan does not play a significant role in their daily lives. Nonetheless, their associations were restricted due to the watchful eye of other Somalis, especially their Somali clientele who might suspect them of nepotism.

TELLING OF CLAN'S USEFULNESS

Despite clan's pervasive role in the diaspora, Somalis contest its influence in their everyday lives. Somalis deny significance of their clan affiliations even as they point out their and their associates' clans. Somalis abroad are embarrassed by clan's ubiquity, which seems antithetical to modernity. As one informant revealed, "Tribe is one of those things that make unprogress." Moreover, the international community and Somalis themselves blame clannism for Somalia's civil war and prolonged strife in the former nation-state. This cultural intimacy shapes clan's continued construction in the diaspora.

Informants claim that clan is less important today than it was in the early to mid-1990s when newcomers were directed to self-identify by clan. Each claim tested an individual's ability to exhibit cultural competence or clan genealogy, and this practice seems antiquated and uncouth. Today, through the practice of telling, Somalis locate one another's clan. Using an array of tactics, Somalis politely tell clan often without naming names, that is, clan names. Telling is structured by three levels of intimacy. First, to outsiders, Somalis claim clan is unimportant and obsolete. Second, clan is just a convenience marker. Third, clan is important but also harmful. Thus, the practice of telling depends on the intimacy shared. Once telling is achieved, individuals are in a position to build clan-based social capital. Membership in a clan or group does not ensure access to social networks. In fact, clan, a form of capital, is not a latent and accruing value. Moreover, success in accessing this capital results from an individual's constant effort at engagement.

Whether Somalis utilize clan for its practicality as a marker, tell clan to legitimize claims or access resources, employ clan stereotypes, or blame clan and persons who are clannistic, "they all contribute, through these little acts of essentializing to making it [clan] a permanent fixture in their lives."[37] Indeed, clan is less explicit than it was 10 to 15 years ago, but it is not less important. Its concealment is an indication of usefulness.

Feasibly, clan identities are particularly robust in welfare states like Finland where the state provides housing, healthcare, education, and child allowances. In this context, there is little incentive for Somalis to unify because their basic needs are met by the state. In other countries, such as Egypt, Somalis tend to promote a nationalist identity to help counteract "their harsh living conditions and limited legal rights."[38] This is not to say that Somalis in Finland find clan ties to be unproblematic. In fact, Somalis consider their rights and obligations toward family, clan, and in Al-Sharmani's terms, *interdependent transnational families* alongside competing ideologies of Finnish autonomy and gender equality.[39] Nonetheless, clan relationships become real as they become useful. Somalis use clan in modern ways; they manage transnational capital through clan networks. That is, Somalis realize and reaffirm clan networks through their use as a resource in the moments of movement, celebration, and crisis.

Acknowledgements

I thank the 186 Somalis who helped me understand the complex dynamics of clan in the diaspora. These individuals will go unmentioned by name because the Somali community in Finland is relatively small and the informants' identity would be easy to discern otherwise. Also, I want to recognize my mentor and long-time friend Dr. Alice B. Kehoe for commenting on this chapter. The American-Scandinavian Foundation funded this research with partial support from the Wenner-Gren Foundation for Anthropological Research. During the course of my field research, I was affiliated as visiting researcher with the Department of Sociology at the University of Helsinki. The Department provided me with office space when such space was a scare resource.

Notes

1. Cerulli, E. (1957). *Somalia: Scritti vari editi ed inediti, Vol. I.* Rome: Istituto Poligrafico dello Stato.

   Cerulli, E. (1959). *Somalia: Scritti vari editi ed inediti, Vol. II.* Rome: Istituto Poligrafico dello Stato.

Cerulli, E. (1964). *Somalia: Scritti vari editi ed inediti, Vol III*. Rome: Istituto Poligrafico dello Stato.

Colucci, M. (1924). *Principi di diritto consuetudinario della Somalia Italiana meridionale*. Florence: Societá Editrice La Voce.

Helander, B. (1988). *The slaughtered camel: Coping with fictitious descent among the Hubeer of southern Somalia*. Doctoral dissertation, University of Uppsala, Uppsala, Sweden.

Helander, B. (2003). *The slaughtered camel: Coping with fictitious descent among the Hubeer of southern Somalia*. Uppsala, Sweden: Uppsala University Press.

Lewis, I. M. (1961). *A pastoral democracy: A study of pastoralism and politics among the northern Somali of the Horn of Africa*. London: International African Institute/Oxford University Press.

Lewis, I. M. (1962). *Marriage and the family in Northern Somaliland*. Kampula, Uganda: East African Institute of Social Research.

Lewis, I. M. (1994). *Blood and bone: The call of kinship in Somali society*. Lawrenceville, NJ: The Red Sea Press, Inc.

Luling, V. (1971). The social structure of southern Somali tribes (Doctoral dissertation, University of London).

Marlowe, D. H. (1963). The Galjaal Barsana of central Somalia: A lineage political system in a changing world (Doctoral dissertation, Harvard University).

Luling, V. (2002). *Somali Sultanate: The Geledi city-state over 150 years*. London, U.K.: HAAN; Piscataway, N.J.: Transaction Publishers. p. 94.

This literature overwhelmingly cites kinship as the basis of Somali social organization and group formation. Somali society is organized into segmenting units based on patrilineal descent. Clan-families are segmented into clans whose members believe they descend from the same apical ancestor. Clans are further segmented into sub-clans.

2. See Gough, K. (1971). Nuer kinship: A re-examination. In T. O. Beidelman (Ed.), *The Translation of Culture: Essays to E. E. Evans-Pritchard* (79-12). London: Tavistock Publications.

   Hutchinson, S. E. (1996). *Nuer dilemmas: Coping with money, war, and the state*. Berkeley and Los Angeles: University of California Press.

   Southall, A. (1970). The illusion of tribe. *Journal of Asian and Afrian Studies,* 5(1), 28-50.

   Southall, A. (1986). Illusion of nath agnation. *Ethnology*, 25(1), 1-20.

Verdon, M. (1982). Where have all their lineages gone? Cattle and descent among the Nuer. American Anthropologist 84, 566-579.

3. See Lewis, I. M. (1998). Doing violence to ethnography: A response to Catherine Besteman's representing violence and "othering" in Somalia. *Cultural Anthropology,* 13(1), 100-108.
4. Burton, F. (1978). *The politics of legitimacy: Struggles in a Belfast community*. London: Routledge and Kegan Paul. Frank Burton's concept of telling elucidates the practice of sectarian differentiation among Catholics and Protestants in Northern Ireland.
5. The Helsinki metropolitan region, inhabited by 1.2 million persons, consists of four municipalities: the capital, Helsinki, and the surrounding cities of Espoo, Vantaa, and Kauniainen. This paper is based on ethnographic research (conducted from 2000-2001; summer 2002; 2003-2004) in the Helsinki metropolitan area, where Somalis overwhelmingly reside.
6. The population sample for this study consisted of 186 Somalis: 77 men and 109 women 18 years and older.

   Surveys were in Somali, Finnish and English and were read aloud to informants by the researcher and responses were recorded by the researcher. While the surveys were structured, in most cases, informal conversations developed during surveys, revealing supplementary information; these data were noted by the researcher.
7. Since the 1990s, Finland has received an unprecedented influx of Somali refugees. There are approximately 8,096 native Somali speakers in the country, making them the fourth largest minority population, and the only sizably significant African population.

   Statistics Finland. (2005). *Ulkomaalaiset ja siirtolaisuus 2004* [Foreigners and international migration 2004]. Helsinki, Finland: Tilastokeskus.
8. *Black Hawk Down*, a Hollywood film released in 2001, is based on the book *Black Hawk Down: A Story of Modern War*. The film is a dramatic portrayal of the Battle of Mogadishu during which nearly 100 U.S. Army Rangers were dropped into Mogadishu in October 1993 by helicopter to capture Somali warlord Mohamed Farrah Aideed. The drop culminated in fighting between the U.S. Army Rangers and hundreds of Somali gunmen. The clash destroyed two Black Hawk helicopters. This film portrays the U.S. Army Rangers' point of view who survived this mission. Somalis worldwide staged protests over the film's debut in cities such as Milwaukee, WI and Minneapolis, MN.

9. Herzfeld, M. (1997). *Cultural intimacy: Social poetics in the nation-state*. New York: Routledge. p.3.
10. Bourdieu, P. (1998). *Practical reason: On the theory of action*. Stanford, CA: Stanford University Press. p. 68.
11. Bourdieu, P. (1984). *Distinction: Critique of the judgement of taste*. (R. Nice, Trans.). Cambridge, MA: Harvard University Press.
12. Burton, F. (1978). *The politics of legitimacy: Struggles in a Belfast community*. London: Routledge and Kegan Paul. p. 38.
13. Bourdieu, P. (1986). The forms of capital. In J. G. Richardson, (Ed.), *Handbook of theory and research for the sociology of education* (pp. 241-258). New York: Greenwood Press. p. 249.
14. Kusow, A. M. (2004). Contested narratives and the crisis of the nation-state in Somalia: A prolegomenon. In A. M. Kusow (Ed.), *Putting the cart before the horse: Invented nationalism and the crisis of identity in Somalia* (pp. 1-14). Trenton, NJ: The Red Sea Press. p. 2.
15. Informants used the terms Bantu and Jareer interchangeably. Jareer is a Somali term for hard-textured hair.
16. Luling, V. (2002). *Somali Sultanate: The Geledi city-state over 150 years*. London, U.K.: HAAN; Piscataway, N.J.: Transaction Publishers. p. 94.
17. Kusow, A. M. (2004). Contested narratives and the crisis of the nation-state in Somalia: A prolegomenon. In A. M. Kusow (Ed.), *Putting the cart before the horse: Invented nationalism and the crisis of identity in Somalia* (pp. 1-14). Trenton, NJ: The Red Sea Press. p. 4.
18. Kroner, G. K. (this volume). Transit or dead end? The Somali diaspora in Egypt. In A. M. Kusow & S. R. Bjork, (Eds.), *From Mogadishu to Dixon: The Somali diaspora in a global context*. Trenton, NJ: The Red Sea Press.
19. Somalis have three names. The first name is a given name. The second name is the given name of the father, and the third name is the given name of the paternal grandfather. Married women rarely change their names after marriage; married women's second and third names retain their patrilineage.
20. Abgaal is a clan of the Hawiye clan-family.
21. Habar Gedir is a clan of the Hawiye clan-family and Air is a sub-clan of Habar Gedir.
22. Bjork, S. (2001). Watched weddings: Circulating videos and transnational community-building amongst Somalis in Finland (Master's thesis, University of Wisconsin-Milwaukee, 2001).

23. Issaq is a clan-family.
24. Dir is a clan-family.
25. Often, Somalis with common names have nicknames to help others distinguish individuals. Nicknames may denote physical characteristics such as body shape, hair, skin color, and eyes, personality traits, or family names. Some nicknames are telling of clan affiliation in terms of clan dialect. I developed my own nicknaming strategy in the field to distinguish between individuals. On my mobile phone, I listed individual names followed by their place of residence. For example, I used nicknames like "Abdi Havukoski" for an informant named Abdi (a common male name), who resided in Havukoski, an area in the city of Vantaa.

26.. Marehan is a clan of the Daarood clan-family. The wedding took place in Koivukylä, an area in the city of Vantaa.

26. Burton, F. (1978). *The politics of legitimacy: Struggles in a Belfast community*. London: Routledge and Kegan Paul. p. 54.
27. Bhoola, F. A. (1989). Household structure, decision-making, and the economic, social, and legal status of women in Mogadishu, Somalia (Doctoral dissertation, Michigan State University).

    Cassanelli, L. (1982). *The shaping of Somali society: Reconstructing the history of a pastoral people, 1600-1900*. Philadelphia, PA: University of Pennsylvania Press.

    Simons, A. (1995). *Networks of dissolution: Somalia undone*. Boulder, CO: Westview Press.
28. According to historian Omar Eno, (e-mail to author, July 7, 2005) Somalis do not have a specific word for persons who hide their clan. Eno notes that, "people normally create a word spontaneously. For example: *Qabiil-diid* (someone who rejects tribalism), *Sheegato* (a newcomer who identifies himself with the natives), and *Tol-laabe* (someone who does not belong to a clan); probably he is hiding it."
29. Majeerteen is a clan of Daarood clan-family.
30. Bourdieu, P. (1986). The forms of capital. In J. G. Richardson, (Ed.), *Handbook of theory and research for the sociology of education* (pp. 241-258). New York: Greenwood Press. p. 250.
31. Bourdieu, P. (1986). The forms of capital. In J. G. Richardson, (Ed.), *Handbook of theory and research for the sociology of education* (pp. 241-258). New York: Greenwood Press. p. 245.
32. Alitolppa-Niitamo, A. (2000). The equator to the Arctic Circle: A portrait of Somali integration and diasporic consciousness in Finland. In E. M. Goździak and D. J. Shandy (Eds.), *Rethinking refuge and*

displacement (pp. 43-65). Arlington, VA: American Anthropological Association.

33. Tuomarla, I. (2001). The Somalis in Finland and in Britain. A comment to Asha-Kin F. Duale. In M. S. Lillius (Ed.), *Variations on the theme of Somaliness* (pp. 291-293). Turku, Finland: Centre for Continuing Education, Åbo Akademi University.
34. Malkki, L. H. (1995). Purity and exile: Violence, memory, and national cosmology among Hutu refugees in Tanzania. Chicago: The University of Chicago Press. p. 8.
35. See also McMichael, C., Manderson, L. (2004). Somali women and well-being: Social networks and social capital among immigrant women in Australia. *Human Organization*, 63(1), 88-99. The authors report that Somali men in Australia play a similar role in Somali associations.
36. Herzfeld, M. (1997). *Cultural intimacy: Social poetics in the nation-state*. New York: Routledge. p. 2.
37. Al-Sharmani, M. (this volume). The poetics and practices of Soomalinimo: The Somali diaspora in Cairo. In A. M. Kusow & S. R. Bjork, (Eds.), *From Mogadishu to Dixon: The Somali diaspora in a global context*. Trenton, NJ: The Red Sea Press.
38. Al-Sharmani, M. (2004). Refugees and citizens: The Somali diaspora in Cairo (Doctoral dissertation, the Johns Hopkins University).

Chapter 7

AMBIVALENT ENCOUNTERS: NEGOTIATING BOUNDARIES OF SOMALINESS, DANISHNESS AND BELONGING

Nauja Kleist

INTRODUCTION

Somalis are one of the most debated immigrant groups in Denmark. Since the arrival of a large number of Somali asylum seekers in the middle of the 1990s, the group has been in the center of political and media attention where stereotypes of Somaliness have been prevalent.[1] These stereotypes are often constructed on a premise that Islam and Somali culture differs greatly from Danish norms, that integration is impossible or very difficult and consequently, that Somalis do not belong in Denmark. In contrast to North America, ideas of 'race' or skin color are not part of Danish official discourses of difference and social stratification.[2] Still, in everyday life, many Somalis experience racist incidents, either on a personal or general level.

In this chapter, I analyze dynamics of Somali inclusion and exclusion in Danish society. My aim is to explore negotiations of the collective categories of Somaliness and Danishness that Somali-Danes might encounter in everyday life. I thereby show how these encounters take part in shaping identities and belonging, or rather perhaps, how they form part of the context and conditions for identification. My main argument is that the circulation of stereotypes of Somali refugees as well as the nationalist version of Danishness as limited to be an exclusive group circumscribes Somali-Danish identification and belonging. Through four case studies, I explore different reactions to stereotyping as well as different coping strategies, including the desire of some Somali-Danes to leave Denmark.

Let me start by making clear that the categories of Somali and Danish as well as Somaliness and Danishness are not natural units with a given content. The categories are, on the contrary, powerful discursive constructions, which are employed in meaning-making (and administrative) processes with real effects. In my usage, Somalis refers to persons who hold or have held Somali citizenship. Somali-Danish refer to Somalis who live in Denmark with the purpose of staying in the country, i.e., excluding short-term visitors, such as tourists or students. I thus neither wish to contribute to discussions of what a Somali or Danish person is or should be, nor to discussions of the nature of Somaliness or Danishness. My aim is to contribute to an analysis of how these categories become meaningful and how they are negotiated in a Danish context. I therefore start by outlining Somali migration to and reception in Denmark.

SOMALIS IN DENMARK

Denmark is a relatively new location for Somali settlement. A few Somali sailors arrived in the late 1960s, followed by a limited amount of refugees and families re-unified throughout the 1970s and 1980s. The majority of Somalis in Denmark arrived in the mid 1990s as asylum seekers from the Somali civil war or as families re-unified. About 13,000 Somali citizens now live in Denmark; the number is about 17,400 with descendants.[3] As indicated above, the reception of Somalis in Denmark has been marked by hostility, and the media exposure of and political attention to the group has tended to focus on fraud, "problems of integration," and outspoken strangeness.[4] This position stands in contrast to Bosnian refugees, who arrived in Denmark at the same time, and who were received and described as "real war refugees" and "like us," (i.e., like Danes). Somalis in Denmark, however, have been relegated to a position of overwhelming difference and marginalization, both in terms of socio-economic position and symbolic representation.[5] This marginalization is also reflected in the fact that Somali citizens in Denmark hold the lowest level of employment among all ethnic groups.[6] Furthermore, the group has been targets of several special measures such as repatriation efforts, DNA-profiling and in relation to so-called correctional educational trips of children and youth to the parents' country of origin.[7]

As in Canada, as Kusow has shown,[8] Somalis in Denmark find themselves stigmatized by their surrounding society. The Danish context, however, is quite different than the Canadian one. While Canada is a declared country of immigrants with deliberate multicultural politics, Denmark is in the middle of a struggle concerning the nature of Danishness vis-à-vis the challenges of immigration, especially of non-Western, Muslim immigrant groups. Furthermore, as mentioned above, there is no official vocabulary of 'race' relations in Denmark, but racism does take place at an everyday level. Somalis in Denmark, as a group of black, African, Muslim, and recently arrived refugees, are positioned in the center of both problematics.

The arrival of a large number of Somali asylum seekers in Denmark in the middle of the 1990s concurred with changes in the political climate concerning immigration and integration. Immigration and integration have been hot political and media issues in Denmark since the late 1960s when guest workers from the South of Europe and Pakistan started to enter the country, but the debates became more central and politicized in the 1990s. The political debate in Denmark has often been characterized as polarized between so-called "immigration opponents" and "immigration romantics." The latter are accused of denying any reality of the challenges of immigration, while the former remain very skeptical towards a multicultural society and fear for the future of the welfare state. During recent years, there has been a growing political majority that believes in tightening immigration and asylum legislation and focusing on the preservation of Danishness and Danish culture.[9] It should be emphasized that there are different positions in these debates and that the nature of belonging and migration is also perceived in different ways. Still, there is a tendency, in my view, to perceive migration from non-Western countries within the framework of what Liisa Malkki has termed the national order.[10] In this perspective, culture, identity, and the nation are seen as overlapping and discrete entities, contained within the territories of nation-states, while migration is seen as a deviation, a threat to cultural and national coherence. While this perspective is not sociologically--or, in my view, politically--tenable, the idea is a powerful one and informs the more populist voices in the Danish debates. In a less nationalist language, but often equally anxious mode, the presence of non-Western immigrants is presented as one the main challenges to the survival of the welfare state. The fact that immigrants are often termed *de fremmede,* i.e. "the strangers," indicates that Somalis are and other migrant groups are positioned as outsiders to the Danish society. My research indicates that Somalis as a group in many ways are seen to be the "strangest of the strangers."

We should, however, be very careful not conflate an analysis of the symbolic representations of Somalis in Denmark with their diverse individual experiences and life situations. On the contrary, the aim of this description is to highlight the shared context and conditions of identification. My suggestion is that the collective stereotype of Somalis that individuals might encounter takes part in shaping how Somaliness and Danishness are made into meaningful categories. I explore this in four stories, which are reconstructed from qualitative, semi-structured life story interviews. The aim of the life stories is to analyze the trajectories of physical and social mobility of the interviewees and to make them "define and explicate to others their own fields of belonging and identification and how these fields are articulated with the socio-cultural and physical boundaries which they experience in their everyday life".[11] Life stories allow us, in other words, to situate the interviews in a wider perspective, as articulated by the interviewees. In the following, I first present three stories, which I discuss in relation to experiences of living in Denmark, before I turn to a last example.

THREE STORIES

These three stories were selected from 50 interviews carried out in the Greater Copenhagen area, Somaliland, and London.[12] The following research questions guided my fieldwork: What is the relationship between the status and standing of Somalis in Denmark and their transnational engagements? How do Somali-Danes articulate and mobilize collective identity? In this chapter, I am especially interested in how Somali-Danes cope with stereotypes in their encounters with Danish society and what it means for ideas of Danishness and Somaliness. Therefore I have chosen four interviewees who articulate different opinions and coping strategies. Furthermore, the interviewees have different experiences in terms of gender, background in Somalia, and arrival situations in Denmark, though they are not representational in the sense of speaking for all Somali-Danes as a group. The fact that they are fluent Danish speakers, that they are employed and/or have pursued a Danish education positions them in a more advantaged situation than many other Somali-Danes. Still, their relationships to Denmark are rather ambivalent. Take Hawa, for instance.

HAWA: "I NEVER THOUGHT THIS WOULD HAPPEN TO ME"

Hawa grew up in a relatively wealthy family in a major town in the southern part of Somalia. When the war broke out, Hawa fled to Kenya and after two years she took a plane to Denmark with just one transit stop. Several of her siblings went to Canada and the United States and the family now lives in three continents. At that time Hawa was nineteen and she was placed in a Danish asylum centre, following the normal procedures. "It was such a terrible time," Hawa tells me. To be assigned a number, instead of her name. To have to stand in a long line to get a meal. To share a small room with several other women who sometimes had male visitors at night. "Things you never thought would happen to you," Hawa says. After three weeks Hawa was moved to another centre with a very bad reputation among the other asylum seekers. "If you don't turn into a prostitute, you'll surely become a drug addict," they told her. Hawa was very afraid and kept asking herself why she had to be moved. In the new centre, however, she accidentally ran into a Danish woman, Kirsten, for whom she used to work in Somalia. Kirsten presented Hawa to her own family and asked them to help her, should she ever need it. It turned out that Hawa did. After a few months, Hawa moved in with Kirsten's family by special permission. This was a turning point. Hawa started studying and later met her future husband, a Danish man with whom she now has two children. In her own words, Hawa feels that she was "very, very lucky to get a Danish family" and get an extraordinary chance. And she has indeed done very well: she has completed her education with very good results, she speaks Danish perfectly, and she works within her field of studies.

FATUMA: "IT WAS EXCITING IN THE BEGINNING"

Like Hawa, Fatuma also arrived in Denmark as a young woman, but through family reunification. Living in Mogadishu, her family was, as Fatuma phrases it, "not rich, not poor, like a normal family with our own house." The family had to flee at the outbreak of civil war and was separated in the course of events. For three months, they received no news of Fatuma's father, but finally learned that he had reached Denmark, and that they should make their way to Ethiopia and then to Denmark by means of family reunification. Unlike Hawa, Fatuma thus arrived with her family and did not experience the difficulties of living in an asylum centre. On the contrary, Fatuma explains:

> It was exciting in the beginning. I was seventeen years old and when you are young girl coming to a new country, you just think of getting to know this country, to learn the language. It was exiting and nothing could prevent me from getting to know Denmark; it was just fun and interesting.

In Denmark, Fatuma went to school and started her education to be a schoolteacher. She is now married to a Somali man and has three small children. Fatuma is not active in community work among other Somalis, but both she and her husband remit money to relatives still living in Somalia. "They think we always have money," she says, but continues that people in Somalia know well that life in Denmark is not always that easy. For Fatuma, it was easy to arrive in Denmark, but she finds that everyday life is proving more difficult. So does Abdirizak.

ABDIRIZAK: "IT IS VERY TOUGH TO LIVE IN DENMARK"

Abdirizak, a man now in his forties, lost his parents at a young age and grew up as an orphan. Thanks to the economic support of an older brother working in Saudi Arabia, he, the only one among his siblings, managed to get an education in Mogadishu. When the civil war broke out, Abdirizak fled Somalia, but had to leave his pregnant wife behind and had no news from her for a long time. Abdirizak's route to Denmark went over Asia before he arrived in the early 1990s. At that time, he finally got in touch with his wife and after a few more years, she arrived in Denmark through family re-unification. This was the first time Abdirizak saw their child. The couple now has five children. The first years in Denmark were difficult, Abdirizak recalls. He wanted to pursue further education, but was told by a social worker to take care of his kids instead. Like Hawa, he never thought he would be a refugee and be dependent on other people's charity and the experience of finding himself in that situation was very upsetting.

> I was 28 years old when I came to Denmark. I was educated, and I had worked in Somalia, and I had my pride . . . but I lost it when I came to Denmark . . . . After I came to the social security office and got social security. I was so. . . No! I would much rather work, but I couldn't find a job. It was so difficult because of language barriers, because there was no work at that time. It was a very tough and difficult situation for me to receive social security. And I got a bit aggressive, because when the social worker said I should do this or that, I thought, "no, they are just saying that because they provide for me." My social worker didn't understand me. She said, "why is he such a hard man?" . . . . It is very tough to live in Denmark, you have to manage your life, otherwise you lose yourself and you don't get any respect, neither from society or your family, if you don't work. But if you work and pay taxes and provide for your family and yourself, there is more independence, there is more pride . . . and satisfaction with your life.

During his first years in Denmark, Abdirizak started to chew *qhat,* a stimulant leave, which is widely chewed in the Horn of Africa. He did, with his own words, waste his time and after a while, he decided that he had to change his situation, no matter what. Abdirizak started doing different odd jobs and some translation work. Now, he has a regular job and is very active in various Somali associations.

THE TWO FACES OF DENMARK

Hawa, Fatuma, and Abdirizak entered Denmark in different ways; they have different backgrounds and family responsibilities and live different lives. Still, all three of them emphasize the difficulties and ambivalence of their lives in Denmark. For Hawa, life in Denmark is of a double nature. She has been, as she said, very lucky to receive that special chance and live with a Danish family; nevertheless, in spite of her language skills and education, she has recurrent experiences of prejudice and discrimination. It is, Hawa says, like Denmark has two faces.

> I have two images of Denmark. The Danes that I know and mix with, my friends. They are like one life, one world, and then the world outside them, which doesn't know me, that generalizes me as . . . as a group, as Somali or a general group . . . Somalia this and that . . . and which means that all of us are generalized into one group, instead of appreciating individuality. That said, it is only the media and the official Denmark that holds that view of us. When I am with my friends, the people who know me, it is something completely different . . . . In a way, you can say that . . . I have two visions of Denmark, one that knows me and who isn't at all afraid of me, and then the ones who don't know me. And sadly, those who don't know me become more and more numerous.

This statement, though phrased in different ways, is recurrent among many of the Somali-Danes I have talked with. That the public collective image, the stereotype of 'the Somali refugee," defines the agenda for how individual Somalis are encountered in Danish society and that this stereotype often overshadows the possibilities for being met as an individual. Fatuma says:

> Well, the first comments you get . . . by Danes who realize you can speak Danish . . . "hey, where are from?," "I am from Somalia," "oh, but you speak Danish!" It's like we cannot do anything at all . . . . So you have to explain all the time, like 'we are not like this, we are human beings as well, we also went to school.

So Hawa, Fatuma and many others spend a lot of time explaining that they are ordinary people, who have gone to school. That they have had ambitions, dreams, and hopes for the future, which the civil war terminated--for a while. That they do their best to be a part of Danish society. But while it is hard enough to be encountered with prejudice and ignorance as an adult, it is becomes really difficult when such encounters not only concern oneself, but also one's children. This is illustrated in the following story.

When it was time for Hawa's little girl to start in daycare, Hawa and her husband made a list of the institutions nearby in order to visit them and they agreed to tick off the institutions when they had contacted them. One day, Hawa called a daycare near by, but she was told that their waiting list was just too long and that there was no need to bother at all. Okay, she thought and forgot about it. She also forgot about ticking the daycare off from their list. However, when her Danish husband came home that afternoon, he started phoning, and phoned the same institution. This time, the message was completely different. "Oh, do come by, we have plenty of space for new kids," the voice on the phone said. This experience made both Hawa and her husband angry and disturbed. Hawa said:

> Imagine that the same child is experiencing two completely different . . . treatments, just because her father is Danish and I am Somali. Also when I walk with her in the streets, very few people say like "oh, she has beautiful hair" or things like that. But when she is with her father, it is like everybody admires her and she turns into another girl. It is the same girl, but she experiences another face of Denmark, if it is her father or her mother who is with her.

The daycare wanting to avoid Hawa and her daughter, as well as people on the street reacting differently to her daughter whether she or husband walk with her, are examples of biological racism as well as so-called new racism. Whereas biological racism relates to the idea that biology and skin color defines the social characteristics of people and thus their worth, in new racism, biology has been replaced and supplemented by ideas of culture and religion,[13] for instance in relation to Islam as an emblem of overwhelming and threatening difference. In a Danish context, where there is no official vocabulary of 'race', new racism seems to be quite outspoken in the more populist debates of non-Western, Muslim immigrants. Still, the two kinds of racism might well feed into and reinforce each other. The black skin color and, for some Somali-Danish women, the style of dressing, becomes a site for ideas of threatening cultural and religious practices, which are transferred to individual Somali-Danes.

For Fatuma, the ongoing debates about immigrants and her own experiences of discrimination have made her doubt whether she can keep on living in Denmark. "I don't mind living in Denmark," she says, and continues:

> The problem is . . . that you think about the future of your kids. Can they have a future here? I know they can go to school, of course, and pursue further studies, but can they feel self-confident, can they feel equal to the Danes? When they are done with the university will they feel that it also their country and that they can do something? It is very important for me that my children do well. So in that way, it is difficult to say that we can live here for the rest of our lives.

For Fatuma and Hawa, then, while asylum in Denmark does provide highly valued security from the civil war as well as health, education and peace, there remains a feeling of insecurity about the future of the children. Abdirizak shares this worry, but also points out that life in Denmark poses big challenges for the adults. While he maintains these challenges are not harder as such for men than for women, he still emphasizes the problem of unemployment and the following lack of respect that many men seem to encounter. This causes considerable frustration, among other things, because the men cannot fulfill the duty of providing for their families, that Islam and widely held cultural gender ideals prescribe.

> The men are not providing for their families, they just receive social security, as do their wives, and it's not a lot of money . . . . They are trying to find employment, but they are not able to because of language barriers and lack of education, it is very hard for them . . . . Sometimes they

> try to communicate with the Danes, but they are turned down, or when they apply for a job, they are turned down and then they start to withdraw, or they feel discouraged and they get so upset. . . . After a while, they think "I don't have any opportunities here, what shall I do? Denmark doesn't need me, so I have to find another place to live." Because you cannot be on social security your whole life, you just cannot, it is a very. . . tough life, a lonely life, an unpleasant life.

Abdirizak is not alone in these frustrations. The difficulties many Somali men have coping with life in Denmark and more generally in the West are widely discussed among Somalis in Denmark and elsewhere. Many Somali-Danish women find themselves socially isolated and busy taking care of their families while having to attend language school, activation or employment at the same time. Still, they have a reputation for coping better, for exploiting and enjoying the possibilities and rights that the Danish welfare state offers.[14] Certainly, this should not lead us to the general idea that all Somali-Danish women do well, while all the men are suffering. The point is the situation of Somali-Danish men is often articulated as especially difficult because of the changes in family and gender relations where many men seem to lose authority and respect. However, as the daycare story shows us, Danish institutions might not be very welcoming toward Somali-Danish women. And in the case of Abdirizak, his family is currently in the process of relocating to the UK--on the initiative of his wife, who is tired of the pressures of daily life in Denmark. Not everybody, however, dreams of leaving Denmark. Ali Mohamed, the final case study I present here, does not see himself moving to the UK or the US.

ALI MOHAMED: DANISH AND TRANSNATIONAL COMMITMENTS

Ali Mohamed lived on a farm in the countryside in Somalia. He had finished high school and started to work in a factory, but had to leave with his family when the civil war approached their home area. After a few years in Kenya, the family raised enough money so that Ali Mohamed could seek asylum in Sweden. While in transit in Copenhagen, however, Ali Mohamed could not proceed, and had to stay in Denmark. After a few months at an asylum centre in Copenhagen, he was sent to a very small island, but later moved back to Copenhagen where he graduated from business school. Ali Mohamed is divorced and lives with two foster children. He supports his mother and siblings in Kenya financially and thus has responsibility for quite a number of people. Ali Mohamed has worked for shorter periods in different firms, and as is Abdirizak, he is very active in a variety of Somali associations, which involve activities that are directed towards both Denmark and Somalia. His engagements include local radio, a local Somali club and several Somali transnational reconstruction projects.

Even though Ali Mohamed does not think that life in Denmark is always easy, he does not want to start all over again in another country. Still, it is no secret, he says, that many Somalis are having a hard time in Denmark. Even if he does not wish to go to the UK, the US or Canada, Ali Mohamed still thinks that many Somalis do better in these countries and he points out that many educated Somalis choose to move on. It is brain drain, Ali Mohamed continues, and bad business for Denmark. He says, "There are certain system barriers, many people are pacified. . . . I don't know who to blame. Is it the Danish society that cannot accept us, or are we the problem?" In his own case, however, he emphasizes his engagements locally in Denmark as well as in Somalia. He explains to me:

> I don't think there is anything preventing us in integrating in our society, on the one hand, and supporting the reconstruction in our homeland, on the other hand. Because all the educated people left Somalia, so it is necessary that we do something. If we don't, there are only warlords left . . . . I am a member of the local integration council and do different things, I mean local things, right, and on the other hand, I think, we should spend some time on supporting our homeland . . . . I think that if you are okay yourself, you should help other people, right.

Ali Mohamed does indeed commit himself to helping out in different places. "We are a part of society," he says and emphasizes that you have to do something yourself. He talks about "our society," Denmark, and "our homeland," Somalia, without any opposition between the two allegiances. Ali Mohamed lives in what Nina Glick Schiller and Georges Fouron have termed a transnational social field: "networks of social relationships that link together an array of transmigrants and individuals in the homeland connected to each other through kinship, friendship, business, religion or politics".[15] Though transnational relations might not be unproblematic, Ali Mohamed's case shows us that simultaneous transnational and local engagements are possible without incorporation in Danish society is impaired. For him, both engagements are central to his life in Denmark. Still, while engagement in Denmark usually is valued from the Somali side, this is not necessarily the case the other way around: Generally speaking, transnational engagements are not encouraged in Danish society.[16] On the contrary, double allegiances and engagements tend to be ignored or seen as disturbing or even threatening for the integration in Danish society.

COMPLICATED IDENTIFICATION

While Ali Mohamed situates himself in a transnational social field that exceeds the national order of belonging and engagements, Hawa and Fatuma seem to regard their relations to Denmark more ambivalently. When I asked them how they think of themselves in terms of being Somali-Danish, Danish, Somali or something completely different, they agreed that this was a tough question and continued with the following conversation:

> Fatuma: You can say that I am from Somalia, but anyway . . . . I have picked up many, many things from the Danes, where I can say that I am a part of the Danish society. . . .
>
> Hawa: I . . . because of my education, my Danish education, my teachers, my friends, they are all Danish. So in a way I feel a part . . . but I would never say that I am Danish. I would say that I am a Somali woman who is a part of Danish society. I don't know why. . . . I really appreciate my education, you know, I am very grateful

> for what I learned and that Denmark received me, when I needed it. I will always do my best for Denmark. But even if I am a Danish citizen, deep down I feel Somali. I tell my husband that if I die in Denmark, he will have to send my body to Somalia. That is what I think.
>
> Fatuma: But then we cannot request that the Danes. . . accept us as Danish, can we?
>
> Hawa: But they need to accept us as are we are, as a part . . . otherwise Denmark will never be multiethnic, if everyone has to become Danish. We will never get blue eyes or blond hair. The Danes have to accept us. In the States there is China Town . . . and that's how it should be, I think. You don't throw away your background and your identity – your former identity – just because you lived here for ten years . . . . Here there is nothing like "I am an African-Dane" or . . . Latin-Dane or Arab-Dane or Pakistani-Dane or anything like that. Either-or and that what's I don't like.

For Hawa, then, one of the barriers of inclusion in Denmark is the exclusivity of Danishness as reserved to white-skinned bodies with blue eyes and blond hair. For her, the absence of hyphenated identities such as African-Dane, excludes her and other non-white persons from being considered Danish.[17] Not everybody, however, would agree that hyphenated identities do not exist. When I asked interviewees to explain their identities, several Somali-Danish parents used the term Somali-Danish to describe their children, who were raised in Denmark, but not themselves. Furthermore, several of the interviewees who were interviewed in Somaliland or London identified themselves as Somali-Danish.[18] Still, the term Somali-Dane or African-Dane is not part of the dominating public discourse of migrants' identities or fields of belonging.

Hawa, then, does not want to fit into the exclusive category of Danishness; she wants to expand it, to reflect the multiethnic reality. Though she considers herself a part of Danish society, she does not see herself as Danish. The question of being a part of society and part of a nation--the tension between civic and national belonging-

-turns into a Catch 22: migrants are expected to become Danish (for instance by dressing and behaving in certain ways), but still cannot be accepted as such, because the dominant understandings of Danishness remain too exclusive. For some, "being or becoming Danish" not only presents itself as an impossible task, but also an undesirable one; it is an invective term to designate reserved and busy people, and in the eyes of some, a threat to Somali culture. This is not what Hawa or any of the other three interviewees express, but it is important to underline that one aspect of the exclusive and narrow Danishness is the prospect of reverse distance. For Fatuma, the lack of inclusion does not turn into contempt for or distance to Denmark, but creates of feeling of never feeling "secure in your heart." She says:

> The hardest thing about life in Denmark is that you know, that you will never . . . feel really secure . . . in your heart, I mean, and say that 'now I am not a stranger any longer, but a part of this country. It was hard when we fled our country. It wasn't because we hated it, it but we had to. And then we came to another country and it is not like that we thought we would be dependent on it all the time. We cannot forget our roots . . . we would like to keep them as well . . . . It is not like Somalis who fled to the States or Canada or the UK. They don't have this pressure that we have in Denmark.

Fatuma, then, expresses the same dilemma: A pressure to give up her "roots," while feeling that she will remain a stranger anyway. Not everybody, however, articulates this dilemma, as Ali Mohamed's example showed us. Nevertheless, it is my impression that the feeling of not really belonging is a common one. One of the responses of this dilemma is a desire to leave Denmark behind and try one's luck somewhere else.

MOVING ON

Fatuma and Abdirizak certainly are not the only ones who desire to move on from Denmark. The exact amount of Somalis who have left Denmark the later years is unknown, but it is estimated that as many as 3,000 Somali-Danes have left Denmark within the last few years to move to cities in the UK such as London, Birmingham, Leicester and Cardiff.[19] Somali migrants not only depart from Denmark, but also from Sweden, Norway, and Holland. Furthermore, there seem to be other migrant groups on the move as well, who, as naturalized EU citizens, make use of the possibility of free movement within the European Union. For Hawa, Fatuma, Abdirizak and many others, the UK and other multicultural societies such as the US and Canada are seen to offer opportunites for a more dignified and equal life. These countries are contrasted to Denmark, where the categories of *andengenerationsindvandrer* (second generation immigrant), *pæredansker* (real Dane) or *de fremmede* (the strangers) etc. are constantly in play, pointing out an insurmountable difference. The UK, Canada and the US are places, the story goes, where it is possible to be a part of society without the skin color or religion is "getting in the way," as it often seems to happen in Denmark. The fact that many Somalis have family members in the UK, that language problems might be fewer, and the idea that jobs are easier to find obviously also contributes to the attraction of these places. Whether London and elsewhere actually offer a better life is indeed another story,[20] but the longing for another life, a life without the perpetual categorization of being a stranger, is widespread.

CONTESTED CATEGORIES OF BELONGING

One way to explain the absence of and resistance to complicated, transnational identifications is proposed by sociologists Zygmunt Bauman and Bülent Diken.[21] According to Bauman and Diken, the stigmatization of strangers is a response to the complexity and insecurity of late-modern life, marked by the uncertainties of economic globalization and societal changes. Bauman suggests that the anxiety of an uncertain present and future are transformed into policies of controlling and policing immigration. Along a similar vein, Diken proposes that the stigmatization of certain migrant groups is a way for receiving societies to handle migrants and their possible ambiguous multi-stranded fields of belonging. Inspired by Georg Simmel's famous article about strangers,[22] Diken claims that migrants' ambiguous identities and fields of belonging are reduced and stabilized into singular, unambiguous categories belonging only there and thus not here. The categories of us and them are, in other words, stabilized, ordered and (re-)established, as is the belonging to national and cultural categories, i.e. *Danish* versus *Somali* and so on. This process works, in other words, counter to transnational fields of belonging and supports an idea that incorporation into Danish society requires singular, unambiguous and non-complex identifications and engagements.

Obviously, this argument is not the only explanation of the ambivalent encounters with Danish society or of the absence of hyphenated identities. The nationalist or reductive version of Danishness is not the only one in circulation or the only one which Somali-Danes might come across. As Hawa said, Denmark has two faces, and while one is based on ignorance and sometimes hostility, the other face is friendly and accommodating. Furthermore, we should remember that the mechanisms of exclusion and oppression within national categories. Indeed, there is no agreement on who and what is recognized, included or excluded in the categories of Somali and Somaliness, or Danish or Danishness. National categories (like other categories of collective identification) are powerful discursive constructions that are constantly renegotiated, but which nevertheless posses a certain sluggishness and, certainly, have real consequences in terms of the rights, protection and possibilities for individuals. Still, the existence or non-existence of hyphenated identities as available categories of identification can be seen as a possible barometer for the inclusiveness or exclusiveness of national and ethnic categories. It might provide us with a hint of the flexibility of the boundaries of belonging and of us-and-them categories, both in relation to the host country and migrant groups.

CONCLUSION

In this chapter, I have discussed ambivalent encounters between Somali-Danes and Danish society and how ideas of Danishness and Somaliness may shape identifications and perceptions of incorporation. I have argued that individuals are often encountered as stereotypes and not met in their individuality. This stigmatizing stereotyping happens both at the general level, by the constant exposure of

Somalis and other Muslim, non-Western migrants as the strangers, as well as in everyday encounters. Furthermore, I have suggested that for some Somalis in Denmark, the seeming impossibility of being an accepted and equal part of Denmark may create a reverse distance where Danishness is rendered undesirable. For others, it creates a feeling of uneasiness, a lack of "security in the heart," and a desire to leave Denmark. This is, inspired by the words of Hawa, the other face of Denmark, or rather perhaps, the othering face of Denmark.

Finally, inspired by theoretical reflections on strangeness and stigmatization, I have argued that stigmatization of migrant groups, can be seen as a way of stabilizing ambivalence by reducing complexity into singular, "frozen" cultures and identities; making hyphenated identities improbable and the categories of Somali and Danish mutually exclusive. One consequence might be that transnational practices in which many Somalis engage, such as remitting money to family members, supporting reconstruction projects, etc., risk being seen as an a priori barrier towards incorporation. My argument is that these processes of negotiating the categories and boundaries of Danishness, Somaliness and incorporation is an important context of Somali identification and belonging that many, if not most, individual Somali-Danes will have to cope with and respond to in their own unique ways.

Acknowledgements

This paper was presented at the annual Danish Congress of Sociology 2005, and, in a Danish version, at the seminar *Den stille integration* (The silent integration). I thank all participants and the organizers for inspiring and challenging questions and comments. Likewise I thank the editors for useful suggestions. Most of all, I thank Hawa, Fatuma, Abdirizak, Ali Mohamed and many others for sharing their stories with me.

Notes

1. Part of the present chapter is a revised and translated version of a Danish paper: *Danmarks to ansigter. Stille integration og stille diskrimination blandt somali-danskere*, M. H. Pedersen & M. Rytter (Eds.).

(forthcoming). *Den stille integration. Nye fortællinger om at høre til i Danmark'*. Copenhagen: A.C. Reitzels Forlag.

2. I put 'race' in adverted commas to underline the point that the idea of 'race' as a biologically given is a social construction, but with real consequences.

   See Kusow, A. M. (2004). Contesting stigma: On Goffman's assumption of normative order. *Social Interaction*, 2, 179-197.

3. Statistikbanken. (2004). Befolkning og valg. BEF3. Retrieved from http://www.statistikbanken.dk. Danmarks Statistik 2004. Udlændingestyrelsen. Udlændingestyrelsen– beretning 2003. pp. 47-48.

4. See Fink-Nielsen, M., Hansen, P., & Kleist, N. (2004). Roots, rights and responsibilities. Place-making and repatriation among Somalis in Denmark and Somaliland. *Stichproben. Vienna Journal of Critical African Studies*, 7, 25-48.

   Fadel, U. H., Hervik, P., & Vestergaard, G. (1999). De "besværlige" Somaliere. In P. Hervik (Ed.), *Den generende forskellighed. Danske svar på den stigende multikulturalisme* (pp. 171-213). Copenhagen: Hans Reitzels Forlag.

   Jørgensen, R. E., & Bülow, V. S. (1999). Ali og de fyrretyve k(roner). En analyse af Ekstra Bladets kampagne "fremmede" og om læsernes opfattelse af forskellighed. In P. Hervik (Ed.), *Den generende forskellighed. Danske svar på den stigende multikulturalisme* (pp. 81-107). Copenhagen: Hans Reitzels Forlag.

5. Fraser, N. (1995). From redistribution to recognition? Dilemmas of justice in a 'Post-Socialist' age. *New Left Review*, 212, 68-93.

   As Nancy Fraser argues, groups might encounter economic and cultural domination at the same time and it is necessary not to conflate these two kinds of injustices. While I both present the socio-economic and cultural aspects of marginalization here, the main focus of the paper remains on the cultural and symbolic perspectives.

6. Statistikbanken. (2004). Befolkning og valg. BEF3. Retrieved from http://www.statistikbanken.dk. Danmarks Statistik 2004. Udlændingestyrelsen. Udlændingestyrelsen– beretning 2003.

7. For other Scandinavian countries see Assal, M. A. M. (2004). *Sticky labels or rich ambiguities? Diaspora and challenges of homemaking for Somalis and Sudanese in Norway*. Oslo: BRIC, University of Bergen.

   Fangen, K. (2004, September). Identity and symbolic ethnicity among Somali immigrants in Norway. Aalborg, Denmark: 9th International Congress of Somali Studies.

Halane, F. W. (2004, September). “Otherness” – a challenge or an obstacle for Somali-Swedish women in Sweden. Aalborg, Denmark: 9th International Congress of Somali Studies.

8. Kusow, A. M. (2004). Contesting stigma: On Goffman’s assumption of normative order. *Social Interaction*, 2, 179-197.
9. Apart from a general tightening of asylum legislation (which has had the explicit purpose of reducing the number of Somali asylum seekers), the requirements of fluency in Danish have been raised, and it has become more difficult to obtain Danish citizenship. At the more general level, Danishness is celebrated in the proliferation of canons of Danish literature and culture, which has been initiated by the Danish government to preserve and strengthen Danish culture.
10. Malkki, L. (1992). National geographic: The rooting of peoples and the territorialization of national identity among scholars and refugees. *Cultural Anthropology*, 1, 24-44.
11. Olwig, K. F. (1999). Narratives of belonging: Life stories in family networks of West Indian background. CDR Working Paper 99.7, 27-48. p. 29.
12. This fieldwork was undertaken for my Ph.D. in Sociology at the University of Copenhagen. Interviewees’ names and details of their stories were changed for reasons of anonymity.
13. Castles, S. (2000). *Ethnicity and globalization. From migrant worker to transnational citizen*. London, Thousand Oaks & New Delhi: Sage Publications. pp. 163-186.
14. I base this claim on my interviews as well as on my participation in various seminars and conferences where gender and family relations have been discussed. An example is the 9th Somali Studies International Conference, Aalborg, Denmark, September 2004.
15. Glick Schiller, N., Fouron, G. (2001). *Georges woke up laughing: Long-distance nationalism and the search for home*. Durham & London: Duke University Press. p. 3.
16. See Østergaard-Nielsen, E. (2002). *Politik over grænser. Tyrkere og kurderes engagement i det politiske liv i hjemlandet*. Aarhus: Magtudredningen.
17. My usage of the term Somali-Dane is not meant to describe how the interviewees think about their identity, but to emphasize that Somalis in Denmark are a part of Danish society.
18. See also Kusow, A. M. (2004). Contesting stigma: On Goffman’s assumption of normative order. *Social Interaction*, 2, 179-197.

19. Nielsen, K. B. (2004). Next stop Britain: The influence of transnational networks on the secondary movement of Danish Somalis. Sussex Migration Working Papers 22, 1-21.

    Nielsen suggests that as many as every four Somalis in Denmark have left or are planning to do. Somali-Danish key persons support this assertion. It is however not possible to demonstrate this statistically, as there are no statistics showing the number of naturalized Somalis leaving Denmark.

20. Harris, H. (2004). The Somali community in the UK: What we know and how we know it. London: The Information Centre about Asylum and Refugees in the UK (ICAR).

    Griffiths, D. (2002). *Somali and Kurdish refugees in London. New identities in the diaspora*. Aldershot: Ashgate.

    Bloch, A., Artfield, G. (2002). The professional capacity of nationals from the Somali regions in Britain. London: Goldsmith College, University of London.

21. Diken, B. (1998). *Strangers, ambivalence and social theory*. Aldershot: Ashgate.

    Bauman, Z. (1998). Europe of strangers. In D. Broen, & K. B. Bertelsen (Eds.), *Europe of strangers. Integration policy in a comparative perspective* (pp.4-14). Copenhagen: The Danish Refugee Council & the Danish Cultural Institute.

22. Simmel, G. (1950). The stranger. In K. H. Wolff (Ed.), *The Sociology of Georg Simmel*. New York: The Free Press.

Chapter 8

"DID YOU SEE HER STANDING AT THE MARKETPLACE?" GENDER, GOSSIP, AND SOCIO-SPATIAL BEHAVIOR OF SOMALI GIRLS IN TURKU, FINLAND

Anu Isotalo

INTRODUCTION

In this chapter, I concentrate on ideals and practices concerning gendered moral and socio-spatial behavior of Somali girls (approximately 17–23 years of age) in the city of Turku in the Western coast of Finland.[1] First, I discuss gendered ideals, expectations, norms and socio-spatial practices described by the Somali girls and women themselves.[2] According to them, what is considered morally appropriate or inappropriate socio-spatial behavior for Somali girls in Turku? I concentrate mainly in places and spaces outside of the home. Second, I examine the role of social networks and gossip, especially with reference to individual and social self-definitions and socio-spatial behavior. Third, I pay attention to differences in girls' behavior in Turku and in the metropolitan area of Helsinki, represented by the interviewees living in Turku. In other words, the focus will not be on descriptions and opinions of everyday life in Helsinki told by those girls and women who live there, but on impressions and interpretations of life styles in Helsinki expressed by girls and women in Turku.

At present, there are approximately 450 Somalis living in Turku. The total population of Somalis in Finland is approximately 8,600.[3] Extracts of interviews below are examples taken from the research material. However, the material does not form a representative sample of attitudes and thoughts of Somali girls and women living in Turku. Somalis in Finland do not constitute a uniform group either in interpretations of Islam, socio-economic status or place of origin previously in Somalia. All in all, however, the examples illustrate *socially recognized* ideals and practices among Somalis in Turku, even if they should not be interpreted as commonly shared, agreed or definitive.

SPACE AND GOSSIP AS SOCIALLY CONSTRUCTED

Depending on the context, gendered socio-spatial aspects of behavior may be considered relevant in estimations of morally good or bad behavior. To begin with, I define briefly some of the crucial concepts related to socio-spatiality. Here *space* is primarily regarded as relational, socially negotiable and culturally produced. *Place* is defined as a socially and culturally constructed space, to which a person has associated personal meanings, experiences and memories.[4] In other words, space is meaningful for a person or a group of persons as a certain kind of space, that is, a place. Accordingly, there can be various simultaneous social spaces in the same physical space.[5] Space is also inseparably connected to time: the marketplace may be regarded as a place for shopping in the daytime, but at night it may be thought of as a dangerous or socially degrading place. For instance, if a girl or a woman is seen standing or "hanging around" at the marketplace, it may implicitly be associated to her (lack of) moral and sexual value. Hence, with the concept *socio-spatial behavior* I refer to socially, culturally and temporally recognised behavior interpreted in relation to and in interaction with other people in places where social encounters and activities occur.

However, in the construction of socio-spatial meanings, the relationship between the organization of space and social bodies cannot be considered as a nonrecursive model where the physical environment is directly seen as influencing the nature and the production of socio-spatial meanings. Rather, the production of socio-spatial meanings must be seen as recursive, such that physical environments influence identities and the movement of bodies, while bodies also produce socially shared space and impregnate it with culture specific meanings.[6] Further, space is constructed in a constant process as gendered as well as gendering. Among Somalis in Turku, this means, first, socio-spatial segregation of different sexes according to religious and cultural tradition. Second, certain places are perceived as significantly gendered (e.g. "a woman's place is at home" or "men often socialize at the center or in the cafeterias"). This, however, does not mean that they are literally considered as such.

The fourth key concept of the research is *gossip*. In everyday talk, the word "gossip" often has negative connotations. It has most usually been considered as malevolent slandering or at least as idle talk.[7] However, in ethnographic research, gossip is perceived as a common social phenomenon among others, not as an exceptional or morally deprived social practice as such.[8] In fact, gossip may have important social functions: it may work as a means to articulate and negotiate socially shared or contested values within different kinds of social spheres and networks (schools, workplaces, small towns, villages, different kinds of social groups etc.).[i] Further, gossip may communicate relevant information about everyday actions and social relations.[10] Thus, in the construction, maintenance, definition, differentiation and (re)production of a social group, gossip may – depending on other factors and the socio-cultural context – have a crucial significance in manifesting and communicating the social and moral boundaries of a community.

Briefly defined, gossip is here regarded as a form of communication, which requires, first, a certain kind of social relation (sender, receiver and object of gossip); second, non-presence of a third party (object); third, accentuation of the extraordinary (for instance unexpected, inappropriate or otherwise noteworthy stories); and finally, often some kind of moral comment or indignation expressed by speaker.[11] As a genre that functions to establish the honor or dishonor of community members, gossip is a field of contestation.[12] Further, gossip within social networks can be considered as an informal strategy to gather and spread information. It may also be used as a means of manipulation. Gossip is social knowledge, and knowledge is closely connected to power. In order to gain some kind of personal advantage, knowledge can be used as a resource in reciprocal exchange.[13]

Some of the informants mentioned a Somali saying "men drink tea and women gossip." Interestingly, in many cultures the tendency to gossip has in folklore and everyday stereotypical representations been especially related to women. Nevertheless, talking about others' affairs is a well-known activity among women as well as among men and children.[14] The interviewees themselves attached different meanings to gossip, and explained it in their own ways. This chapter is based on the interpretations of these explanations, thoughts and opinions. I examine gossip mainly as a means of informal social control of socio-spatial behavior: more thorough consideration of power aspects, social relations and the status of gossipers (gender, age, possible motives) as well as the analysis of different functions of common talk and gossip remain beyond the focus of the chapter.

AN IDEAL SOMALI GIRL AND GENDERED EXPECTATIONS

There are expectations about socially acceptable behavior in every culture. These ideals are often somehow gendered and inconsistent with actual everyday practices. Rules of Islam were mentioned as significant moral markers for decent behavior and clothing for Somali girls. An ideally good Somali girl, according to the interviewees, behaves shyly and politely. She does not speak "too much," both in general and especially when communicating with boys and men. By this she also expresses her modesty and premarital abstinence from sexual relations. She wears a scarf and a skirt, reads Koran, prays regularly and wants to be successful in her studies. Further, she respects her parents and other older people, helps her mother with the housework, and takes care of smaller children in the family. Instead of spending time in the city with no reason, a good girl stays at home.

However, the research material reflects a variety of opinions on practices of everyday socio-spatial behavior. Rather different or even opposite ideas were justified on religious grounds. Regarding clothing, for example, some of the informants referred to "devotion of the heart" in stating that being a good Muslim is a matter of a pure heart and pure thoughts, not a matter of using a veil. They did not use a scarf regularly, especially when spending time in the metropolitan area of Helsinki. Other informants stressed that inner devotion is expressed by using a veil and skirt: for them, other choices were signs of sexual moral indecency. Wearing tight trousers and no scarf was also associated with "becoming (too) Finnish." Further, some interviewees explained that young Somali girls in their puberty wanted to try different things, and saw it as part of their youth. Those who did not prefer to wear a scarf may after a few years change their opinion. In this way it was interpreted as an understandable part of a process of growing up and to becoming a girl and a woman.[15]

I suggest that representations of decent behavior for Somali girls can be described by the metaphor of a girl "being closed." She is "closed" because of her moderate behavior towards men, her covering style of clothing, and her socially expected positions ("inside") in the gendered space.[16] Immoral behavior, on the other hand, is attached to social and bodily openness, e.g. noticeable talkativeness in the presence of men, as well as an indifferent attitude to either the rules of covering body figures or conventions of socio-spatial behavior within and outside of domestic spheres.

FINNISH CONTEXT AND CONCERNS ABOUT CULTURAL SOCIO-SEXUAL CHANGE

For Somalis in Finland, ethnicity, religion and "socio-sexual" gendered ideals and practices have become significant markers of social boundaries between Finnish and Somali culture. With the concept socio-sexual I refer to those forms of gendered behavior (i.e. verbal and non-verbal communicative patterns), which in certain social and cultural context are interpreted as expressions of sexual meanings, and, because of that socially accepted and/or suitable or forbidden and/or indecent. There are different standards for males and females in many cultures. For instance, boys' initiatives towards girls and their seeking of sexual experiences may in everyday humorous talk be explained—and socially justified—by the commonly recognized phrase "boys are boys." A boy's behavior may also increase, not spoil, his reputation as "a boy who knows how to handle girls." In contrast, the same kind of active behavior for a girl towards boys may be regarded indecent and detrimental for her sexual reputation.[17] In other words, socio-sexual expectations may be notably gendered.

There are differences in social norms concerning Somali girls and their Finnish peers, too. In contrast to a Somali ideal, it is common for Finnish adolescent girls to spend time outside the home or household environments. Spending time in the city center, in cafeterias, pubs or discos are considered socially recognized and accepted ways of meeting peers. The objectionable Finnish "they" for Somali girls may be, then, manifested in the behavior of those Finnish girls and women who take a "too open" attitude towards boys and men, wear overly revealing clothes, drink alcohol in nightclubs, and have pre-marital sex. Consequently, Somali girls growing up in Finland, attending Finnish schools and getting to know the Finnish youth culture, encounter situations in which they are—constantly and repeatedly—faced with differing views on gendered valuations of behavior.[18] One interviewee talked about a Somali girl without scarf and skirt as follows:[19]

> She is proud and she doesn't listen to what other people [Somalis] say. She just accepts what they all say. And little by little, things get worse, and every day she hears "they said this and this and this about you." And it gets worse. Now it can be that she is wearing trousers but has done nothing bad. She has only taken off her skirt and wears trousers, nothing else. But they may say that if she is wearing trousers, she has given up on her faith, or that she has changed from a decent girl into a whore. She was not a whore, but if some people say "whore whore whore" and she hears it, it can be that she gets tired of what other people say. And then she may even become a whore. Or goes after what they have already named her for.[20]

The interviewee both interprets the reason for a girl not conforming to rules of clothing and describes the defining power of social networks in Turku. According to her, the decision to wear trousers may in everyday talk be understood as a sign of losing her religion and sexual moral decency. Moreover, partly because of social disapproval and gossip, a girl may adopt her socially and morally degraded position as "a whore." In this extract, it is possible to perceive the idea of a self-fulfilling prophecy.[21] According to the theory of self-fulfilling prophecy, a person begins to behave in line with social expectations laid upon her. Here, one bad choice is assumed to lead to another, and the result will be socially and individually detrimental for the person in question. The idea and fear of "gradual worsening" in Finland was one recurring theme in interviews, too. However, as discussed above, this was not the only interpretation concerning dress codes. Ideas of gradual worsening may also be examined in discussions about dangers of becoming "too Finnish." In several examples in the research material, "to become Finnish," meant the same as "to become worse." There were, however, also positive connotations of Finnishness mentioned, e.g. having a good education, getting a permanent job or speaking fluent Finnish.[22]

It seems that in diaspora the clothing as well as the behavior of Somali girls and women has become a more important sign of individual and collective commitment to religion, culture of origin, and moral standards.[23] In the Finnish socio-cultural context, the interpretation of departures from gendered rules and expectations may also differ from that in Somalia.

> I: That is interesting when you said that in Somalia, culture was, cultural customs were strong, and when you came to Finland, something changed. Could you tell me something more about it?
>
> R: For example the clothing. In Somalia, before you were married, you didn't have to wear scarf.[24] Here it became like, even if you were so young girl you had to put it immediately. People are afraid of that; they change. I don't know what they are afraid of. I am not trying to forget my own growing up and my own culture. I try to keep them; I am a Muslim and I try my best to behave according to all rules, but I do not want to change everything in my life, like I should try to be something that I am not. I cannot live like that. But there are some people who try to show that they are Muslims [hits her hands together]. They are so strong [hits her hands together], so and so and plaa plaa plaa. I cannot stand that.
>
> I: Mm. What do you think? Why do they try like that?
>
> R: People are very afraid

I: What are they afraid of?

R: That they will change. Or if you don't know, if you change into something you are not. But I think it is stupid to have that kind of fear.

I: Are people afraid of someone's opinions too, like if someone [Somali] is observing how they live here?

R: Yes, people always talk and we are [a] small [group]. We are a small minority here, those who live here [in Turku]. It is true that people always talk, and children become evaluated. How you raise them, what kind of people they will be.[25]

The woman stated that Somalis are worried about losing their religious and cultural identity in Finland. Previously in Somalia, seeing a girl without a scarf was not similarly regarded as a sign of social change or a threat to cultural continuity. Those interviewees, who (or whose friends or relatives) had traveled to Somalia during summer vacation told that they were surprised when they noticed certain differences between behavior of Somalis living in Finland and in Somalia. According to them, Somalis in Finland (here especially in Turku) followed gendered rules and social segregation between girls and boys more strictly than many Somalis they met in Somalia. Consequently, they were amazed by their impression of Somalis, as if they were becoming "more Somali" in Turku than they were in Somalia.[26] What to think of "Somali culture" cherished in diaspora if that differs so much from "culture in Somalia"? How to relate them?

It seems that in the case of Somali girls in Turku, deviations from (re)constructed traditional gender ideals and practices may easily be considered as signs of assimilation to Finnish majority culture—particularly to its non-desirable forms, for example, too liberal attitudes towards free time activities, girls' revealing clothing and premarital sexual experiences.[27] Further, expectations concerning Somali girls may constitute a constructed and reactive ideal in the Finnish context—one that recreates not necessarily what was truly practiced in Somalia, but what was an ideal.[28] This may be examined as an example of hybrid ideal created by a diasporic community.

By definition, hybrid ideals are constructed in relation to the homeland and the host environment. In diaspora, immigrants may create a more idealist value system in reaction to what is perceived as an overwhelming majority culture. In other words, the ideals may be constituted and reproduced also through the force of exclusion and abjection of certain features of the host culture.[29] In this case, intensification of ideals may serve to dissociate Somali culture from the assimilative power of the Finnish culture: In order to cherish Somali traditions in the diaspora, the immigrants may create more explicit norms and social expectations for the "true membership" of the community—who is, in this sense, defined as a "real" Somali, who has "changed" too much. Hence, any ideals are neither natural nor given, but the result of *discursive constructions* in a certain socio-cultural context.[30] These constructions, nevertheless, have real effects, as in the case of a Somali girl in Turku losing her sexual moral reputation because of gossip about her behavior outside of the home.

This chapter is not focused on Somali boys, but some kind of comparative aspect expressed by the interviewees may be considered relevant here. According to interviewees, Somali boys are allowed to move more freely than girls. One woman, after stating that a concern for good reputation is more apparent for a girl, said:

> Even if a boy drinks alcohol, his reputation stays the same. They [the Somalis] may say "okay, he has adopted the Western way of living." Sometimes they may say nasty things about him. But if a girl harms her reputation, she cannot cure the damage, not in a hundred years. "She was wild and then she married him." Same thing after thousand years. "She was a whore and [then] she married him."[31]

Another girl said that Somali girls are regarded fragile, as "glass, which gets broken very easily".[32] Boys, in contrast, are represented as being much stronger. She talked about different expectations for boys and girls, and criticized the double standards.

> The worst is always expected from a girl. That she ends up in bed with someone, that she ends up being married to a Finn, that she totally forgets her religion. That she is hanging around with Finnish people, that she takes more of their culture. The worst of all, Somali guys *do* these things, but there are no expectations for them.[33]

However, it seems that the image of "strong boys" and "fragile girls" has in a way changed in diaspora. According to the informants, parents are still more concerned about their daughters and the way they behave. They often explain this by stating that it is always the girl who is in danger to become pregnant outside of wedlock, which would be detrimental for her and her family's honor. Nonetheless, at the same time, some of them have become more anxious about their sons—not least because of their questionable free time activities outside the home, i.e. hanging around with gangs, drinking alcohol, and getting into trouble in the city. In addition, the concern for Somali girls was also regarded as a form of taking care of them and protecting them from dangers. Some of the interviewees stated that Somali boys would need the same kind of care and protection, too.[34]

MORAL GEOGRAPHIES: CITY AS A SOCIAL SPACE AND GIRLS' REPUTATION

Before presenting some interpretations of socio-spatial behavior and (female) gendered expectations, it is necessary to mention some basic facts about Turku. Somalis are the largest black minority group in the city of 175,000 inhabitants.[35] Because they are a relatively small ethnic minority, they often recognize each other by appearance. The city center area with shopping malls, restaurants, banks and bars is quite small. Almost all the city buses take their passengers around the marketplace, which is at the core of the center. Many Somali girls and women use public transportation between the center and suburban areas, where they live. Hence, Somalis are able to observe each other quite easily, for instance while sitting in a cafeteria near the market place (mostly men) or waiting for a bus.

According to culturally gendered ideals, Somali girls should stay at home instead of spending time outside domestic environments. However, it is quite normal for a girl or a woman to be seen in the center because of necessary daily comings and goings to school, work, bank, social office or shopping malls. Her behavior can be defined as exceptional if she is seen too often, too late or in "susceptible" company. In the next example, a girl describes the consequences for a Somali girl of being repeatedly "out of her place" in the center. According to her, this kind of girl both violates the honor of her family, and ends up to be an object of sexual and moral evaluation of other Somalis in Turku.[36]

> I: So do the girls usually go around in the city?
>
> R: It actually depends on the person. There are lots of girls who are at home, who are not involved with, who don't even remember what is going on in the city. And don't know anything. There are girls who go freely to the city and see there whatever they like. And even stay for a long time, late in the city. Yes, there are, but it is a choice for them to make. They have it bad, then. Bad name in the town.
>
> I: What does it mean, bad name? What do you mean?
>
> R: Bad name means that it is bad for her family. She has brought it. People say: "what is she doing in the city at this time of the day?"
>
> I: Is it like she is a bad girl?
>
> R: Bad girl, yes. If she is late in the city or today she walks with one boy, tomorrow again in a gang, she is like spending time there, not going there for a reason.
>
> I: So this [idea of] badness is associated with boys and men? That she is a bad girl, she is walking, spending a lot of time there and it can be that she is in contact with men, in contact with boys?
>
> R: Yes, and that, it can be, women can also complain that the girl is not nice anymore. Or is not good. That she has been in the city like this and this and some people have

> seen her and heard about her matters. That there are lots of her fingerprints, you know. There are many descriptions of her, and she has been seen.[37]

Social norms for behavior outside of home arise notably from the ideal of a Somali girl's premarital virginity and sexual purity. If a girl seemed to be spending time in the city, it harmed her sexual and moral reputation. She was evaluated as "a loose girl", whose socio-spatial behavior—and possibly her clothing style, too—was associated to lack of modesty and indecent sexual openness. Altogether, it was not only a question of her reputation, but the honor of her family, too.[38]

According to the interviewees, exceptions from socially shared, gendered socio-spatial expectations in Turku may be interpreted as signs of a girl's sexual impurity and immodest behavior, as demonstrated by expressions such as "town girl," "marketplace girl" (*gabadh suuqa)*, "whore" (*sharmuuto, dhilo*), and questions like "Why was she standing there at the marketplace, was she after a man or was she waiting for her boyfriend?"[39] Referring to the interview material, I suggest that in public spaces in Turku, Somalis outside of the girl's family have the possibility to define and label her either as sexually and morally indecent or decent enough. Consequently, this undermines the inviolability and the honor of her family, and opens up its private boundaries to the judgements of others.[40] Bad reputation may have relevance e.g. at the age when a girl gets married, as mentioned by one girl. A girl should avoid shame in order to be honored and socially valued.

> I believe that if some man sees a girl who spends time in the city, wears trousers and has no scarf, he thinks he can't marry that girl. There's no future with her. He would actually like to be with her, have fun, but a future together, I don't think so. That is because she has no shame.[41]

There was also variation in the opinions about socially acceptable behavior for Somali girls outside of the home. Differing opinions may be at least partially explained by previous social practices in Somalia related to socio-economic status and educational background. There were, for instance, differences in ideas about girls going to have coffee in the city center with their friends. Some of the interviewees stated that it is not appropriate or honorable for a Somali girl to go to cafeterias at all. The others saw no harm, except the possible consequences of gossip.[42]

GOSSIP AND SOCIAL CONTROL

Talking about other people's affairs was mentioned to be a part of everyday socializing among Somalis in Turku. According to the interviewees, Somali girls are one quite common topic: who has been seen talking or spending time with whom, who has a new boyfriend or maybe will get married soon, who is seen often in the center, who wears overly revealing or tight clothes or does not wear a scarf. In the next extract, the interviewee describes her experiences after meeting her friends in a cafeteria in Turku. She compared her leisure time activities in Africa and in Finland and found some crucial differences. These differences were also related to sharpening of social norms and ideals discussed above.

> R: And every afternoon [in Africa] I went for a coffee with my cousins. Nobody ever said anything to me there. Nobody told me what is it that becomes worse if I do that. And I did not know, then. But when I moved to Finland I was, I thought that things would be the same than before in Africa. But in Finland it was different.
>
> I: So in Finland it is more like…
>
> R: More, in Finland they [Somalis] understand more about everything. Really. More than we when we were in Africa.
>
> I: Mm. Did you mean that in Finland there is more or less understanding?
>
> R: Some understand more, some understand less. But still, my mother has never said to me "don't go there, don't do anything." My mother does not have time to tell me what is right, what is wrong. But she tells me at least about reli-

> gion, what you cannot do and things like that. But about cafeterias nobody told me. [In Africa] I always went with my cousin and mother trusted on that. I came to Finland and I thought that it's the same thing here. I went. When I was seen there in the cafeteria everybody talked to mother about that. Then I said [to her] "well, you heard my name, I won't go to a cafeteria anymore." If I nowadays go to a cafeteria, I don't go to those places where I can be seen, so that people [Somalis] know where I was. Not anymore. I go to have a coffee, but somewhere else, where people cannot see me.[43]

All the interviewees were aware of the possibility of becoming an object of observation at the center of Turku. They named certain cafeterias and places, which were known to be famous among Somali boys and men. Many of the girls stated that if they went to a cafeteria, they stayed away from those places where they knew Somali men would used to go. This is because they wanted to avoid the risk of being a topic of the men's coffee table, and after that, the subject of circulating gossip about their possible motives to spend time in a cafeteria ("what are they/is she looking for?").

The interviewees gave different explanations to lively gossip in Turku.

> I: You said that Somali women talk a lot about each other's things. Why is that?
>
> R: They don't have enough things to do. If they had something to do they won't, they wouldn't have time. But they don't have anything to do other than childcare and shopping. And then in a shop [a grocery store] they meet someone and then they talk about the happenings of the day and the highlights of the week. And then they go to the bank and meet someone else, and then they go to the social welfare office and see someone and then they come home and the telephone rings.[44]

This extract is an example of interpretation of gossip as a way of spending time, to have some extra activity and entertainment.

Some of the informants also regarded unemployment and lack of studying possibilities as an explanation for lively circulating gossip in Turku.[45] The following example illustrates not only lively gossip, but also the role talking about other people may have in starting a discussion.

> R: It's like, nowadays we say FM [radio channel], they tell immediately. It's like [news] from the radio, they tell right away, you know everything.
>
> I: To whom do they tell, why do they tell?
>
> R: [before the year 2000] If I walk in the street or in the shopping mall, somebody sees me and they go and tell my brother. "I have seen [her name] walking in the street." Why, what is the meaning? Nothing, but he wants to have a reason to start to talk.[46]

Besides radio channel, gossip was humorously compared to an advertisement or to two of the local newspapers in the interviews. In other words, gossip was regarded as an important information channel, even if not a reliable or totally accepted one.

> I: But why are girls not seen in the city? I mean girls with no children or family, young women?
>
> R: They don't want that. They save their honor. You are like a whore if you are seen somewhere in that way. And it's the girls' problem that Somalis gossip too much. Even if you have been alone in a hamburger restaurant, they say "yes, she was surrounded by two men, she was with two men."
>
> I: But why do they gossip about these kinds of things, what do you think?
>
> R: They gossip because they only want to cause problem, nothing else.[47]

In this example, the woman explained gossip as a way of causing problems (maybe also as a means to express jealousy as mentioned by a few interviewees, or differences between sexual morality of a speaker and immorality of a girl being talked about). The interviewee considered gossip as a problem for Somali girls, because they could end up having a bad reputation with no real cause, only by being seen in the center, especially in the evenings. Later in the interview the woman stated that fear of wrong gossip was one reason for Somali girls in Turku to control their behavior. With reference to this view, one girl told that she avoided going to the city center because "there are invisible eyes everywhere" and she may easily become a subject of gossip.[48] By "invisible eyes" she meant Somalis who may always observe her without her knowing it.

In general, Turku was considered to be a small town, where talk spread quite quickly and easily. According to interviewees, "the older generation," adult Somali men and women were interested in the behavior of young Somalis in Turku. Those Somali boys and men who spent their time in the city center during daytime or in the evenings were mentioned among the possible observers, too. Also the girls themselves talked about other girls' clothing styles or gossip about possible new relationships, changes in someone's behavior or future weddings in Turku.[49] At any rate, interest as well as non-interest in gossip was first and foremost a question of personal preferences.

To conclude, estimations about socio-spatial behavior of Somali girls in Turku seemed to be a powerful source of gossip, not least because of worries about socio-cultural and religious change as well as change in gender roles among Somalis in the diaspora. I suggest that the fear of gossip may work as an informal social control of socio-spatial behavior of Somali girls living in the relatively small city of Turku. In other words, the process of "policing" through gossip seemed to serve as a way to stress and reproduce gendered (here: female) ideals.

MORAL TOPOGRAPHY OF FINLAND: DIFFERENCES BETWEEN TURKU AND HELSINKI

In the interviews, informants expressed interesting comparisons between Turku and the metropolitan area of Helsinki.[50] Compared to Turku, there were significant tones of moral degradation associated with interpretations and descriptions of life in Helsinki: According to the impressions of the interviewees, the everyday lives of Somali girls in Helsinki were freer, less moral, and more Western or Finnish.[51] However, this idea was by no means generalized to all Somali girls in Helsinki. One girl criticized the social change she had perceived in the metropolitan area. According to her, the individual lifestyle was preferred to previous communal sharing and care, and—like the Finns—"many minded only their own business."[52]

> I: Have you noticed any differences between Helsinki and Turku if you think of Somali girls?
>
> R: In my opinion, girls living in Turku follow more rules. They wear a skirt and a scarf, but not in Helsinki, half of them don't do that. [This statement is either her estimation, or a way to illustrate and stress her point.]
>
> I: Why is that, what do you think?
>
> R: I think that here in Turku parents see, this is a small town and girls will be seen. But Helsinki is a large city, and they don't know each other. That's why they are dressed like that.[53]

All the interviewees stated that one notable difference between Helsinki and Turku is the way Somali girls dress. According to this interviewee, social control is diminished in Helsinki by the fact that all Somalis do not know each other in the same way they do in Turku, which is a notably smaller city. Nevertheless, in Helsinki there are, of course, social networks among Somalis and parts of the city where they know each other, at least by appearance. Moreover, it is also possible that a Somali girl walking in the center of Helsinki after 10 p.m. may be asked by a Somali man: "what are you doing here at this time?"[54] Thus, despite differences between Helsinki and Turku, there were networks of social control in Helsinki, too. Some of the interviewees also expressed the idea of a more superficial and consumerist way of life in Helsinki. According to their opinion, Somalis paid more attention to Somali culture and the religious rules of Islam in Turku—a view possibly disagreed by many Somalis living in Helsinki.[55]

Hence, in relation to girls' socio-spatial behavior and clothing, the metropolitan area was considered as a place for social and cultural change. Somali parents may also be concerned about the possible change in their daughter's behavior if the family moved to Helsinki.[56] One girl stated that they don't want to [move]. They say: "my daughter becomes worse if we move there."[57]

Another often mentioned difference between Turku and Helsinki concerned the frequency of social events organized by the Somalis. Because of the large Somali population in Helsinki, there were more festivities, weddings, concerts and other activities taking place during weekends than in Turku. Some girls said that they travelled to Helsinki to spend time with their friends or relatives. It was then possible to take part in festivities, too. Some of them told they sometimes wore trousers and no scarf during their stay. A few also mentioned they had been in discos in Helsinki: They explained this by stating that they liked to have fun with their friends in ways that were not socially possible in Turku; if they went to a nightclub or a disco in Turku, they would quite probably meet Somali boys or men there. According to one interviewee, "the whole city" would soon know about the girl's behavior, which would be interpreted as socially degrading for her and her family.[58] In this sense, spending time in Helsinki gave more alternatives for free time activities. The chosen ways of socializing with peers in the weekends were possible to be kept secret from the family, too. Nevertheless, the choices actually made depended on the person and her attitudes towards the opinions of her relatives, too—and, this applies to girls in Helsinki as well as in Turku.

The interviewees also compared Helsinki and Turku in terms of the dynamics of gossip. Some of them explained that social control was loosened in Helsinki because there were a plenty of issues to talk about.

> R: [In Helsinki] gossip goes around much slower. Before the first story gets half away, another one starts to circle. And then the first one is forgotten. Then, when the second gossip gets half away, the third one is born. It goes around half circle.
>
> I: How are things in Turku?
>
> R: (Laughs) It goes all around, and then the next thing happens after a year, after two years. It goes around another three years and the next thing happens and it goes around for the next three years.[59]

In this example, the interviewee referred to Helsinki as a larger area with a larger Somali population. The gossip had no such an authority as in Turku, where a girl knew that "once a topic, a long time a topic." Later in the interview the girl also stated that Turku was too small a town for her because of the feeling of constant observation. Because of this, she expressed her willingness to move away from Turku.[60]

In conclusion, according to the interviewees, it was possible for a Somali girl to move more freely in Helsinki. In their opinion, girls were not recognized among the large Somali population in the same way as in Turku. Consequently, they did not end up being an object of gossip because of their behavior. Thus, life in Helsinki was regarded notably different from life in Turku, and, depending on the respondent, either something to hope for, or an example of moral degradation.

CONCLUSION

In this chapter, I have considered the impeccable behavior of Somali girls in Turku as socio-spatially and sexually valued. According to the research material, socially and morally acceptable behavior was associated with socio-sexual modesty, according to which the social status was also defined. Due to the small number of

Somalis in Turku, gossip could serve not only as a source of useful information, but also as a means of informal social control. I have examined aspects of social networks and gossip especially in the case of Somali girls. I suggest that through selective moral and social inclusions and exclusions (e.g. valuing something approved and something disapproved) the socially recognized "general opinion" has significance in the construction of social, moral and ethnic boundaries of Somali community (communities) in Turku and in Finland.[61] However, these boundaries are neither fixed nor static.

The significance and intensification of certain cultural ideals and gendered expectations may be considered in relation to questions of cultural continuity and change in Finland. It seems that in the diaspora the more or less explicit ideal or role for girls and women as "keepers of culture" has been paid more attention to in social evaluations of decent behavior and maintenance of religious values and Somali culture.[62] In the context of Turku, "in their own village within the city,"[63] many Somalis knew each other by appearance. Because of quite dense social networks, then, it was possible to discuss gendered ideals concerning girls in relation to perceived everyday choices done by them.

Notes

1. The research material consists of 26 interviews (HLI-index) and field diaries (KP-index) based on participant observation (e.g., at homes, city center, mosque, and festivities). The interviewees have been living in Finland approximately for three to over ten years. All the interviews were carried out in Finnish. I thank the Somali girls and women who commented on this chapter. I also thank Laura Stark for useful theoretical comments on the themes of gossip and gender.
2. In this chapter, "a girl" refers to an unmarried Somali girl, and "a woman" to a married Somali woman. (About the concepts of Muslim girls and women in the anthropological research see Harris, C. (2005). *Control and subversion. Gender relations in Tajikistan.* London & Sterling, Virginia: Pluto Press.) The same difference between "a girl" and "a woman" is also made in Somali. *Gabadh* refers to an unmarried girl, a virgin, while *naag* indicates that the person in question is or has been married, that is, is not a virgin (anymore).

The age scale of the interviewees is approximately from 17 to 35 years of age. The majority of them are under 24 years old.

3. Statistics Finland. (2004). Somalinkieliset ja Somalian kansalaiset Turussa 31.12.2004 [Somali speakers and Somali citizens in Turku 31.12.2004].

   Statistics Finland. (2005). Väestörakenne 2005 [Population Structure 2005].

4. Koskela, H. (1994). "Tila on kuin tuhat lävistävää silmää" – Ajatuksia tilakäsityksistä, kaupunkipeloista ja tilan kokemisesta ["Space is like a thousand penetrating glances" – Thoughts on perceiving space, fears in the city and experiencing space]. *Naistutkimus*, 7(4), 22–33.

5. Lefebvre, H. (1991). *The production of space*. Oxford & Cambridge: Blackwell.

6. Saarikangas, K. (1998). Tila, konteksti ja käyttäjä. Arkkitehtonisen tilan, vallan ja sukupuolen suhteista [Space, context, and user. On relations between architectonic space, power and gender]. In K. Saarikangas (Ed.), *Kuvasta tilaan. Taidehistoria tänään* [From picture to space. History of art today] (pp. 247–298). Tampere: Vastapaino.

7. Koskinen, I. (2000). *Väritetty totuus. Juorut arkielämässä* [The coloured truth. Gossip in everyday life]. Helsinki: Helsinki University Press.

8. By definition, gossip and rumor have different meanings, even if the difference between the definitions is by no means clear-cut. Briefly defined, the former takes place among people in networks or groups. The latter refers to unsubstantiated information, that may pass in wider networks (and areas) than gossip. Gossip may proceed into circuits of rumor and vice versa. (See Stewart, P. J., & Strathern, A. (2004). *Witchcraft, sorcery, rumors, and gossip*. Cambridge: Cambridge University Press. pp. 38-39.

9. About meanings and functions of rumors and gossip in society, see Fine, G. A., & Turner, P. A. (2001). *Whispers on the color line. Rumor and race in America*. Berkeley and Los Angeles: University of California Press.

10. See Koskinen, I. (2000). *Väritetty totuus. Juorut arkielämässä* [The coloured truth. Gossip in everyday life]. Helsinki: Helsinki University Press.

    Goodman, R. F., & Ben-Ze'ev, A. (1994). *Good gossip*. Lawrence: University Press of Kansas.

11. Bergmann, J. (1997). Moraalin paikallisesta luonteesta nyky-yhteiskunnassa [On the local nature of morals in contemporary society]. *Sosiologia*, 34(3), 231–241.
12. Kapchan, D. (1996). *Gender on the market. Moroccan women and the revoicing of tradition.* Philadelphia: University of Pennsylvania Press.
13. Stark-Arola. L. (1998). *Magic, body and social order. The construction of gender through women's private rituals in traditional Finland.* Helsinki: Finnish Literature Society.
14. Koskinen, I. (2000). *Väritetty totuus. Juorut arkielämässä* [The coloured truth. Gossip in everyday life]. Helsinki: Helsinki University Press.
15. HLI(03)01; HLI(04)02; HLI(04)03; HLI(04)12; HLI(04)13; HLI(04)18; HLI(05)01; HLI(05)03A.
16. Traditionally, a Somali girl has also been "closed" by infibulation. Infibulation (pharaonic circumcision) is a type of female circumcision commonly practiced in Somalia. In this operation, a part or all of the external genitalia are excised and the sides of the vulva are stitched together in order to narrow the vaginal opening.

    Talle, A. (1993). Transforming women into 'pure' agnates: Aspects of female infibulation in Somalia. In T. V. Broch-Due, I. Rudie, & T. Bleie (Eds.), *Carved Flesh/Cast Selves. Gendered Symbols and Social Practices*, (pp. 83–106).Oxford: Berg.

    World Health Organization. (2000). Female genital mutilation. Retrieved August 17, 2005, from http://www.who.int/mediacentre/factsheets/fs241/en.

    There are also different types of less extensive operations without sewing of the vaginal opening under the definition of "sunna" circumcision. (About socio-sexual meanings of female circumcision in Somalia, see Johnsdotter, S. (2002). *Created by God. How Somalis in Swedish exile reassess the practice of female circumcision*. Lund: Department of Sociology, University of Lund; Talle, A. (1993). Transforming women into 'pure' agnates: Aspects of female infibulation in Somalia. In T. V. Broch-Due, I. Rudie, & T. Bleie (Eds.), *Carved Flesh/Cast Selves. Gendered Symbols and Social Practices* (pp. 83–106).Oxford: Berg.

    See Salmela, A. (2004). Pysyvyyttä muutoksessa ja muutosta pysyvyydessä. Turussa asuvat somalinaiset islamin ja yhteisöperinteen välittäjinä [Constancy in change, change in constancy. Somali women as mediators of Islam and community tradition in Turku]. In O. Fingerroos, M. Opas, & T. Teemu (Eds), *Uskonnon paikka. Kirjoituksia uskontojen ja uskontoteorioiden rajoista* [The place of religion. Essays on boundaries of religions and religious theories] (pp. 279–311). Helsinki: Finnish Literature Society.

For socio-cultural meanings and control of female openness, see Boddy, J. (1989). *Wombs and alien spirits. Women, men and the Zâr cult in Northern Sudan*. Madison, WI: University of Wisconsin Press; Stark-Arola. L. (1998). *Magic, body and social order. The construction of gender through women's private rituals in traditional Finland.* Helsinki: Finnish Literature Society.

Talle, A. (1993). Transforming women into 'pure' agnates: Aspects of female infibulation in Somalia. In T. V. Broch-Due, I. Rudie, & T. Bleie (Eds.), *Carved Flesh/Cast Selves. Gendered Symbols and Social Practices* (pp. 83–106).Oxford: Berg; Tapaninen, A. M. (1996). Kansan kodit ja kaupungin kadut. Etnografinen tutkimus eteläitalialaisesta kaupungista *[Homes of the folk and streets of the city. An ethnographic study on a city in the Southern Italy].* Helsinki: Finnish Anthropological Society.

17. Andersson, Å. (2003). Inte samma lika. Identifikationer hos tonårsflickor i en multietnisk stadsdel [Not the same. Identifications of teenage girls in a multi-ethnic quarter of a town]. Stockholm: Symposium.

    Lees, S. (1986). *Losing out. Sexuality and adolescent girls.* London: Hutchinson.

    Salmela, A. (2006). Somalitytön sosioseksuaalinen liikkumatila ja seksuaalisuudesta puhumisen tavat [Somali girls, socio-sexually defined space, and ways to talk about sexuality]. In T. Kinnunen, & A. Puuronen (Eds.), *Seksuaalinen ruumis* [Sexuality and body]. Helsinki: Gaudeamus.

18. Salmela, A. (2004). Pysyvyyttä muutoksessa ja muutosta pysyvyydessä. Turussa asuvat somalinaiset islamin ja yhteisöperinteen välittäjinä [Constancy in change, change in constancy. Somali women as mediators of Islam and community tradition in Turku]. In O. Fingerroos, M. Opas, & T. Teemu (Eds), *Uskonnon paikka. Kirjoituksia uskontojen ja uskontoteorioiden rajoista* [The place of religion. Essays on boundaries of religions and religious theories] (pp. 279–311). Helsinki: Finnish Literature Society.

    Østberg, S. (2003). Norwegian-Pakistani adolescents. Negotiating religion, gender, ethnicity and social boundaries. *Young* 11(2), 161–181.

19. The extracts are mostly translated into English in correspondence with original speech in Finnish. Accordingly, some translations are not grammatically correct.
20. HLI(03)01.
21. Merton, R. K. (1968). *Social theory and social structure*. New York: Free Press. p. 477.
22. HLI(03)01; HLI(04)02; HLI(04)04; HLI(05)01; HLI(05)02.
23. See Berns McGown, R. (1999). *Muslims in the diaspora. The Somali communities of London and Toronto*. Toronto: University of Toronto Press; De Voe, P. A. (2002). Symbolic action: Religion's role in the changing environment of young Somali women. *Journal of Refugee Studies*, 15(2), 234–246; Tiilikainen, M. (2003). *Arjen islam: Somalinaisten elämää Suomessa* [Everyday Islam: Life of Somali women in Finland]. Tampere: Vastapaino.
24. There were regional and social differences in the expected dress codes.
25. HLI(03)02.
26. HLI(04)15; HLI(04)16; HLI(04)18; HLI(05)03A; HLI(05)05.
27. See also Niemelä, H. (2004). Islam elämänvalintojen ohjaajana somalialaisten maahanmuuttajatyttöjen arjessa [Life choices guided by Islam in the everyday life of Somali refugee girls]. *Nuorisotutkimus*, 22(2), 61–65.
28. Of course there were regional and social differences in social expectations, too.
29. For themes of exclusion and abjection in the constitution of the subject, see Butler, J. (1993). *Bodies that matter. On the discursive limits of "sex."* New York & London: Routledge.
30. I thank the editors for stressing this point in their comments.
31. HLI(04)11A.
32. HLI(04)04.
33. HLI(04)04.
34. HLI(04)06; HLI(05)02.
35. Statistics Finland. (2005). Väestörakenne 2005 [Population Structure 2005].
36. See also de Vries, M. (1995). The changing role of gossip: Toward a new identity? Turkish girls in Netherlands. In G. Baumann & T. Sunier (Eds.), *Post-migration ethnicity. Cohesion, commitments, comparison* (pp. 36–56). Amsterdam: Institute for Migration and Ethnic Studies.

37. HLI(03)01.
38. Lees, S. (1986). *Losing out. Sexuality and adolescent girls*. London: Hutchinson.
39. HLI(04)03.)
40. See Stark-Arola, L. (1998). *Magic, body and social order. The construction of gender through women's private rituals in traditional Finland*. Helsinki: Finnish Literature Society.
41. HLI(04)13.
42. HLI(03)02; HLI(04)06; HLI(04)15; HLI(04)17; HLI(05)02.
43. HLI(04)18.
44. HLI(04)04.
45. HLI(04)04; HLI(04)07; HLI(04)15; HLI(05)02.
46. HLI(04)05B.
47. HLI(04)11A.
48. HLI(04)04.
49. HLI(04)03; HLI(04)11A; HLI(04)15; HLI(05)02; HLI(03)A.
50. There were 8,593 persons who spoke Somali as their first language in Finland in 2005. Eighty-two % of them lived in the metropolitan area (i.e. Helsinki, Espoo, Kauniainen and Vantaa). Statistics Finland. (2005). Väestörakenne 2005 [Population Structure 2005].
51. This kind of division in terms of moral geography has been acknowledged in many researches focused on value-laden meanings associated to "morally too liberal" metropolitan areas versus "more idyllic" smaller towns or rural areas.
52. HLI(05)05.
53. HLI(04)13.
54. KP(05)15.
55. HLI(03)02; HLI(04)03; HLI(04)04; HLI(04)07; HLI(04)13; HLI(04)18.
56. Many Somalis have moved from Turku to Helsinki. Helsinki has been preferred to Turku because of more multicultural atmosphere, larger Somali population, more lively social life, and better possibilities to get a job.
57. HLI(04)03.
58. HLI(04)11A; HLI(04)13; HLI(04)18; HLI(05)03A.
59. HLI(04)04.
60. See also de Vries, M. (1995). The changing role of gossip: Toward a new identity? Turkish girls in Netherlands. In G. Baumann & T.

Sunier (Eds.), *Post-migration ethnicity. Cohesion, commitments, comparison* (pp. 36–56). Amsterdam: Institute for Migration and Ethnic Studies.

61. See also Goodwin, M. H. (1990). *He-said-she-said. Talk as social organization among black children.* Bloomington and Indianapolis: Indiana University Press.
62. See also Nisula, T., Rastas, A., & Kangaspunta, K. (1995). Perinteen puhtaus ja somali-identiteetti. Pakolaistytöt kulttuurinsa vaalijoina [The purity of tradition and Somali identity. Refugee girls cherishing their culture]. *Nuorisotutkimus,* 13(2), 18–29.
63. HLI(05)05.

Chapter 9

CONTINUITY AND CHANGE: SOMALI WOMEN AND EVERYDAY ISLAM IN THE DIASPORA

Marja Tiilikainen

INTRODUCTION

In the conditions of refugee life and diaspora, the significance of religion for individuals may either grow or diminish, or even stay as it was before exile. Despite differences regarding religious views, Somali women and their families in the diaspora share the challenge to more consciously than before consider the importance of their Muslim background in their new life as a minority in a non-Muslim society. In addition to localized everyday lives in resettlement countries, experiences of civil war and transnational ties provide us with further understanding about religion for Somali women in the diaspora.

By definition, life in the diaspora is largely determined by a continuous relationship to a previous home country.[1] This relationship is maintained, for example, through memories, a desire to return back home and the maintenance of personal ties to the homeland. Research on transnationalism and diaspora is increasingly focusing on the relationship between transnationalism and religion.[2] In this chapter, I will highlight the various, multilayered religious processes in the diaspora by focusing on Somali women in Finland. How are religious practices and interpretations interlinked with the everyday life of Somali women in Finland? In this context, what kinds of meanings do these women give to Islam? How do they negotiate and recreate their religious and cultural identities in relation to their transnational lives?

This chapter is based on ethnographic data I gathered among Somali women in Metropolitan Helsinki from 1996–2002 for my Ph.D. research in comparative religion and medical anthropology.[3] Most women who participated in my research were mothers of small children. The number of my main informants was 22, many of whom I met, interviewed and observed repeatedly during several years at homes, health care settings, mosques and women's gatherings such as weddings. I found the informants by a snowball method, by participating in a Somali women's group and from a health care center. The language used during fieldwork was mainly Finnish, sometimes also English or Somali. As my knowledge of Somali language is elementary, some discussions and interviews were conducted with the help of an informant's friend or relative. Moreover, in this chapter I will draw on my recent five-week period of fieldwork in Northern Somalia (commonly referred to as Somaliland) in the summer of 2005. As part of my on-going study on transnational healing practices I observed and interviewed several healers and patients who came from the diaspora to visit them. All the names in this chapter are pseudonyms.

EVERYDAY CHORES AND CONTINUITY

For historical, political and geographical reasons Finland has not traditionally hosted large immigrant populations. However, 1990 marked a turning point in the history of immigration to Finland. At that time, asylum seekers from Somalia began to enter Finland; their arrival changed the whole scene of Muslims and immigrants in general.[4] By the end of 2004, the largest groups of non-Finnish citizens originated from Russia, Estonia, Sweden and Somalia. The number of native Somali speakers was 8,096; women numbered nearly half. The number of children is significant as almost 46 percent (3,696 people) of Somali speakers were under 15 years of age.[5] Most Somalis in Finland are originally from Southern Somalia. Since their arrival, Somalis have been the largest Muslim group, the largest refugee group and also the largest African group in Finland.[6] The majority of Somali families live in Metropolitan Helsinki. Somalis have experienced discrimination and racism in Finland.[7]

In addition, the unemployment rate among them is high, around 61 percent in 2004.[8]

The everyday life of Somali women in Finland is filtered through Islam, but at the same time, Islam is filtered through women's everyday life. Somali mothers actively interpret Islam, and make compromises and choices regarding religious requirements in order to manage their everyday tasks of overseeing the household and caring for children. Interpretations concerning Islamic food regulations offer an example of Somali women's agency.

In Somali families, making food is primarily women's responsibility. In Finland, Somali women have adopted new influences into their food culture, making it necessary to rethink the meaning of Islamic food codes; in a non-Islamic, industrialised country the risk to eat foods forbidden by Islam is greater than in Somalia. When Somalis first arrived in Finland, they were not always aware that Finland was not a Muslim country, and may have accidentally eaten pork. Moreover, it may be difficult to distinguish what belongs to Christianity (and is hence forbidden) and what does not; a Somali woman explained how she mistakenly took chocolate from Father Christmas in a shopping mall without realizing that the long-bearded man was part of Christmas (and, according to her understanding, a crucial part of Christianity).

Daily cooking takes a lot of women's time since many families prefer fresh food to industrial ready-made food products. One reason for this preference lies in the difficulty of finding out the content of the food and making sure it has no forbidden ingredients. In Finland, Islamic prohibitions concerning the use of alcohol, pork and blood products are, however, followed differently by individual women, and at times by the same women according to the situation. All Somali women who participated in my research told me that they did not use pork. Among them, however, are those who just refuse to eat pork meat, and those, who also refuse products made with gelatin which may possibly contain pork. As follows, women might also refuse vaccines and medication containing gelatin. Women following food regulations in the strictest sense usually prefer ritually slaughtered *halal* meat to meat available in ordinary Finnish shops. But, again, even these women may compromise when needed; if there is no time to visit an ethnic shop or a shop in a mosque, meat from ordinary shops might be purchased and consumed as well. Along these lines, chicken may be bought from ordinary shops, while all other meat has to be ritually slaughtered halal meat. Or, Somali mothers who usually purchase halal meat may buy canned baby food for their young children.

Observance of food regulations may also be influenced by external opinions, even pressures. A young woman described her uncertainty and search for the right way:

> The first time I heard of these additional substances, that there is some pork in them, was in 1995. I was in Sweden to my aunt's place and there was a big sheikh, who lives in Sweden. He goes around, talks to people.... He is a Somali. He came to my aunt's place and they stayed two or three days with us, and then he gave some lectures on Islam. Then he gave us a bunch of paper, where there were 35 or more....We must not eat cheese. Why? Because to make the cheese, they use some bacteria which they get from the testicles of cows and other animals. And then, he told us, because when they killed this cow, they did not kill but they have this electric shock, it dies that way, they didn't slaughter it. So, eating something which is not slaughtered in Islam is forbidden. Because they get the bacteria that way, it will be forbidden to eat cheese. (Laughs) Okay, that was cheese. And so, 35 or more things.... How can you live with this? We tried. My aunt had an eight-year-old son, he said, I can't live without cheese. He was crying, how come we cannot eat cheese? But then, we decided not to eat anything. We look everything, if there was any additional substance which was from pork, everything, cheese, bread. He told us about the bread, that we should not eat bread, and he told us about some kind of flour, which has something added to it, and almost everything. So, for three days we did not eat that much food. We decided, okay, we don't have to eat pizza, we don't have to eat anything. We have to forget about these things and try to have more traditional food.... But then we decided to forget all about that! My uncle said, forget about that. My aunt said, no, it is forbidden. He

> says, forget about that and buy everything! And we bought everything without looking. And since then I don't look anything, I don't care. Just pork and blood, and if there is some food which they add wine when it is cooked, I don't eat.... It is so difficult and boring to go around with this big list.... You cannot live like that.[9]

According to Somali hospitality, upon entering a home, a visitor is served something to drink and eat. Eating is a profoundly social activity and food is an inseparable part of all social activities and events, including meetings, parties and rituals. As a woman explained, food even tastes better when it is shared with others. Women in particular are interested in food: food is prepared together, women meet their friends by food, food is talked about and food carries memories. Continuous cooking is tiresome, but good cooking skills are something women are proud of.

Between women, food is often served and eaten with the right hand from a common tray. As a woman explained, eating by hand is in accordance with Prophet Mohammed's instructions. In parties and other social events where guests are served, bad service may indicate an inflamed relationship. Hence, through preparing and serving food women can also use power. Furthermore, food is one way to show respect to husbands and other male relatives: When a husband invites a guest home, he utilizes his wife's cooking skills and possibly other female relatives in order to show his position and hospitality. Hence, men depend on women's resources--in this sense, women enable men's agency.

While immigrant men are often in charge of official rituals within religious institutions, immigrant women commonly play a central role in home-centred, unofficial rituals.[10] Through religious and cultural rituals, immigrant women, in this case Somali women, can produce ethnicity and strengthen the cultural identity of their family. Even cooking can be counted as a religious activity: By preparing and serving ethnic food, women can strengthen religious and cultural identities of their families and friends, and also take part in official religious ceremonies in congregations.[11] For example, Ramadan is a sacred time when food and the absence of food have special meaning. During Ramadan, mothers are busy preparing special foods. Moreover, they sometimes prepare extra food which their husbands may take to a mosque or elsewhere for single men. This is voluntary alms, *sadaqo*. Somali women also prepare food shared in religious and cultural rituals (e.g., reading the Koran for a sick person, *saar* rituals or weddings).

In a culturally, socially and religiously alien environment, after the turmoil of civil war, Somali women's and mother's everyday routines at home such as preparing food, keeping the house and taking care of small children, have probably helped women to create a sense of continuity, order and control in the middle of otherwise chaotic experiences and uncertainty. Daily acts, linked with religious observance, daily prayers and religious sacred times have helped them build a home in the diaspora that creates bridges between the past, present and future.[12] Like Hibo, a mother of three children, said:

> Religion belongs to everything. When I go to toilet, I first step with my left leg, but when I enter mosque, I step first with my right leg; before I start eating I say *bismillahi*; I pray five times a day; I do not use any items of pork origin… The meaning of religion for me is exactly the same as it was in Somalia.[13]

For Hibo, the meaning of religion in the diaspora is the same as it was in Somalia. Nevertheless, for many women, the meaning of religion has totally changed in exile.

EXILE AND RELIGIOUS CHANGE

> I am a Muslim, yeah, but actually, since I came to Europe, that feeling is going. Because nobody is talking about religion, nobody talks about Islam. When we are in a Muslim country, you feel more that you are a Muslim. But here…. In Kuwait, for example, people are very religious. In that part of the Islamic world people are very religious and their culture is more based on Islam and they are so strict. So, when you go there, everybody talks about Islam and everybody uses the word Allah. You will hear the word Allah hundred times a day. But here, I never hear it![14]

As Zahra describes, religious change in the diaspora may mean a diminishing role of the religion. Living in a non-Muslim and highly secular society, without tight ties to a religious community, along with individual autonomy and freedom of choice, highly valued in Finnish society, may result in weakening of religiosity in an individual life. However, in case of Somalis, the religious change more commonly implies increased importance of religion.

> If Somalis had believed or obeyed what Allah and our Koran say, the war would not have begun. Because Islam says, do not kill and do not steal anything which belongs to another person. But people did not obey this. Those who now fight and rob in Somalia, they do not know the religion.... Religion is the most important thing in my life. If Allah forgives us and shows what religion is and people study to become good Muslims, then there will be peace.[15]

The elderly woman quoted above gives an explanation for the civil war, which many Somalis in my research sample basically seemed to share: Somalis' previous ignorance towards religion was followed by God's punishment. From the point of view of Somali Muslims, civil war and ensuing social suffering can be seen as a trial, punishment or will of God. Hence, explanations for the outbreak of war, as well as a vision for a better future, can be found in Islam. The war has brought a sense of collective guilt for Somalis. Experiences of civil war, the death of relatives and friends, and forced migration have, in many cases, resulted in religious awakening. Faadumo, a mother of four children, is an example of religious awakening in the diaspora:

> My relation to religion has changed totally: When I moved to Finland, my life was full of time because I had no work and I did not go to school. I had to study religion a lot, and I have learnt quite a lot about it--what I have to do, what I must not do. I had knowledge about Islam even before, but it was not enough. You always have to search for more knowledge, knowledge that you need yourself such as the role of women, what women cannot do, and what they have to do.[16]

For Faadumo, religious awakening also means a moral act in relation to the arbitrary war. According to her, the outbreak of war woke up many Somalis; they started to think about the Doomsday, the coming death and the importance of religion. Many Somalis started to read the Koran and they learned that Islam forbids killing. After her religious awakening, Faadumo started to pray regularly, study Islam and visit a mosque on weekends. She took part in seminars and other events organised by a mosque and her children regularly attended a Koran school. Gradually, her knowledge of Islam increased and she started to teach Islam to other Somali women who gathered at her home.

Faadumo's religious change was also visible in her dress. She told me that in Somalia she did not use to cover her head and during her first year in Finland wore jeans. But, at the time of her religious awakening, she started using jilbaab, a large veil to cover her body. She explained: "In Islam, it is forbidden for a woman to use trousers, jeans. Women have to use this kind of loose clothes." Faadumo is not a rare example; jilbaab has become common among Somali women throughout the diaspora[17] and also increasingly in Somalia before, during and after the civil war.[18] As a woman explained, "Jilbaab came during the war from Egypt, Iran and Saudi-Arabia. It is a new fashion. Previously we had garbasaar or guntiino. Dire is transparent and everything can be seen."

In Finland, Somali women often stress that the use of jilbaab or another kind of hijab is directly related to their increased religious knowledge. New veiling is not only related to religious identities; according to a young woman, veiling is also seen as necessary for maintaining Somali women's cultural identity in an alien environment:

> Changes have happened when people came to a strange country and everything was different. They just want to keep their culture and identity…. And this is the reason they use these clothes which differentiate them from other people. They want to keep all such things which are related to Somali culture…. They feel that if they do not maintain their religion, they cannot remember anymore. So, this is the only way they can practice and maintain their religion. If they do not practice, they will gradually forget.[19]

In addition to religious and cultural identities, a veil has been even connected to an identity as a mother: "Now when I am older, I feel a bit shy. And as I have an own child now, I feel it is better to look like a mother, and not like a young girl anymore," a woman explained. But also more practical reasons such as economical and environmental aspects, for example cold climate in Finland, have been mentioned in relation to increased veiling.

In an interesting way, Somali women in Finland negotiate a proper dressing code. Although jilbaab seems to be commonly accepted as a decent way to dress, the use of niqab, a face veil, divides women's opinions. Some women have underscored that although the use of niqab is religiously good and rewarding, it is not obligatory. Some women have explained that the Prophet's wives used niqab and moreover, a beautiful woman should cover her face from the eyes of men. Other women, instead, have rejected the use of niqab because it is difficult to use in Finland. They have explained that because Finns find the niqab strange, it would be impossible or at least very difficult for women who wear the niqab to study or work. The niqab has also been viewed as unpractical, and even dangerous and risky. A woman criticized:

> Women should keep on our own culture.... All this (veiling), I did not see it before. All these people, they are just ordinary people.... In Somalia we only have normal garbasaar, but now they started to use bigger veils, like in Saudi Arabia. Yes, this is a new thing which did not exist earlier.... When they now cover the face, they cannot see anything when they walk. It is difficult. It is not obligatory to use a face veil. It is difficult: at the railway station there are escalators, and if you do not see anything, what happens if your gear gets stuck, and you cannot move and stop the escalators.... I find it so difficult to understand. It is not obligatory to put on a niqab, I do not like it. And it is not safe for a child either, if her mother gets stuck in stairs....[20]

Naturally, there are Somali women who do not cover their heads at all or only occasionally, and many others prefer other kinds of veils to jilbaab. In particular, young Somali girls combine Western clothing often donning long skirts and various fashionable scarf styles. Dressing is also contextual. At women's parties, especially during Somali weddings, Somali women in Finland wear their most beautiful, colourful, fashionable and transparent clothes along with jewellery, which they cannot use in daily life.

Women who do not wear hijab may face pressure from the Somali community. Zahra told me how some of her male classmates had asked her to veil:

> They came and asked me to put hijab. They said you have to put hijab when you want to study and there are men, and this is our culture and our religion.... One man asked me, do you have a religion. Yes, I told him. Then he said, why don't you put hijab? ....I used to tell them, okay I know and thank you for telling me. But then, for one month or three months they were telling me every day. I told them, this is none of your business.... Then one day, one of the girls who wore jilbaab came and said to me, some of these men asked me, because we are girls, to talk with you. I have never seen something like that all my life, never.... So I told them, hey listen, this is none of your business and if I want to put hijab, I will put it. Not for you, just for my God. If you don't want to see me then, you should control your eyes. Actually Islam says you should not look.... If you see a very religious person, if you are a woman and this a man, he will not even look into your eyes. He has to see you, but he cannot watch you like admiring you, she is so beautiful.... That is something you do by yourself, you have to control yourself, you have to control your eyes.... I became angry because one of these men, when he was trying to advise me, he said to me I was not religious, I was too bad, I used to go with Finnish ladies, I used to do this and that bad thing, like I drink or used to go to discos.... Then I told him I do not do, I do not go anywhere, but I do not like to cover my hair.[21]

The quotation is revealing in several ways. First, it shows how Somali women themselves can use religious argumentation to define their role and life in Finland. Second, it notes another role of religion in the diaspora: Islam is also used as a border between a moral Somali community and an immoral Finnish community. For many Somalis, characteristics of Finnish society such as alcohol abuse, free socializing of boys and girls, different ways of dressing and nakedness, and youth's disrespectful behaviour towards parents and elders symbolize an immoral, sinful society. Through Islam, it is possible to try to maintain, create and strengthen a bastion of morality. In this process, a Somali woman's veiled body seems to gain important communal meanings. Moreover, the religious community may become a place of esteem and safety in contrast to the larger Finnish community, where experiences of discrimination and humiliation are common.[22]

Moral aspects of religion also seem to gain importance in the larger Somali diaspora community. Generally speaking, Somalis in Finland equate religiosity with goodness and morality. Islam has often been one uniting factor among Somalis and even in the present civil war situation, Islam is hoped to lead to peace and reunification of the Somali people. Muslim identity may be seen as more important than identity as a Somali, like a path to a global home for all Muslims. Islam is a fragile tie, connecting the past and today, on which common trust and a new communality may be built. Third, the quotation above reveals that Islam in Finland is a contested field: It is not clear who has the power and authority to define "correct" Islam. In my research, tension regarding different religious interpretations has raised between women and men, and also between older and younger generations. Local Islamic interpretations in Finland are intertwined with global processes in the Islamic world, particularly Islamic movements in Somalia.

The rise of Islamic movements in Somalia began in the 1970s as part of an international Islamic revival and in reaction to Somalia's tangled internal and international policies.[23] In the 1990s, Islamists were divided in two main groups: *Jama'at al-Islah*, which identifies with the Egyptian Muslim Brotherhood, and *al-Ittihad al-Islami*, which is close to the puritanical *Wahhabi* and *Salafiyya* movements of the Arabian Peninsula. In Somalia, the influence of Islamic movements has been strongest in cities. Nowadays, their presence is observable among Somalis in the diaspora.[24] Every now and then,

Somali women in Finland have referred to these movements by disclosing conflicts between, on one hand, their own religious ideas and everyday life, and on the other hand, the religious interpretations of "men with long beard and short trouser legs," as they have phrased it. An attempt to find a common nucleus for all Muslims, and to separate cultural and religious fields from each other, is part of today's Islamization process. In this process, Somali women's saar is contested.

WORLD OF SPIRITS

Somali saar (*zar*) belongs to a wider spirit possession phenomenon, which I.M. Lewis calls *zar-bori*-cult.[25] The saar spirit healing cult is syncretistic. In addition to Islamic and Christian influences, it has preserved its pre-Islamic and pre-Christian features.[26] This spirit possession phenomenon is widely known on the East African coast and its hinterland. Despite different cultural and historical characteristics, the basic structures are usually quite similar.[27]

Spirit possession refers to different states in which a spirit, for one reason or another, has entered a person. Spirits can cause illnesses and symptoms, which in Somalia typically include fainting, falling down, vomiting, feebleness, bodily pains, general malaise, depression, violent bodily agitation, epilepsy and often also madness.[28] In Somalia, saar, which includes many different cults, is common among all social classes. Different spirits such as *mingis*, *sharax*, *wadaaddo* and *boorane*, have their own specific ritual practices, which may also vary in different areas and groups. Healing rituals often include special incense types, different dance styles, and music and animal sacrifices.[29]

Saar can be seen as part of the religious, spiritual and moral order of the Horn of Africa even though today many Somali Muslims reject any connection between saar and Islam.[30] Generally speaking, in many East African Muslim communities, where everyday life is divided according to gender, the existence of spirits is a cultural fact. Furthermore, research has shown that women in particular seem to be prone to spirit possession.[31] Diseases caused by spirits and their treatment have often been seen as women's and other marginal groups' counter culture. I.M. Lewis,[32] for instance, regards saar as a deprivation cult, through which marginalised Somali women try to enhance their position. According to other interpretations, saar has been seen as a complementary cultural practice for Islam and men's public role in Islamic rituals,[33] or as an inseparable part of women's cultural values, moral principles and everyday life as Muslims.[34]

In the Islamic world, spirits are generally referred to as *jinn*.[35] After Islam spread to Somalia, traditional saar spirits were often classified as a kind of jinn so that they could fit better into Islamic categories.[36] According to women who practice saar, the basic difference lies in how the relationship between a human and a spirit is seen: Jinn are regarded as something one should try to get rid of (mainly by reciting the Koran), but a relationship with a saar spirit ideally develops into a lifelong, mutually beneficial acceptance and agreement.[37] What happened to saar when families fled from Somalia and found asylum in far away countries like Finland? Did spirits follow Somali women to the diaspora? The following description of a saar ritual is based on my own observation in Finland.

> The mingis ritual was arranged in a cultural center in metropolitan Helsinki. Twelve Somali women, mainly from Southern Somalia, had been invited. The oldest woman was over 50 years of age and the youngest less than 20. Calaqad had a recorded cassette from a mingis ritual in Somalia. As the cassette played, women tried to sing along to the tape. A plastic salad bowl and a brush used for washing dishes were brought from the kitchen and used for drumming. Women did not seem to know or remember the words of the songs well. Sometimes they only listened to the cassette, and at times they drummed and clapped their hands.
>
> After a while, Calaqad fell into a trance, her facial expression changed, and she moved wildly around, singing and dancing. A spirit was present and spoke through Calaqad. In trance, Calaqad seemed very determined. Every now and then, she showed with her hands that the other women should clap and sing stronger, and at other times, she looked challenging, even threatening. She hit other women on their backs, commanded them to dance, and

> even choked one of the women. While dancing she took a bottle of perfume, waved it on her head and splashed strong-smelling perfume on the others.
>
> After the spirit of Calaqad had appeared, other women started falling into trances, too. A spirit showed itself in different ways: one of the women waved her scarf powerfully, another woman waved her hands, and yet another looked aggressive. Some of the women fell down, while others just danced wildly and afterwards looked somehow confused. Later Calaqad explained that mingis can be felt in the legs or in the head. Mingis can also cause pain in the legs, neck or upper back when it appears. To ease the condition of the women who were in trance state, Calaqad might go and hit their upper backs, step with bare feet on their legs, and bend their necks forcefully to different directions.
>
> One of the women seemed to suffer from severe chronic rheumatoid arthritis. Calaqad diagnosed mingis to be the reason for her illness. Calaqad covered the head of the sitting woman with a scarf. The patient inhaled incense and fell into a trance. Her head fell backwards, and her fingers and hands cramped and became stiff aside her body. Calaqad addressed the spirit of the woman and asked: "Who are you? Tell who you are and we will fulfil all your wishes. Do not harass this weak person anymore." During the trance, a spirit told Calaqad that the woman had received the spirit from her mother, her husband and his mother. After a while, the spirit of Calaqad shouted loudly "*Xabash*!"[38] Calaqad pointed at the ill woman and shouted that her whole family had Xabash. After the diagnosis, three women helped the woman to dance, even though she had difficulty walking because of her disease.[39]

Calaqad, a leader of the mingis cult, got mingis in Somalia already in the 1970s, while she was pregnant with her second child. She believes that she got the spirit from her mother, who had both mingis and boorane spirits. Her husband, who worked in Arabic countries, paid for a ritual, which was arranged for the first time in the beginning of the 1980s. A seven-day-long ritual was the first stage of initiating into the ritual. For five years she was well, after which the second ritual was arranged. The third ritual took place in the 1990s, when she already lived in Finland. The woman travelled to Somalia to visit her ill mother and during the same trip she searched for a cure for herself. She collected money from relatives, including her brother who lives in Canada, to pay for her travel and ritual. Participating in a ritual as a patient is also a learning process; step by step a patient learns to deal with the spirits, and may become a teacher her/himself. After the third ritual she became Calaqad. As signs of her position, she has a silver bracelet, *birmad*, a ring with a red stone and a particular metal coin, *sharuq*.

Calaqad has not been able to afford to travel to Somalia for another ritual. Instead, she takes care of mingis at home by herself: she burns different kinds of incense, wears beautiful clothes,[40] cleans and decorates the house, and makes food she desires and shares it with her family. She listens to what the spirit inside her wants. She has a cassette recording from a mingis ritual in Somalia. Every now and then, she arranges a small ritual with some female friends, and they heal each other. She gets special incense from her relatives and friends who live in the Arabian Peninsula and Somalia. Perfumes needed in a mingis ritual nowadays are also available in a Somali owned shop in Helsinki.

Somali women told me that the presence of the spirits can be felt, for example, as itching on skin. Mingis inside a person can be peaceful for a long time, but if a person does not pay respect to the spirit, it may get angry and cause ill health. Symptoms connected to mingis and other saar spirits include: fears at night; general malaise and unhappiness; tiredness; loss of energy; restless and sleepless nights; unwillingness to eat or talk; anger; a tense feeling in the chest; aching bones, muscles and lower limbs; and even a sensation of paralysis in limbs. If attention is not paid to mingis, symptoms can become worse and lead to an inability to move, madness, and even death.

According to some Somali women, once a person has been possessed by saar, she/he will usually never get rid of the spirit. Hence, women took their spirits along when they crossed Somalia's borders.

It is possible, however, that in the diaspora spirits do not disturb much, but are relatively peaceful for long periods of time. Elisa Pelizzari noted a Somali male Calaqad, who was in exile in Kenya and who had lost his healing skills.[41] He felt that spirits had left him and were gradually staying further and further away. Instead, for some Somali women, spirits appeared for the first time in Finland. One woman, for instance, told that she had often seen sharax rituals in Somalia and that her mother in Somalia had a sharax spirit. She herself, however, had not had any symptoms and she was unaware of her own spirit until she went into trance during a ritual for which I was also present. Afterwards, when we talked, she was afraid and told me that she had thrown away a cassette with sharax music, which she had sometimes listened to at home. Now she had decided to arrange a big feast for sharax in Somalia when she travels there. Another woman explained that she had not even seen saar dances before, but despite that she went into trance during the same ritual.

Nowadays, Somali *umma* in Finland strongly oppose the practice of saar as it is seen as a non-Islamic cultural practice. This same change can also be seen also in Somalia, where saar, and also Sufi traditions have been rejected by Islamists.[42] Jinn, instead, have a legitimate role as part of the history of Islam. This has led saar to have gone "underground" in Finland. Women possessed by saar spirits usually keep quiet, because most husbands, sheikhs or other "religious people" do not accept them. One woman explained: "Religious people do not like mingis because they think that in the ritual jinn are asked to come and then they are worshipped. On the contrary, religious people think that jinn should be avoided and got rid of." And another woman commented: "I have heard Somali men in Finland say, if a woman has problems, she has to go to a doctor and then we also read the Koran, that's all." According to these women, reading the Koran does not usually solve problems caused by saar spirits, but can even make spirits angrier. I was told about a woman who experienced religious awakening after entering Europe, and since then denied the existence of mingis spirits. As a result, all her three children who were born in Europe became mentally ill or disabled. In the end, the mother acknowledged the existence of mingis, but her children who were born in the West, do not believe in spirits.

In addition to Islamic resistance, lack of suitable locations, money, and expert knowledge have made it difficult to arrange saar rituals. Moreover, there are many Somali women in Finland who do not believe in spirits or their influence. A Somali woman, for example, stated that she did believe in the existence of jinn as such, since they are mentioned in the Koran, but she could not believe in their power over a human being.

Despite the fact that the mosques turn away from saar, women who participate in spirit possession rituals do not believe that saar and Islam are incompatible. Saar is part of women's life as Muslims, although some women have underscored saar to be part of their culture, not religion. For example, saar rituals were interrupted at prayer times and Calaqad always watches very carefully to be sure that her own children pray regularly. During the month of Ramadan, saar cannot be arranged. Based on my data in Finland, the relationship between Somali women and saar spirits has to do with questions about illness, healing, and alleviating suffering. In addition, the existence of saar concerns women's memory and identity.

In Finland, saar rituals have mostly been on a small scale, and have taken place in secret in private homes. I observed a saar ritual in Finland twice. Another way to get a proper cure is to travel abroad to another European county where the Somali community is larger than in Finland or to the Horn of Africa where saar rituals can be easily arranged. In addition, other traditional and religious treatments are more easily accessible in Somalia. Lack of religious experts and healers in the diaspora seems to be among those reasons why Somalis from Europe and the United States visit Somalia.

During my fieldwork in the Hargeysa area during the summer of 2005, I observed the consultations and treatments given by local religious and other traditional healers, and also interviewed diasporic Somalis who relied on these treatments. This data confirms that the practice of saar is in decline also in Somalia, although rituals are still arranged. However, the number of religious healers that treat problems related to jinn, witchcraft and the evil eye with the Koran and the Prophetic tradition has increased. I was also told that problems related to jinn are nowadays very common, which was not the case before the war. According to my interpretation, this change in healing traditions reflects a wider social, political and religious change in Somali society.

CONCLUSION

For Somali women in Finland, local and transnational dimensions are intertwined with their everyday lives and interact in complex ways. Thus, everyday life in Finland is tied to a scattered, transnational family where the homeland is present in many ways. The role of Islam and the multiple meanings and processes attached to it are likewise complex, and cannot be understood detached from the life world of Somali women. On one hand, the everyday life of Somali women in Finland is "sieved" through Islam, but on the other hand, Islam is also sieved through women's everyday. Women actively interpret religion and make different choices inside the Islamic framework. In addition, the civil war along with the current political and social situation in Somalia coupled with Islamic movements and their influence, add another fiber into Somali women's life in exile.

In conditions of civil war and diaspora, Islam has for many Somalis become a more conscious part of life than what it had been. In a religiously, culturally, and socially new environment, Islam may work as a moral and also practical compass in everyday life for Somali refugee women.[43] Many Somali women in Finland regard Islam as an important factor not only in terms of religious reproduction, but also for cultural reproduction and maintenance of ethnic identities.[44] For Somali women, Islam may signify continuity and resource, but also change and challenge, even pressure.

In Finland, Somali men active in mosques define and recreate the new Somali identity, based on "normative" or "correct" Islam, purified from cultural practices. Moreover, many Somali women are gaining Islamic knowledge by taking part in religious teaching, and their example further influences other Somali women. In particular, young Somali women who have not lived amidst Somali cultural heritage like their parents often find it easy to draw sharp distinctions between religion and culture. For their mothers and grandmothers, this change is not necessarily easy.

Through Islamization male knowledge easily becomes normative, and women need to develop strategies to resist the eradication of traditional female knowledge.[45] In the case of traditional female rituals such as saar, transnational networks may offer Somali women a means of resistance in the midst of new Islamic interpretations. Hence, it is important to further examine the various changing relationships between religion and the everyday lives of Somali women, and also men, in exile. For Somali families, reconstructing lives and identities in the diaspora, particularly in the aftermath of civil war, is an ongoing and open-ended process.

Notes

1. Safran, W. (1991). Diasporas in modern societies: Myths of homeland and return. *Diaspora*, 1(1), 83-99.
2. Leonard, K. I., Stepick, A., Vasquez, M. A. & Holdaway, J. (Eds.). (2005). *Immigrant faiths: Transforming religious life in America*. Walnut Creek, CA: AltaMira Press.

   Ebaugh, H. R. & Chafetz, J. S. (Eds.). (2000). *Religion and the new immigrants: Continuities and adaptations in immigrant congregations*. Walnut Creek, CA: AltaMira Press.

   Ebaugh, H. R. & Chafetz, J. S. (Eds.). (2002). *Religion across borders. Transnational immigrant networks*. Walnut Creek, CA: AltaMira Press.

   Levitt, P. (2001). *The transnational villagers*. Berkeley: University of California Press.

   Warner, R. S. & Wittner, J. G. (Eds.). (1998). *Gatherings in diaspora: Religious communities and the new immigration*. Philadelphia: Temple University Press.
3. Tiilikainen, M. (2003a). *Arjen islam: Somalinaisten elämää Suomessa* [Everyday Islam: The life of Somali women in Finland]. Published dissertation, Tampere: Vastapaino.
4. Old ethnic, cultural and religious minorities of Finland have consisted of indigenous Sami people, Roma, Jews, and Tatar Muslims. During the 1990s, the overall number of foreign citizens in Finland increased rapidly. In addition to growing numbers of refugees and asylum seekers, another significant group were Finnish-speaking Ingrians from the former Soviet Union, who were granted the status of returning emigrants. Furthermore, many immigrants moved to Finland due

to family ties or studies. Labour migrants have always constituted a very small proportion of Finland's immigrants. By the end of the year 2004 there were 108,000 foreign citizens in Finland (Statistics Finland 4.11.2005).

5. Statistics Finland (2005). Retrieved from http://tilastokeskus.fi/tup/tilastotietokannat/index_en.html.
6. The estimated number of all Muslims in Finland is about 30,000, including Finnish Tatars and converts to Islam.
7. Jasinskaja-Lahti, I., Liebkind, K., & Vesala, T. (Eds.). (2002). *Rasismi ja syrjintä Suomessa: Maahanmuuttajien kokemuksia* [Racism and discrimination in Finland: Experiences of immigrants]. Helsinki: Gaudeamus.
8. Ministry of Labour. (2005). Retrieved from http://www.mol.fi/mol/fi/99_pdf/fi/04_maahanmuutto/08_mahanmuuttotilastot/tilkint.pdf.
9. Zahra (personal communication, May 21, 1997).
10. Ebaugh, H. R. & Chafetz, J. S. (Eds.). (2002). *Religion across borders. Transnational immigrant networks*. Walnut Creek, CA: AltaMira Press. pp. 385-399.
11. Ebaugh, H. R. & Chafetz, J. S. (Eds.). (2002). *Religion across borders. Transnational immigrant networks*. Walnut Creek, CA: AltaMira Press. pp. 385-399.

    See also Levitt, P. (2001). *The transnational villagers*. Berkeley: University of California Press. p. 169.
12. See also McMichael, C. (2002). 'Everywhere is Allah's place': Islam and the everyday life of Somali women in Melbourne, Australia. *Journal of Refugee Studies,* 15(2), 171-188.
13. Hibo (personal communication, February 20, 1997).
14. Zahra (personal communication, May 21, 1997).
15. Dahabo (personal communication, October 31, 1997).
16. Faadumo (personal communication, May 1, 1997).
17. See also Berns McGown, R. (1999). *Muslims in the diaspora: The Somali communities of London and Toronto*. Toronto: University of Toronto Press. p. 39.
18. See also Helander, B. (1994). Somalisk islam som världsbild och enande kraft. In I. Svanberg and D. Westerlund (Eds.), *Majoritetens Islam: Om Muslimer utanför arabvärlden* (pp. 122-137). Stockholm: Arena. p. 131.
19. Asha (personal communication, April 7, 1997).
20. Halimo (personal communication, October 12, 1997).

21. Zahra (personal communication, May 21, 1997).
22. Schiffauer, W. (1988). Migration and religiousness. In T. Gerholm & Y. G. Lithman (Eds.), *The New Islamic Presence in Western Europe* (pp. 146-158). London: Mansell.
23. I talk about global Islamic revival on a very general level. In different contexts the phenomenon has been given different names such as Islamism, Islamic fundamentalism and radicalism. With "Islamic movements" I refer to such movements, which also have political goals.
24. Berns McGown, R. (1999). *Muslims in the diaspora: The Somali communities of London and Toronto*. Toronto: University of Toronto Press. pp. 33-39.
25. Lewis, I. M. (1991). Introduction: *Zar* in context: The past, the present and future of an African healing cult. In I. M. Lewis, A. Al-Safi, & S. Hurreiz (Eds.), *Women's medicine: The Zar-Bori-cult in Africa and beyond* (pp. 1-16). Edinburgh: Edinburgh University Press for the International African Institute.
26. Lewis, I. M. (1991). Introduction: *Zar* in context: The past, the present and future of an African healing cult. In I. M. Lewis, A. Al-Safi, & S. Hurreiz (Eds.), *Women's medicine: The Zar-Bori-cult in Africa and beyond* (pp. 1-16). Edinburgh: Edinburgh University Press for the International African Institute.
27. Boddy, J. (1989). *Wombs and alien spirits: Women, men, and the Zâr Cult in Northern Sudan*. Madison, WI: University of Wisconsin Press.

    Lewis, I. M. (1991). Introduction: *Zar* in context: The past, the present and future of an African healing cult. In_I. M. Lewis, A. Al-Safi & S. Hurreiz (Eds.), *Women's medicine: The Zar-Bori-cult in Africa and beyond* (pp. 1-16). Edinburgh: Edinburgh University Press for the International African Institute.

    Lambek, M. (1993). *Knowledge and practice in Mayotte: Local discourses of Islam, sorcery, and spirit possession*. Toronto: University of Toronto Press.

    Nisula, T. (1999). Everyday spirits and medical interventions: Ethnographic and historical notes on therapeutic conventions in Zanzibar Town. TAFAS 43. Helsinki: The Finnish Anthropological Society.
28. Lewis, I.M. (1998). *Saints and Somalis: Popular Islam in a clan-based society*. London: HAAN Associates. p. 109.

    Janice Boddy (1989:145) has described similar symptoms among Sudanese women: nausea, persistent headache, anorexia, lassitude, apathy and depression, sleeplessness, anxiety, unspecified aches, being easily saddened, fertility problems, and blindness or paralysis without apparent organic cause.

29. Antoniotto, A. (1984). Traditional medicine in Somalia: An anthropological approach to the concepts concerning disease. In T. Labahn (Ed.), *Proceedings of the second international congress of Somali studies* (pp. 155-169). Hamburg: Helmut Buske Verlag. p. 164.

    Ahmed, A. M. (1988). Somali traditional healers: Role and status. In A. Puglielli (Ed.), *Proceedings of the third international congress of Somali studies* (pp. 240-247). Roma: Il Pensiero Scientifico. p. 241-242.

    Pelizzari, E. (1997). Possession et thérapie dans la Corne de l'Afrique. Paris: L'Harmattan.

30. Lewis, I. M. (1991). Introduction: *Zar* in context: The past, the present and future of an African healing cult. In I. M. Lewis, A. Al-Safi, & S. Hurreiz (Eds.), *Women's medicine: The Zar-Bori-cult in Africa and beyond* (pp. 1-16). Edinburgh: Edinburgh University Press for the International African Institute. p. 3.

    See also Boddy, J. (1989). *Wombs and alien spirits: Women, men, and the Zâr Cult in Northern Sudan*. Madison, WI: The University of Wisconsin Press. p. 278.

31. Boddy, J. (1989). *Wombs and alien spirits: Women, men, and the Zâr Cult in Northern Sudan*. Madison, WI: The University of Wisconsin Press.

    Lewis, I. M., A. Al-Safi, & S. Hurreiz (Eds.). (1991). *Women's medicine: The Zar-Bori-cult in Africa and beyond*. Edinburgh: Edinburgh University Press for the International African Institute.

    Nisula, T. (1999). Everyday spirits and medical interventions: Ethnographic and historical notes on therapeutic conventions in Zanzibar Town. TAFAS 43. Helsinki: The Finnish Anthropological Society.

32. Lewis, I. M. (1971). *Ecstatic religion: A study of shamanism and spirit possession*. London: Routledge.

    Lewis, I. M. (1998). *Saints and Somalis: Popular Islam in a clan-based society*. London: HAAN Associates.

33. Nisula, T. (1999). Everyday spirits and medical interventions: Ethnographic and historical notes on therapeutic conventions in Zanzibar Town. TAFAS 43. Helsinki: The Finnish Anthropological Society. pp.160-163.

34. Boddy, J. (1989). *Wombs and alien spirits: Women, men, and the Zâr Cult in Northern Sudan*. Madison, WI: The University of Wisconsin Press. p. 276.
35. See Ashour, M. (1989). *The Jinn in the Qur'an and the Sunna*. London: Dar Al-Taqwa.

    Philips, A. A. B. (1997). A. A. B. Philips (Trans.) *Ibn Taymeeyah's essay on the Jinn (Demons)*. Riyadh: International Islamic Publishing House.
36. Lewis, I. M. (1998). *Saints and Somalis: Popular Islam in a clan-based society*. London: HAAN Associates. p. 28.

    See also Boddy, J. (1989). *Wombs and alien spirits: Women, men, and the Zâr Cult in Northern Sudan*. Madison, WI: The University of Wisconsin Press. p. 278.
37. Pelizzari, E. (1997). Possession et thérapie dans la Corne de l'Afrique. Paris: L'Harmattan.

    Tiilikainen, M. (2003a). *Arjen islam: Somalinaisten elämää Suomessa* [Everyday Islam: The life of Somali women in Finland]. Published dissertation, Tampere: Vastapaino.
38. *Xabash*, which literally means Ethiopian, is one of the *mingis* spirits. According to Somali women, it is the worst of all spirits. Particularly in Northern Somalia *saar* is also known by a name *saar xabashi*, which may refer to the Ethiopian origin of the cult (Lewis 1991:10).
39. Tiilikainen, M. (Fieldnotes, June 1, 2002).
40. Different spirits are fond of different colours. For example, *Maame*, which is one of the main spirits of *mingis*, likes the colour red and often women possessed by *Maame* wear red clothes.

    Luling, V. (1991). Some possession cults in Southern Somalia. In I. M. Lewis, A. Al-Safi, & S. Hurreiz (Eds.), *Women's medicine: The Zar-Bori-cult in Africa and beyond* (pp. 167-177). Edinburgh: Edinburgh University Press for the International African Institute. p. 168
41. Pelizzari, E. (1997). Possession et thérapie dans la Corne de l'Afrique. Paris: L'Harmattan. p. 168
42. Kapteijns, L. (2000). Ethiopia and the Horn of Africa. In N. Levtzion & R. L. Pouwels (Eds.), *The History of Islam in Africa* (pp. 227-250). Athens, OH: Ohio University Press. p. 244-245
43. See also Tiilikainen, M. (2003b). Somali women and daily Islam in the diaspora. *Social Compass* 50(1), 59-69.

44. Compare Ebaugh, H. R., & Chafetz, J. S. (Eds.). (2000). *Religion and the new immigrants: Continuities and adaptations in immigrant congregations*. Walnut Creek, CA: AltaMira Press.

    Warner, R. S. (1998). Immigration and religious communities in the United States. In R. S. Warner & J. G. Wittner (Eds.), *Gatherings in diaspora: Religious communities and the new immigration* (pp. 3-34). Philadelphia: Temple University Press.

45. Evers Rosander, E. (1997). Introduction: The Islamization of 'Tradition' and 'Modernity'. In D. Westerlund and E. Evers Rosander (Eds.), *African Islam and Islam in Africa: Encounters between Suufis and Islamists* (pp. 1-27). London & Uppsala, Sweden: Hurst & Company in co-operation with the Nordic Africa Institute. p. 6-7

Part III

North America

Chapter 10

TRADITION AND THE INNER CITY: SOMALI WOMEN IN REGENT PARK, TORONTO

Rima Berns-McGown

INTRODUCTION

Diaspora is primarily an act of imagination. The attempt to (re)create a meaningful life in a strange place, holding on to the values and narrative that made sense in the "homeland," can be made especially challenging by the harsh reality of socioeconomic hardship. This essay, based on a series of in-depth interviews conducted in early 2004, investigates the border between the "traditional" Somali home and the inner city social housing project. It examines how differences between the home and the surrounding community are perceived, managed, and mitigated by the Somali mothers who see themselves as the guardians of the home and its values. In doing so, it examines how integration into the wider community is perceived to be affected by the social housing experience.

For this study, in-depth interviews were done with fifteen women in the neighborhood of Regent Park, Toronto in January and February, 2004. Residents were contacted via a rolling interview technique. The women were between the ages of 18 and 60 years old. Most had been in Canada for about 10 years, and almost all had experience in living in other parts of Toronto before they arrived in the housing project. Interviews were done in small groups at a local community center. All the women understood English; most could speak it. In the case of two women, translation was provided by a third. It was important to them to know that their names would not be used in the finished article.

Somalis began arriving in Toronto, and other Western cities, in significant numbers in the early 1990s, following the ouster of Dictator Siad Barre and the consequent civil war that marked the dissolution of Somali civil society. The vast majority arrived as refugees, even though many of the early arrivals, in particular, had been people of means with businesses, educations, and professions in Mogadishu. Almost 15 years later, a number of whom live in socially-assisted housing, including Regent Park, one of the most readily identifiable public housing developments in the city.

Social housing developments such as Regent Park are relatively insular and are separated from the surrounding neighborhoods by invisible barriers and complex codes of conduct. They are plagued by reputations for inner city problems, including gang violence, cycles of poverty, drug and alcohol abuse, and teenage pregnancies. Many of the problems associated with social housing projects stem from ways of life that are alien to the traditional values Somalis tended to cling to after immigration. Somali immigrants have tended to become more religious in the West as they have struggled to maintain their identities.[1] Although they have, for the most part, redefined their practice of Islam in the process-becoming Western, not Westernized, Muslims-this Islam is nonetheless based upon values they see as traditional.

CONTEXT

It is most important to understand a group of refugees in terms of the context of their departure from their homeland and their arrival in the new. In a world of porous borders and rapid communication, all refugee groups can be said to be in a diaspora-separated from their geographical or imagined homelands, but still carrying with them the lives that fuelled their departure. While it is not possible to fill in the full context of the circumstances surrounding Somali refugees' departures, or all the salient aspects of their political and social lives before and during the exodus, certain points need to be borne in mind.

Somalis are not as homogeneous a people as they have frequently been depicted, both in the media and by scholars, and there are significant cultural and even language differences between the northern pastoralists and the southerners with their more mixed economy, and between the histories that have accompanied each tradition. Ironically, this has been better understood after Somalia's civil breakdown, given that the disintegration of established orders has provided the impetus and opportunity for a re-creation of some of Somalia's cultural myths.[2]

Somalia's refugees have come from all regions of the country: north, south, and the interior. They are drawn from the cities of Mogadishu and Hargeisa, from the towns as well as the countryside, and from all classes. They include urbanites of all professions: pastoralists and farmers, the privileged and the impoverished, the well-educated and the uneducated.

The challenges of diaspora forced Somalis to re-examine their identity as Muslims and their practice of Islam, both out of a realization that, in the face of an array of competing faiths and a culture of secularism, they could not take Islam as they had understood it prior to migration for granted, and also-and more importantly-out of a fear of "losing" their children to the dominant North American culture. Mothers, especially, have wrestled with the questions of how to instill Somali and Muslim culture in their children.

The position of women has been changing in Somali society and diaspora communities. Women have been instrumental in keeping shattered Somali families and communities together, both in the diaspora and in the homeland. They have been at the forefront of the redefinition of Somalis' practice of Islam as it has occurred in the diaspora in the years since mass migration, and in the transfer of ideas back into the homeland.

Critical among the latter is the understanding that female genital cutting-also called female circumcision or female genital mutilation-is not integral to Islam, and therefore need not play a central role in defining a Somali woman. This was a new understanding for Somali women, gained for the most part in the West once they had begun to study Islam more consciously, and caused a re-examination of the practice of female genital cutting, both in the diaspora and over time, at home.[3] As such, women have played, and continue to play, an enormously influential role in the developing Somali sense of self and identity.[4]

INNER CITY NEIGHBORHOODS AND SOCIAL HOUSING PROJECTS

As Murdie and Teixeira write, "access to a neighborhood where the newcomer feels comfortable and housing which is adequate, suitable and affordable" is critical to the integration of immigrants and refugees, especially in the early stages of their resettlement.[5] Newcomers face particular barriers in their search for such housing, barriers which vary according to the ethnicity and degree of "newness" of the refugee group in question. Discrimination by landlords on the basis of color or religion, language problems, lack of familiarity with the city and the housing market, household size and, of course, limited means, all contribute to refugees' difficulties in finding satisfactory housing.[6]

Somalis in Toronto have faced all of these barriers, in addition to the difficulties imposed by post-traumatic stress and the fact that households were frequently headed by single mothers. Complicating their difficulties was the fact that, given the inter-clan strife that had fuelled the civil war and was the reason for their flight in the first place, Somalis preferred to live in close proximity to other members of their sub-clans or, at least, clan-family members with whom they had not recently had disputes. This was a tremendously sensitive point for Somalis in the early years of their arrival in Toronto and other western cities. Researchers have commented on the large number of community support organizations that were very quickly established by Somalis.[7] This "impressive number of community support facilities" was the legacy of mistrust and pain among immigrant Somali sub-clans in the early years, and rapidly became a feature of life in every city in which they settled. For this reason, as well, and as increasing numbers of Somalis from the interior as well as the larger Somali cities and towns began to arrive, Somalis have settled in concentrated pockets in various neighborhoods throughout Toronto.

Public housing in Toronto accounts for about 11% of the total housing stock in the region.[8] No new social housing has been built since 1997, due to withdrawal of provincial and federal funding, and the waiting list is long, upwards of 40,000 households and ten years' waiting time.[9]

It is important to understand, as well, that even concentrated pockets of public housing, such as Regent Park, are not ghettos in the sense that this term is used in large American cities. Regent Park is located in the near center of the city of Toronto, and is bounded by River Street to the east, Shuter Street to the south, Gerrard Street to the north, and Parliament Street to the west. It is bordered by Cabbagetown, one of Toronto's more desirable urban neighborhoods. Cabbagetown is not a uniformly wealthy neighborhood; sex workers are plentiful on its night streets, as are, at all hours, homeless shelters, food banks and many of the poor who use them. But many of the neighborhood's old Victorian homes have been renovated by wealthy urbanites, and it is a lively restaurant and arts quarter. Moreover, Regent Park, and other similar neighborhoods, is considered safe to walk and drive through during daylight hours. There are no abandoned buildings within them.

Regent Park was purpose-built as a social housing community in 1948, one of the oldest in Canada. It was meant to create a "modern, car-free, spacious and pleasant" environment for low-income Torontonians.[10] Low-rise buildings face onto small quadrants, and there is no through-traffic. Nor, however, are there shops or street-facing buildings within the residential spaces, and cultural, education, health and sports facilities are all on its borders. This has recently been seen as a problem. The inward-facing buildings contribute to a sense that the neighborhood is both physically and socially isolated. Present revitalization plans for Regent Park focus on attempting to more successfully integrate the neighborhood into its surroundings, and introducing commercial and community facilities into the midst of the housing units.[11]

As Andersen has written, neighborhoods that are segregated from their surroundings--however "pleasant" the gardens between the buildings--run the risk of being "excluded from the mental maps of possible living environments for the majority of the urban population."[12] The likelihood of this happening is particularly strong "when visible signs of social and physical decay appear...and especially if they receive bad press." Both of those factors have contributed to Regent Park's isolation. Importantly, Andersen notes, "segregation is not a simple consequence of social inequality, but a product of both social and spatial differentiation."[13]

This segregation occurs as people begin to stigmatize a given neighborhood-and its residents. As immigrants and refugees become more knowledgeable about the social and physical geography of their new homes, the stigma becomes yet another hardship of dislocation they need to overcome. As Anderson describes it, nobody wants to live in an excluded, stigmatized place. Residents of the segregated neighborhood carry a sense of shame about their place of residence. When they move into neighborhoods like Regent Park, they must erect barriers between their sense of dignity and the stigma of living in a rundown neighborhood whose buildings reflect no sense of residents' pride and which has one of the highest rates for violent crime in the city.

CONVERSATIONS WITH WOMEN IN REGENT PARK

The predominant concern of Somali immigrant women, in 2004 and as much as ten years earlier, is to ground their children firmly within a Muslim and Somali cultural tradition, and not to lose them to what they perceive is a smorgasbord of alien cultures. The fact of living in an inner city neighborhood like Regent Park, with its stigma, its poverty and its violence, complicates but does not change that essential challenge. On the other hand, there have been attitudinal changes among Somali women in the almost ten years since the first interviews were done.

In the mid-1990s, women still felt very new and the situation very raw. There was little community knowledge to draw upon, since most refugees had arrived in Toronto fewer than five years beforehand. Everyone was scrambling. There was an overwhelming desire to return home at the earliest opportunity, and every hope that the day when that would be possible was not far off. Somali refugees were reeling from the effects of the violence to themselves, their property, and their families that they had witnessed in Somalia and in the course of their flight. They were struggling to establish themselves logistically in their new homes. Most of all, they were struggling to establish themselves within a new mental landscape, and this was the most daunting consideration of all.

It was in this regard that they experienced a real fear of the unknown. It was apparent that their children were not experiencing culture shock to the same degree that they were. They hit the ground running, as it were, and rapidly determined what clothing, behavior, and attitudes would equip them for life as Canadian children and Canadian teenagers. This is not to say that they abandoned their Somali or Muslim identities. In fact, interviews with teenagers indicated that they had a strong sense of who they were, and that each one had thought through a set of compromises and had determined where to draw the line between accommodation to the norms and behavioral expectations of teachers and peers on the one hand, and of parents on the other. What was striking, in fact, in interviews with teenagers and with parents was that the teenagers were much more stalwart in protecting their Somali and Muslim identities than fear allowed their parents to trust them to be.[14]

At the time, parents were particularly scornful, and afraid, of the constraints Canadian society put upon them by preventing their use of corporal punishment in disciplining their children. Interaction with Canadian authority figures-teachers, social workers, and police-led them to the uncomfortable conclusion that in an altercation with their children, the assumption would be made that they were physically abusing the children, who would then be removed from the home.

> ...In Somalia if you abuse your kids, society will alienate you. This is a terrible sanction, so the system corrects for people who would hurt their kids. Some kids use this system [in Canada] to gain additional freedom. The major thing is if the institution is there for the kids' welfare, and the parents are there for the kids' welfare, there is one objective, so the major thing is to mediate misunderstandings between parents and institutions.

> The thing is, parents who have taken their kids 20,000 miles from a war-torn country would never hurt their kids. Parents who have had to face danger-hunger, lions, fear, uncertainty, murder, the trauma of leaving everything behind and braving immigration to a new country-these people have faced things that social workers in Canada will never begin to understand – all to keep their children safe. Why would they then hurt their children? Of course they would not.[15]

These concerns remain, and yet resignation has replaced the panic that dominated accounts of a decade earlier.

> It's hard with kids, especially teenagers. Back home you have a whole village or a large family taking care of the kids. Everyone looks out for everyone's kids, tells them what's wrong and what's right, tells them to listen to their parents. Here there are other influences. And you can't discipline them. If you spank them, they'll take your kids away and put them in foster homes, and then they are worse when they come back. The foster homes don't do them any good. (Saida)

> We are abused, not the kids. (Ina)

> My kids were here six years before I managed to get here from Mogadishu. When I got here, we were two different families. They already knew everything about the new country; I was still living with old ideas, the old ways of doing things. The kids said, "you are wrong, Mom. Wake up and smell the coffee." (Lul)

The other women laugh at her use of the Canadian expression:

They say, "Chill, Mom."

The women laugh again. They are laughing at themselves, at the expression and what it means and how the kids were speaking, literally and metaphorically, a different language. They repeat it, imitating their children's way of talking and body language, and their own shocked reaction at first hearing the expression and their gradual understanding that the meaning of the word "chill," to be cold, was not how it was being used, which was "relax, Mom, don't get so uptight."

> The kids got used to everything quickly, even if they come from Somalia. It takes the moms a lot longer. (Asha)

> There are no more tears. Our eyes are dry. We are tired of crying. (Fadumo)

> It is very hard. This is on top of all the stress of what we came away from and then trying to survive here. The kids are not in your hands. You can't control them the way you could back home. The problem is the system as well as the kids themselves. Take health care. We tell our girls, "no sex"; they tell our girls "safe sex." Girls and families are uncomfortable talking about these topics. Sometimes, if a girl is over 18, abortions happen without the parents even knowing about it. (Deeqa)

> Also the police and social workers are less concerned with keeping families together than with "protecting" the rights of the kids. Sometimes they are sympathetic. I know a case where the police came to the home where the girl had called '911' and they saw it was a nice home. The girl had nice parents and a nice room. And they said to the girl, you are lucky, so you can either stay here and listen to your parents, or starve on the street. She left but two days later she was back; she saw how lucky she was. But not all police are like that. (Mariam)

Many parental concerns are not connected to the neighborhood the families live in, and have to do with the simple desire of their children to be Canadian teenagers, and to 'fit in' with their peers.

> The kids want to fit in so they do whatever they want. They pull their pants down over their hips when they leave the house; the girls take off their hijab. (Safia)

> Inside the house, they listen to you, but outside it's a different story. You can't force them to pray or to wear hijab. (Zahra)

> Also, most women here are single moms, so the parenting is very unbalanced. It's especially hard with teenage boys. We worry all night when they are out. We can't stop them, can't control them. They are out of control. (Fosia)

Other aspects of parenting are exacerbated by the poor neighborhood and its particular problems.

> The thing you are scared of is that they will drop out of school. Many kids-not Somali kids so much-drop out of school. And in this area, you are scared of drug dealing. (Saida)

None of the women interviewed chose to move to Regent Park. All of them were on the formidable waiting list for public housing, and all of them were frightened when, at last, a house was given them, and they learned it was within the Regent Park neighborhood.

> The guns and knives are very hard to take. We ran away from the bullets back home so it's very hard to come and find it here. (Mariam)

> I lived in Scarborough before and I was very afraid when I came here. (Kinsi)

> We came because we got a two-bedroom house; we had waited for eight years for that, but we didn't want to come here. We were scared and not happy when we heard that the house was here. (Anab)

Their fears were quickly realized by what they saw.

> In Scarborough it was nice and quiet. Here it is scary. There are drugs being sold in the parking lot and it is not so quiet. (Halwo)

> One day I was walking with my ten-year-old, it was the middle of the day, and a teenage boy came up to us. He was staggering and muttering something, I couldn't tell what, it sounded like blah-blah-blah. Suddenly I saw that he had a huge knife sticking into his stomach. Then he fell down, onto his front, and the knife pushed out the back of him. My son was terrified and started to cry. (Safia)

> Seven months ago we heard shooting just outside the building, in the parking lot, and we saw a boy had been killed by a gun. It was just suppertime. My mother was so scared. The kids in our family don't go out at night. They are afraid, so they make sure they are home before it is dark if they can. (Kinsi)

> We are all appalled by the shootings that happen. We left this at home and we don't want to witness it here. (Fadumo)

For all their fears, the women were confident that it was possible to win what they saw was yet another battle for their children's safety and well-being.

> It's hard and they are hard to raise but if you're strong, you can do it. (Lul)

> You have to yell a lot. But they do listen. (Anab)

The women have developed a series of strategies for countering negative outside influences. Most important is the constant effort to create a strong religious household and to set a good example for the children. The women all wear hijab, maintain strong ties to the mosque, and pray regularly at home. They do their best to have their children pray and their daughters wear hijab. They take pains to observe Muslim dietary requirements.

All of the women feel strongly about having the children live at home as long as possible, preferably until they are married. And all of them have made education for all of their children the highest priority.

I teach the kids religion…that's important: religion, culture, language. I was afraid that the teenagers would want to be like other kids, not living with family. I explain that it is important to keep them at home as long as possible, until they are married. (Lul)

I try to keep them very, very busy. I send my kids to Qur'an school five days a week and on Saturdays and Sundays they play basketball at the Center Neighborhood House. Their coaches are Somali. You want to keep them busy all the time so that when they come home they eat and then it's time for bed. (Safia)

I send my kids to Qur'an school for an hour five days a week. (Khadija)

Staying in school is the most important thing. (Mariam)

No matter what they're doing, we never stop explaining. When that boy was knifed in front of my son, my son wanted to know if that would happen to him. I told him, no. Whatever you do, don't quit school, I said. If you do, you end up with those bad kids who have nothing better to do; they sell drugs to get money but then maybe they use the money for themselves, to buy clothes or something, and then if you owe some money to other guys and you don't have it to give to them, you end up with a knife in you. (Safia)

If you respect your kids, they will respect you. Sometimes you make a mistake, and you must be able to apologize. Teach them by example. (Fosia)

And we are all yelling all the time, yelling, yelling, yelling. (Fadumo)

You have to be flexible with the children. You must be friends with them, and explain things to them. Listen to them. Allow them to go to a friend's house and explain when they need to come home. (Halwo)

Yes, too much screaming won't work. (Safia)

Some people kick their kids out if they've done something wrong but that doesn't help. The kids all know they can come to my place if there's a problem. The kids all have their own keys. I never know who's going to be there in the morning. Often in the morning I find a strange pair of shoes and it turns out a friend has come to stay. Mom, says my child, his mom kicked him out. So I take them in. But in the morning I always call the parents and tell them to take their kids back. Even if they've done something wrong, it doesn't help to kick the kids out. (Deeqa)

Sometimes we promise to buy our kids expensive shoes or clothes if they try hard in school or behave well. Air Jordans or Nike or something. The kids are aware of the sacrifice we make when we do that. They know we have very little money. (Lul)

The mothers do feel that the community can claim success. With enough hard work, children tend to stay in school and do remain loyal to their parents. Moreover, they generally do not jettison their cultural foundations or their religion.

Both my sons finished high school here. (Ina)

My Somali neighbor has four kids. Every one of them is at the University of Toronto; they all live at home. (Fosia)

All my children are in school. My older sons are studying electrical engineering and my daughter is studying to be a daycare worker. Everyone is finishing high school and university. (Halwo)

The kids know how to ask questions about pork or alcohol. They won't eat pork and they watch out for each other. (Khadija)

My 11-year-old son made a grilled cheese sandwich with cheese I bought. The neighbor's girls was over – she's 13

> – and she said, "oh, he can't eat that. See this ingredient? That's pork." So we gave it to another neighbor who is not Muslim. We didn't want to throw it away because it's good food. (Safia)

The women believe that their presence in the community is to its overall benefit. They cite the opening of the community mosque in 1997, the community center, and the *halal* food stores that serve them as evidence of supportive structures that have been strengthened because of their needs, their demands, and their presence, or that exist because of them. They believe that they have seen an improvement in the health of the community in the time they have been there.

> It's much better with the mosque here. It's the mosque for all Muslims in the neighborhood: Somalis, Yemenis, Bengalis, Arabs, Indians…We all cooperate. For instance, we take turns making food for *afur*, the evening break fast during Ramadan, and for Eid. (Halwo)

> Regent Park has changed for the better because there are lots of Muslims here. Also because of the neighborhood stores that sell halal food and the mosque. There are also French families here, who are very nice and not Muslim. It depends on the people, not their religion. There's less drugs and less violence than there used to be. (Ina)

> I heard it used to be worse in '95. There were more drug deals then. Taxis used to refuse to come here. The neighborhood has changed for the better. (Lul)

The women believe that their presence, and their orderly lives as Muslims and as people who are ferocious at ensuring their children remain in school, have been instrumental in bettering the neighborhood. But at the same time, they don't demand that their children associate only with other Muslims or with other Somali children. This, too, is a shift from their perspective a decade ago, when, for the most part, they were convinced that that kind of separation was critical to their ability to keep their children's religion and culture.

> The kids are friends with everyone. It doesn't matter whether their friends are Muslim or Somali or whatever. That's not what's important. What's important is whether they're nice kids and they have nice families. If they have good families, then it's okay for them to be friends. (Zaynab)

> They have friends from all over: white, Chinese, black, Somali, everything. It's not good to force kids to be friends only with Somali or Muslim kids. This is Canada. (Safia)

> The kids doing drugs are mostly Jamaican. But there are good Jamaicans too. We are friends with everyone. (Mariam)

> The mothers, too, have friends from all different ethnic groups.
> My daughter's best friend is Chinese. Her mom and I are friends too. The boys bring all their friends to our house to eat and watch TV. Lots and lots of them, from all over. (Zahra)

In spite of misgivings over such issues as schools' teaching of sex education or medical authorities' insistence on placing their children's privacy above their desire as parents for information, the women said they have been supported by the schools and other institutions.

> The schools are very supportive. They send letters home about Eid and all other holidays, so you hear about everything....all religious holidays, Chinese New Year, everything. (Lul)

The women did not equate their experience of Regent Park with their experience of Canada. They see Regent Park as a particular neighborhood with particular problems, but they don't associate those problems with their experience of Canada or of Toronto. They see their stay in Regent Park, where they are exposed to its particular problems as a temporary one. Already, as their children graduate from high school and begin to move to other, more affluent, parts of the city, they see their future elsewhere.

> Canada is good for all of us. Muslim people don't have a hard time in Canada. I have a friend in Denmark; it's awful there. You can't work in the supermarket or anywhere if you wear hijab. Here, lots of girls work in all kinds of places. There's no problem with hijab at all. (Fosia)

> I feel like Canada is my home. There are good opportunities for kids. (Khadija)

Finally, the women were adamant that one of the benefits of having to cope with the Regent Park experience is that it forced them to work together, despite whatever might have happened to their various clan-families in Somalia. The lingering issue of clan-consciousness was extremely divisive and destructive in the early years of Somali migration to the West. These women maintain that, however people may still feel in other parts of Toronto, living in Regent Park meant that they needed to band together and support one another, no matter where in Somalia they came from, or what clan-family they are.

> We are all supportive of one another. We are mostly single moms, and often we don't have other family here. So we support each other, no matter what our clan is. We are Regent Park East African women banding together. We woke up pretty quickly about the need to help each other here. (Asha)

> People don't care so much about back-home problems. Some still think about it, but less and less. (Deeqa)

DISCUSSION AND CONCLUSION

The comments of the women are fascinating for what they have to say about integration and accommodation to circumstances, particularly in the light of earlier interviews.

Regent Park had a reputation for violent crime and for being a place where dropout rates were high and where drugs-and their accompanying evils-were in plentiful supply. None of the women interviewed wanted to move to Regent Park. As Andersen described, it is a socially and spatially segregated neighborhood that falls outside the scope of where "normal" people want to live. They may have been refugees who were faced with particular difficulties, but they consider themselves "normal" people. They did not consider it a suitable neighborhood, in Murdie and Teixeira's words, and it was not what they had traveled thousands of miles and many years to reach. They were dismayed and frightened at the notion of moving to a neighborhood where the threat of guns and knives was very real; this was precisely what they had left Somalia to get away from. Yet the economic realities of their new lives meant that they had no choice but to rely on the waiting lists and space allocations of the Metropolitan Toronto Housing Authority, and they could not afford to say no to the allotted unit.

This meant accommodating themselves to yet another hardship, another barrier that stood between them and a peaceful and comfortable new life. Most women interviewed in 1995 wanted nothing more than to be able to go home. The women of Regent Park recognize that the political reality of Somalia means that there will not, in the foreseeable future, be a safe, orderly home to return to, and that there is no choice but to adjust to life in the diaspora, perhaps for the rest of their lives. In other words, they recognize that their new situation is much more permanent than they thought it would be a decade earlier.

Their response to life within Regent Park was to create strong borders between what they saw as the potential anarchy of the world of the street, and the safety and security of the home. For the most part, they have continued to be more devout than they had been at home: praying, wearing the hijab, insisting that their children follow their examples in religion from an early age, sending them almost daily to the mosque for religious lessons after school. Knowing that they cannot control their children outside of the home, particularly once they reach adolescence, they nonetheless insist on controlling, to the extent that it is possible, the religious and moral climate of the household. Therefore they insist that within the home, their children dress modestly and join in family prayers and religious celebrations on special occasions. They monitor television programs and language. They attempt to impose a moral framework on their children that contrasts with the "anything goes" attitudes that they are concerned their children are exposed to at school and in the courtyards. They attempt to direct and control the friends their children keep. They are not concerned that these friends all be Somali or even Muslim, but rather that they hold values that the mothers recognize as similar to their own-that they value their families and their education. Above all, it is important to the mothers that their children stay in school, and that they live at home until they marry.

There is flexibility to *how* they attempt to do these things. They are resigned to the fact that they do not have all the tools at their disposal that they once would have had in Somalia. They do not have an extended family of uncles to enforce their teaching-corporally or simply through strong male example-and this is particularly a problem with teenage boys. They are afraid to use any kind of corporal discipline, for fear of having their children taken from them. But they have broadened their range of verbal approaches. They yell, they explain, they befriend, they even bribe with expensive brand-name clothes. The latter case is particularly remarkable because Somali culture is a strictly hierarchical one, one in which it would be out of the question to put the desires of children before the needs of adults. But in these cases, the women recognize how much currency a name-brand clothing item carries for a child. And they also recognize, therefore, that in the right circumstances, buying such an item for a child makes an ally of the child, and buys a certain amount of willingness to comply with parental wishes in return.

In addition, the women recognize-and this is in marked contrast to mothers' attitudes nine years ago-that while their children may not retain their modest Muslim dress outside the house, it is not a sign that they have forgotten their culture or their religion. The headscarves may be tucked into backpacks, the pants may be yanked downwards below the hips, the tops may creep up away from the pants, but this, the mothers recognize, is because the kids need to get along with their peers. And at the same time, the mothers believe that there are lines the teenagers will not cross: they will not eat pork or drink alcohol or do whatever it is that they, as individuals, believe would amount to a betrayal of their religion or their culture. This is particularly interesting because nine years ago, interviews with teenagers made it clear that each teen defined for him or herself what was acceptable in terms of the balancing act between adherence to religion and accommodation to Canadian practices, but their mothers were afraid that all religious adherence went out the window when the child went out the front door. A decade later, these mothers can see their children's proud adherence to their own culture. They are able, therefore, to have more trust in them than did earlier interviewees.

Moreover, none of these parents believe, as many parents did nine years ago, that only in keeping their children in the company of other Somalis and other Muslims could they ensure the kids' retention of culture, religion and values. They now believe that the core values they deem important-caring for family members and staying in school among them-are to be found across ethnic groups, religions and cultures. While they say that their closest friends are other Somali women, they also claim friends from other religious and ethnic groups, and recognize that they have much in common with them.

Importantly, they explicitly state that this ability to befriend people from other religious and ethnic groups-to see them as individuals instead of representatives of other groups-and to thrive within an ethnically plural context is an important part of what they understand as being Canadian. It is something that they see themselves as having absorbed. Correspondence with friends and relatives in other Western countries has led them to believe that it a factor of Canadian, not Western, life.

This is true, as well, of their ability to express themselves freely as Muslims and to be supported by the schools in their endeavor to have their children raised as Muslim and to have their cultural and religious needs recognized institutionally. They expressly indicated their satisfaction with their ability to live as Muslims and to be recognized-in schools, in health centers, in work places-as such. This is not to say that being Muslim in Canada is not problematic. Problems they encounter include such issues as the insistence of schools and health professionals on dealing with sex education as a matter suitable for public discussion, or the fact that, if a girl is over 18, her parents are not consulted by health professionals. This means, for example, that a young woman, still living at home, can have an abortion without the consent or knowledge of her parents. The notion that a person (male or female) has full legal agency at the age of 18, and that privacy requirements preclude the involvement of family members, runs counter to their sense of how families are meant to work. Yet they recognize that these are questions of societal framework, and are not intended to denote lack of respect for traditional Muslim values or the people who hold them.

Finally, they believe that their commitment to family, education and religion-the things they believe keep their children safe, off the streets, away from drugs and their associated problems, and in school-are beneficial to the Regent Park community. The women have a strong sense that the order that they and other like-minded women, many but not all of whom are Muslim, have brought to the community have contributed to its improvement. They claim that the stigma of the neighborhood has lessened in recent years, and its reputation improved, and that they have made a strong contribution to that. In the years since their arrival in Regent Park, the mosque and the halal food shops have contributed to the support they need as a community, and they, in turn, have contributed to improve the community around them. They believe that they are, in effect, reversing what Andersen calls the "dynamic process" that involves the exclusion of a community.[16]

And indeed, while this study cannot prove causality, crime statistics support the women's anecdotal evidence. In 1997, the year the mosque opened on Parliament Street, there were eight murders in Regent Park, as well as 469 robberies, 1484 non-sexual assaults and 1051 reported instances of break-and-enter robberies. By 2002, the most recent year for which the Toronto Police have posted statistics, there were three murders, 273 robberies, 1367 non-sexual assaults and 582 break-and-enter incidents.[17]

It is not possible to conclude from this that the presence of Somalis and other Muslims in Regent Park is responsible for the decrease in violent crime in the neighborhood over the past five years. But it is possible to conclude, from the statistics and the impressions of the crime analyst who works full-time at Toronto Police's 51 Division, that their presence has not increased violent crime levels, and that if there have been tensions between Somalis and other groups, it has not expressed itself in increased violent crime.

It is also possible to conclude from the interviews that immigrant integration, while complicated by the perceived hardship of being allocated housing in an "unsuitable" neighborhood, is not thwarted by it. Somali women, are, for the most part and to the extent that these women are representative of their peers, appear able to impose their values upon their children, to make them aware of their cultural and religious heritage, and to keep them in school through high school and even into post-secondary colleges and universities. The hardship of being together in a relatively challenging neighborhood has, furthermore, had the advantage of causing these women to forget the inter-clan grievances they carried with them from the homeland, in recognition of the fact that their ability to thrive in their new homes requires their cooperation, and that this is no time or place to harbor resentments.

Notes

1. Berns McGown, R. (1999). *Muslims in the diaspora: The Somali communities of London and Toronto*. Toronto: University of Toronto Press.
2. Ahmed, A. (1995). *The invention of Somalia*. Lawrenceville, NJ.: Red Sea Press.

   Besteman, C., & Cassanelli, L., (Eds.). (1996). *The struggle for land in southern Somalia: The war behind the war*. Boulder, CO: Westview Press.

   Cassanelli, L. (1982). *The shaping of Somali society: Reconstructing the history of a pastoral people*. Philadelphia: University of Pennsylvania Press.
3. Lacey, M. (2004, June 8). *New York Times*, p. A3.
4. Berns McGown, R. (1999). *Muslims in the diaspora: The Somali communities of London and Toronto*. Toronto: University of Toronto Press.

   Berns McGown, R. (2004). Transformative Islam & shifting gender roles in the Somali diaspora. In A. M. Kusow (Ed.), *Putting the cart before the horse: Contested nationalism and the crisis of the nation-state in Somalia* (pp. 117-133). Trenton, NJ: Red Sea Press.

5. Murdie, R. & Teixeira, C. (2000). Towards a comfortable neighbourhood and appropriate housing: Immigrant experience in Toronto. Toronto: Joint Centre of Excellence for Research on Immigration and Settlement. p.8.
6. Chambon, A., Hulchanski, J., Murdie, R., & Teixeira, C. (1997). Access to housing in a Canadian city: Experiences of three immigrant groups. Toronto: Urban Affairs Association Conference. p. 16.
7. Chambon, A., Hulchanski, J., Murdie, R., & Teixeira, C. (1997). Access to housing in a Canadian city: Experiences of three immigrant groups. Toronto: Urban Affairs Association Conference. p. 16.
8. Murdie, R. & Teixeira, C. (2000). Towards a comfortable neighbourhood and appropriate housing: Immigrant experience in Toronto. Toronto: Joint Centre of Excellence for Research on Immigration and Settlement. p. 39.
9. Ibid., p. 39.
10. As described in the history of Regent Park, Retrieved from http://www.regentparkplan.ca.
11. Toronto Community Housing. The Regent Park revitalization plan, Retrieved from http://www.regentparkplan.ca.
12. Andersen, H. (2003). *Urban sores: On the interaction between segregation, urban decay and deprived neighbourhoods*. London: Ashgate. p. 126.
13. Andersen, H. (2003). *Urban sores: On the interaction between segregation, urban decay and deprived neighbourhoods*. London: Ashgate. p. 126.
14. Berns McGown, R. (1999). *Muslims in the diaspora: The Somali communities of London and Toronto*. Toronto: University of Toronto Press. pp. 101-135.
15. Berns McGown, R. (1999). *Muslims in the Diaspora: The Somali communities of London and Toronto*. Toronto: University of Toronto Press. pp. 107-108, "Rashid."
16. Andersen, H. (2003). *Urban sores: On the interaction between segregation, urban decay and deprived neighbourhoods*. London: Ashgate. p. 128.
17. Toronto Police Services, Statistical reports, 1997-2002, Retrieved April 1, 2004, from http://www.torontopolice.on.ca/publications/#reports.

Chapter 11

THE SOMALI PRESENCE IN THE UNITED STATES: A SOCIO-ECONOMIC AND DEMOGRAPHIC PROFILE

Franklin Goza

INTRODUCTION

Prior to 1991, very few people of Somali decent resided in the United States. However, with the onset of the 1991 Somali civil war this situation was to rapidly change.[1] Since that time, tens of thousands of Somali refugees have relocated to the United States, making them the largest African refugee group in this country and one of the unique sets of newcomers to ever enter this nation. As relatively little is known about this disadvantaged and growing group, this chapter will discuss why it is important to carefully examine their situation. It will also trace the rapid recent increase of Somalis in the U.S., as well as their contribution to the rapidly growing population of U.S. residents born in Africa. The focus of this study will then document their socioeconomic situation as captured by the 2000 U.S. Census of Population.

THE SOMALI ARRIVAL TO THE UNITED STATES

African immigration to the United States has increased dramatically over the past three decades rising from 80,779 during the 1971-80 period, to 176,893 from 1981-90, and to over 354,000 between 1991 and 2000.[2] The 2000 U.S. Census of Population counted 881,300 people born in Africa, the majority of whom entered between 1990 and 2000. This upsurge was due to several factors including: (1) the passage of favorable immigration legislation (e.g., the 1965 Immigration and Naturalization Act); (2) the political and socioeconomic turmoil that has besieged many African nations over the past few decades forcing many Africans to emigrate to or seek refuge in other countries including the U.S.; and, (3) the increased movement of thousands of African students attending U.S. colleges and universities over the last three decades.

The Somali contribution to the flow of Africans began as a slow trickle in the early 1980s. The 1990 U.S. Census of Population counted only 2,070 people born in Somalia. Immigration and Naturalization Service (INS) statistics reveal that in the early 1980s less than 100 Somalis were admitted per year.[3] These early entrants comprised part of categories 1 (i.e., skilled labor migrants) and 3 (i.e., students) mentioned above. However, most of those to follow would constitute part of category 2—those fleeing political and socioeconomic turmoil in their homeland. Table 1 reveals that the first Somali refugee entered the U.S. in 1986 and that by 1996 this number had increased to nearly 6,500. By 2004, the last year for which data are available, over 56,000 Somalis had entered the U.S. as refugees. Similarly, the number of Somalis who entered the U.S. as immigrants steadily increased from 1985 to 2004, totaling more than 35,000 people. Some of these immigrants were highly skilled and able to take advantage of the skilled labor opportunities mentioned above. Still others were able to enter because of family reunification preferences.

Regardless of how they enter, the number of Somalis in the U.S. continues to increase. The enduring social turmoil and political and economic uncertainties in Somalia will likely continue to generate additional refugees and asylum seekers for years to come. Furthermore, many others are expected to arrive via family reunification preferences as they are sponsored by next of kin who either possess U.S. passports or are permanent residents. In sum, the uniqueness of these newcomers and the fact that relatively little is known about them make it imperative to study and understand their situation, especially since any knowledge we acquire may well be directly applicable to other similarly disadvantaged refugee and immigrant populations that may arrive in the future.

TABLE 1. THE IMMIGRATION STATUS OF SOMALIS ENTERING THE UNITED STATES FROM 1985-2004

Year	Refugee Arrivals	Immigrants	Non-Immigrants	Granted Asylum	Persons Naturalized
1985	x	139	x	x	x
1986	1	139	x	16	x
1987	4	197	x	14	x
1988	13	183	x	79	x
1989	68	228	x	128	x
1990	52	227	x	204	x
1991	305	458	x	117	x
1992	1,690	500	44	122	x
1993	2,802	1,088	36	233	130
1994	3,508	1,737	x	565	154
1995	2,506	3,487	x	285	211
1996	6,436	2,170	x	531	306
1997	4,974	4,005	x	699	171
1998	2,951	2,629	634	1,315	306
1999	4,320	1,710	889	2,344	816
2000	6,026	2,465	1,030	1,982	1,247
2001	4,951	3,026	1,003	1,247	1,168
2002	238	4,537	440	435	1,791
2003	1,993	2,448	288	138	2,237
2004	13,331	3,929	383	144	2,714
Totals	**56,169**	**35,302**	**4,747**	**10,598**	**11,251**

Source: Tables 3, 15, 17, 23 and 32. U.S. Department of Homeland Security: various years.

AN OVERVIEW OF THE 2000 US CENSUS OF POPULATION DATA ON SOMALIS

To learn as much as possible about Somali residents of the U.S. the 2000 Census of Population was analyzed. To begin, three distinct Somali subgroups were created. The first consists of those born in Somalia—the first generation immigrants. The second consists of those who were not born in Somalia, but who indicated their primary ancestry was Somali. As will be revealed below, this subgroup consists primarily of second generation immigrants. The third subgroup is comprised of those whose primary language was Somali, but who were not born in Somalia nor were of Somali ancestry. This subgroup is somewhat enigmatic as over 85% were born in either Ethiopia or

Kenya. Perhaps some of these individuals lived in areas historically considered part of Somalia, but because of relatively recent political demarcations found themselves residing within the boundaries of other East African nations. Still others may have never even resided in the Horn of Africa because of their ancestors' earlier out-migration from the area. Unfortunately, census data will not enable us to specifically determine the precise migration histories of these individuals.

Table 2 shows that the 2000 U.S. Census of Population counted approximately 36,600 people born in Somalia, over 8,300 people with Somali ancestry not born in Somalia, and over 5,600 Somali speakers not born in Somalia nor of Somali ancestry. Together these three subgroups total more than 50,000 individuals.

Table 2. Country of Birth for the Somali Sub-Groups in the US, 2000

	Born in Somalia		Somali Ancestry		Somali Speaker	
Country	Frequency	Percent (%)	Frequency	Percent (%)	Frequency	Percent (%)
Ethiopia	x	x	341	4.1	3,780	75.2
Kenya	x	x	1,377	16.6	495	9.9
Other	x	x	1,354	16.0	615	10.9
Somalia	36,595	100.0	x	x	x	x
United States	x	x	5,240	63.0	749	14.9
Total	**36,595**	**100.0**	**8,312**	**100.0**	**5,639**	**100.0**

Source: 2000 U.S. Census of Population

Before discussing the situation of those included in the census it is important to note that many Somalis residing in the U.S. were missed by this census. This information is based on numerous interviews conducted with Somali community leaders. There are many reasons for the Somali undercount. Sometimes they were mistaken for African Americans. Other times, like African Americans, they were undercounted as they too often reside in urban inner city neighborhoods and are relatively poor, precisely those population segments most likely to be under-enumerated.[4] In addition, many Somalis are fearful of government officials, even those from the Census Bureau. Nonetheless, over 50,000 individuals with connections to Somalia were counted by the 2000 census. As such, the data to be analyzed herein represent the most complete count of Somalians in the U.S. currently available.

Table 2 also shows the countries of birth for those not born in Somalia. Over 63% of those with Somali ancestry were born in the United States. As such, nearly two-thirds of this group is at least second generation Somali-American. Another 17% were born in Kenya followed by 4% born in Ethiopia. Both of these countries are home to large refugee camps that have housed Somalis for many years. As such, it is possible that many born in those two countries will have experienced some time in a refugee camp prior to relocating to the U.S. As mentioned above, over 85% of the Somali speaking subgroup was born in either Ethiopia or Kenya. The other 15% were born in the U.S.

BASIC DEMOGRAPHICS OF SOMALIS IN THE US

Table 3 shows year of arrival to the United States for the three subgroups. This table shows that less than two percent of those born in Somalia entered the U.S. prior to 1980. Between 1980 and 1990 an additional seven percent arrived, while the majority (91%) entered after 1990. The other two Somali subgroups mirror the Somali born pattern, but to a lesser degree, as over 80% of each of these groups arrived after 1990.

Table 3. Year of Entry into the United States for the Somali Sub-Groups, 2000

	Born in Somalia		Somali Ancestry		Somali Speaker	
Year of Entry	Frequency	Percent (%)	Frequency	Percent (%)	Frequency	Percent (%)
before 1950	16	0.0	x	x	x	x
1950 to 1954	41	0.1	x	x	x	x
1955 to 1959	54	0.1	x	x	x	x
1960 to 1964	67	0.2	x	x	x	x
1965 to 1969	133	0.4	x	x	x	x
1970 to 1974	63	0.2	95	3.1	69	1.4
1975 to 1979	285	0.8	20	0.7	37	0.8
1980 to 1984	1,101	3.0	219	7.1	506	10.3
1985 to 1989	1,566	4.3	257	8.4	395	8.1
1990 to 1994	7,399	20.2	615	20.0	1,245	25.5
1995 to 1999	23,886	65.2	1,759	57.3	2,519	51.5
2000	2,004	5.5	107	3.5	119	2.4
Total	**36,595**	**100.0**	**3,072**	**100.0**	**4,890**	**100.0**

Source: 2000 U.S. Census of Population

Table 4 shows the age and sex distributions of the three Somali subgroups collapsed into ten year intervals. In all three groups there are more men than women. However, these differences are not large as the male totals range from 51 to 53%. As such, these results reveal sex distributions that are generally well balanced for all subgroups.

Table 4. Age Distribution by Sex for the Somali Sub-Groups, 2000

	Born in Somalia				Somali Ancestry				Somali Speaker			
	Males		Females		Males		Females		Males		Females	
Age	N	%	N	%	N	%	N	%	N	%	N	%
0 to 9	1,783	9.2	1,626	8.4	3,057	69.6	2762	70.5	330	11.4	676	24.6
10 to 19	5,326	27.4	4,194	21.6	587	13.4	512	13.1	588	20.3	518	18.9
20 to 29	5,129	26.4	4,645	23.9	178	4.1	231	5.9	504	17.4	457	16.6
30 to 39	3,707	19.1	3,160	16.3	131	3.0	324	8.3	859	29.7	629	22.9
40 to 49	2,129	11.0	1,851	9.5	296	6.7	50	1.3	458	15.8	168	6.1
50 to 59	575	3.0	871	4.5	85	1.9	0	0.0	112	3.9	144	5.2
60+	790	4.1	809	4.2	60	1.4	39	1.0	43	1.5	153	5.6
Total	**19,439**	**100**	**17,156**	**100**	**4,394**	**100**	**3,918**	**100**	**2,894**	**100**	**2,745**	**100**
Mean		**26.5**		**27.8**		**11.0**		**9.7**		**28.5**		**25.8**
Median		**25**		**25**		**5**		**4**		**30**		**22**
Std. Dev.		**15.1**		**15.8**		**15.1**		**13.1**		**14.2**		**17.3**

Source: 2000 U.S. Census of Population

The summary statistics presented on the bottom Table 4 reveal important demographic distinctions among subgroups. To begin, the Somali ancestry group was the youngest of the three. More specifically, their modal age was 0 as over 1,100 children, more than 13% were less than a year old. In addition, 70% of this subgroup were less than 10 years old and another 13% were between 10 and 19. Thus the mean age of this subgroup was 10 years as old and 83% were under 20 years of age. This age distribution provides important evidence that the Somali ancestry group can effectively be labeled second generation Somali-Americans.

Between the other two subgroups, those born in Somalia and the Somali speakers, the mean age was 27 years. Likewise, approximately 45% of both subgroups were between the ages of 30 and 49. However, this is where similarities end. The age and sex distributions of the Somali born are relatively balanced, with roughly equal numbers of men and women and small numbers of the aged and very young. Among Somali speakers, however, the age and sex distributions are extremely unbalanced and there is not a single individual under the age of five.

In none of the three subgroups did the population over the age of 50 constitute more than 8%. In other words, the Somali American population is extremely young. This age structure will have important consequences for the future of this group. For instance, the 63% of the Somali ancestry group born in the U.S. will grow up knowing the U.S. as their home. Consequently, their experiences and attitudes will be very different from those of their parents and other older Somalis. Likewise, the relatively young age distribution of this population bodes well for the future since many are young enough to successfully adapt to the requirements of life in an extremely distinct social context, something that is known to become more difficult the older one is at time of relocation.

PLACE OF RESIDENCE

Table 5 shows the ten states with the largest Somali populations. Minnesota had the highest percentages among all three subgroups. In 2000 over 51% of the Somali speakers and approximately one-fourth of the two other subgroups resided there. Since 1991 Minnesota has become the focal point for the Somali community in the United States. Some newcomers arrived directly from refugee camps, while secondary migrants relocated to this area because of its good employment prospects and established refugee service agencies.

Table 5. The 10 Largest Somali Populations by Metropolitan Areas for the Somali Sub-Groups, 2000

	Born in Somalia		Somali Ancestry		Somali Speaker	
State	Frequency	Percent (%)	Frequency	Percent (%)	Frequency	Percent (%)
Minnesota	10,024	27.4	2,058	24.8	2,263	51.6
Georgia	3,668	10	820	9.9	272	6.2
Ohio	3,454	9.4	794	9.6	88	2
Washington	3,098	8.5	795	9.6	869	19.8
California	2,635	7.2	766	9.2	549	12.5
Virginia	2,615	7.1	746	9	179	4.1
Massachusetts	1,706	4.7	220	2.6	16	0.4
New York	1,353	3.7	157	1.9	84	1.9
North Carolina	1,277	3.5	76	0.9	0	0
Missouri	805	2.2	292	3.5	63	1.4
Other States	5,960	16.3	1,588	19.1	1,256	28.7
Total	**36,595**	**100**	**8,312**	**100**	**4,383**	**100**

Source: 2000 U.S. Census of Population

Georgia was the second most popular state among the Somali born (10%) and those with Somali ancestry (10%). Next came Ohio and Washington as each contained between 8 and 10% of these subgroups. Among Somali speakers, however, Washington (20%) and California (12%) ranked second and third, respectively, as preferred places to live. Both California and Virginia also had significant numbers of the Somali born and those with Somali ancestry.

Table 6 shows the ten metropolitan areas with the highest numbers of Somali residents. The Minneapolis/St. Paul area had the largest populations for all three subgroups. Approximately 20% of those born in Somalia and of Somali ancestry lived there, as did 36% of the Somali speakers. These data reveal that the de facto capital of Somali life in the US, at least in the year 2000, was the Minneapolis/St. Paul metropolitan region. Next was Atlanta, Georgia, home to approximately 10% of the Somali ancestry and Somali born subgroups, as well as 5% of the Somali speakers. Columbus, Ohio ranked third among those born in Somalia (9%), but fifth among those with Somali ancestry (7%) and sixth for the Somali speakers (2%). Seattle and Washington, D.C. also had sizeable Somali populations. The former had the second largest collection of Somali speakers (15%) and the third highest number of those with Somali ancestry (10%). Meanwhile, Washington, D.C. had the third most Somali speakers (6%), fourth most with Somali ancestry (9%) and fifth most Somali born residents (8%).

Table 6. The Top 10 Metropolitan Areas with the Largest Somali Populations for the Somali Sub-Groups, 2000

	Born in Somalia		Somali Ancestry		Somali Speaker	
Metropolitan Area	Frequency	Percent (%)	Frequency	Percent (%)	Frequency	Percent (%)
Minneapolis/St. Paul, MN	8,030	21.9	1,560	18.8	2,056	36.5
Atlanta, GA	3,640	9.9	820	9.9	272	4.8
Columbus, OH	3,454	9.4	619	7.4	88	1.6
Seattle/Evert, WA	3,084	8.4	795	9.6	843	14.9
Washington, DC/MD/VA	2,920	8	720	8.7	351	6.2
Boston, MA	1,650	4.5	220	2.6	16	0.3
San Diego, CA	1,448	4	512	6.2	89	1.6
Rochester, NY	801	2.2	134	1.6	171	3
Buffalo/ Niagara Falls, NY	732	2	96	1.2	0	0
Portland/Vancouver, OR	327	0.9	168	2	334	5.9
Other	10,509	28.7	2,668	32.1	1,419	25.2
Total	**36,595**	**100**	**8,312**	**100**	**5,639**	**100**

Source: 2000 U.S. Census of Population

Since 2000, however, a great deal of secondary and tertiary migration has occurred as Somalis relocate in search of various types of opportunities (e.g., affordable housing, employment, education and health care). As such, it is unlikely that the population distribution in 2007 remains as it was in 2000.

One consequence of such searching is that since 2001 at least 1,000 Somalis relocated to the small town of Lewiston, Maine from Atlanta.[5] Prior to 2000, there were no Somalis present in this community. Yet today this population segment continues to expand. Another example of a small town witnessing significant growth in its Somali population is Barron, Wisconsin. Since 2001, over 400 Somalis relocated to this small city in northern Wisconsin where many found work at a local meat processing plant.[6] The 400 Somalis represent 13% of this community's population. Similarly, many other former Twin Cities residents have relocated to the Minnesota cities of St. Cloud and Rochester. Parallel patterns of dispersion are also occurring in other locales. One such place is Columbus, Ohio. Former residents of this city have relocated to Cleveland, Toledo and Dayton, as well as numerous small communities within a 100 mile radius of Columbus.

Not all secondary migration is to new locations. Some is to metropolitan areas that have large and established Somali communities. For example, even though Columbus is losing some Somalis to other cities and towns, its Somali population continues to grow since it serves as an important magnet for Somalis from throughout the U.S. and Canada. Various estimates place the number of Somalis residing in the Columbus area at between 20,000 and 30,000[7] making it the nation's second largest Somali concentration.[8] Furthermore, this population continues to grow daily because of secondary migration from other parts of the country.[9] In addition, because of the close ties between the Columbus and Toronto Somali communities, numerous Canadian families and individuals have also relocated to the Columbus area. The most recent newcomers are Somali Bantus, an ethnic minority the U.S. Office of Refugee Resettlement specifically targeted for resettlement.[10] During 2004 between 10,000 and 15,000 Somali Bantu were resettled throughout the U.S. Although initially dispersed to many states, large numbers have since relocated to the Columbus region.[11]

Hence, Somalis continue to relocate throughout North America as they search for better opportunities and more favorable conditions. Such shifting patterns of population distribution will probably continue until solid social roots and perhaps ethnic communities have become established.

FAMILY STRUCTURE

Because refugee families oftentimes become fragmented, it is useful to examine Somali family structure in the U.S. To begin, Table 7 illustrates marital status for Somalis age 18 and over. Among the Somali born the never married category was the most common marital status (36%), while almost as many were married with their spouse present (34%). An additional 14% were married but their spouse was absent. Somewhat surprisingly less than 4% of this group were widowed. While it is possible that some former widows have remarried, the figure provided by the census data is lower than that observed among other refugee populations such as the Southeast Asians.[12]

The results for the Somali speaker subgroup were similar to those of the Somali born. Their most common marital statuses were married with spouse present (39%), never married (33%), and married with spouse absent (10%).

The Somali ancestry subgroup was the group most likely to be married with spouse present (52%) and least likely to be married with spouse absent (4%). They were, however, the group most likely to be divorced, as over 14% were in this situation. This figure was nearly twice as high as it was for the next highest group, the Somali speakers (8%). These results not only suggest that those born or raised in the U.S. have been less traumatized than the other subgroups, witness the high percentage of intact couples, but that they are also more Americanized, one consequence of which is that they are more prone to divorce than other subgroups.

Table 7. Marital Status for the Somali Sub-Groups for Those 18 and Over, 2000

	Born in Somalia		Somali Ancestry		Somali Speaker	
Marital Status	Frequency	Percent (%)	Frequency	Percent (%)	Frequency	Percent (%)
Married, spouse present	8,799	34.3	813	51.9	1,470	38.9
Married, spouse absent	3,546	13.8	59	3.8	380	10
Separated	1,240	4.8	53	3.4	320	8.5
Divorced	1,733	6.7	222	14.2	307	8.1
Widowed	989	3.8	58	3.7	72	1.9
Never Married	9,383	36.5	360	23	1,233	32.6
Total	**25,690**	**100**	**1,565**	**100**	**3,782**	**100**

Source: 2000 U.S. Census of Population

Another family structure variable contained in the census data is number of household members related to the respondent. Table 8 reveals that the modal category (18%) for the Somali born was zero. This response was almost as high for the Somali speakers (16%) but was much lower among those with Somali ancestry (4%). These results suggest two things. The first is that many among the Somali born and the Somali speakers find themselves somewhat isolated from their families, a finding consistent with the family disruptions that may occur among refugees. The other is that because the Somali ancestry subgroup is very young, of necessity they will reside with other older relatives, such as parents, grandparents or siblings.

Table 8. Number of Own Family Members in the Household for the Somali Sub-Groups, 2000

	Born in Somalia		Somali Ancestry		Somali Speaker	
Number of Family Members in Household	Frequency	Percent (%)	Frequency	Percent (%)	Frequency	Percent (%)
0	6,733	18.4	367	4.4	884	15.7
1	3,955	10.8	514	6.2	690	12.2
2	3,495	9.6	1,063	12.8	318	5.6
3	4,270	11.7	1,270	15.3	906	16.1
4	3,318	9.1	1,451	17.5	945	16.8
5	4,778	13.1	1,617	19.5	367	6.5
6	3,306	9	923	11.1	481	8.5
7	3,004	8.2	443	5.3	841	14.9
8	1,288	3.5	382	4.6	54	1
9	1,235	3.4	270	3.2	64	1.1
10	602	1.6	12	0.1	0	0
11	72	0.2	0	0	89	1.6
13	539	1.5	0	0	0	0
Total	**36,595**	**100**	**8,312**	**100**	**5,639**	**100**
Mean		**4.74**		**5.16**		**4.62**
Median		**4**		**5**		**5**
Standard Deviation		**2.98**		**2.15**		**2.61**

Source: 2000 U.S. Census of Population

In Somalia extended families often reside together. As such households can be rather large. This practice continues in the U.S. as nearly 19% of the Somali speakers and Somali born resided with seven or more relatives. As such, Table 8 reveals two important tendencies. The first is for some individuals to live apart from all other family members, likely through little choice of their own but rather due to the complications of the refugee relocation experience. The second pattern, in keeping with Somali tradition, is to reside with many relatives, often in an extended family type of situation.

Individual relationships to the head of household, another census variable, are revealed in Table 9. Several noticeable patterns emerge. First, most people are either the head, the spouse of head, or a child of the head. These three relationship types account for at least 74% of all three subgroups. Among those of Somali ancestry, however, they account for more than 92%. This is because more than 76% of this group are children of the head. When considering this information together with their young ages and their U.S. births it becomes obvious that this subgroup primarily consists of the Somali second generation.

Table 9. Relationship to Head of Household for the Somali Sub-Groups, 2000

	Born in Somalia				Somali Ancestry				Somali Speaker			
	Males		Females		Males		Females		Males		Females	
Relationship	N	%	N	%	N	%	N	%	N	%	N	%
Head	7,424	38.2	4,850	28.3	574	13.1	271	6.9	1,424	49.2	344	12.5
Spouse	533	2.7	3,619	21.1	147	3.3	219	5.6	63	2.2	658	24.0
Child	6,548	33.7	5,603	32.7	3,336	75.9	3,103	79.2	923	31.9	1,120	40.8
Parent	83	0.4	431	2.5	19	0.4	39	1.0	43	1.5	90	3.3
Sibling	996	5.1	679	4.0	35	0.8	0	0.0	90	3.1	115	4.2
Other Relative	1,393	7.2	1,030	6.0	215	4.9	205	5.2	76	2.6	209	7.6
Non-Relative	2,462	12.7	944	5.5	68	1.5	81	2.1	275	9.5	209	7.6
Total	**19,439**	**100**	**17,156**	**100**	**4,394**	**100**	**3,918**	**100**	**2,894**	**100**	**2,745**	**100**

Source: 2000 U.S. Census of Population

True to Somali tradition, within all subgroups men are much more likely to be the household head than the head's spouse. Consistent with refugee status and the family disruptions that often occur, 28% of the women born in Somalia were household heads. This figure is more than twice that of the next highest subgroup, the Somali speakers. These female household heads exhibited various marital statuses: 11% were widows, 20% were divorced, 22% were never married, and 38%, although married, were not living with their spouses. Many of these family situations are also likely related to the complications of the refugee relocation experience.

Table 9 also reveals that one additional result that is consistent with the trauma of refugee relocation. That is, nearly 13% of the Somali speaking men and 10% of those born in Somalia resided with non-relatives. While some may opt to live this way, for others it indicates the lack of family members with whom to reside. Were non-relatives such as these added to the total number of relatives residing together (see Table 8), those figures would appreciably increase and more closely approximate the true size of Somali households in the U.S.

SOCIAL ASSIMILATION

Table 10 documents the English speaking ability of those over the age of five. This five category ordinal measure ranges from does not speak English to speaks only English. The modal category for all groups on this self-reported measure is speaks English very well. The Somali ancestry subgroup speaks the best English, which is not surprising given that most were born in the U.S. Among this subgroup over 17% speak only English, while over 90% speak English well or better. Among the two other subgroups this figure is 15 to 18% lower. When considering those with limited English ability, results again conform to expectations. Approximately 25% of the Somali speakers and those born in Somalia either do not speak English or do so poorly. The corresponding figure among those with Somali ancestry is much lower, at less than 10%.

Table 10. English Speaking Ability, by Somali Sub-Group, for Those 5 and Older, 2000

	Born in Somalia		Somali Ancestry		Somali Speaker	
English Ability	Frequency	Percent (%)	Frequency	Percent (%)	Frequency	Percent (%)
Does not speak English	2,050	5.7	142	3.4	252	4.5
Yes, but not well	7,842	21.9	267	6.4	1,153	20.4
Yes, speaks well	11,709	32.8	1,229	29.3	1,655	29.3
Yes, speaks very well	12,637	35.4	1,837	43.8	2,579	45.7
Yes, speaks only English	1,490	4.2	719	17.1	x	x
Total	**35,728**	**100**	**4,194**	**100**	**5,639**	**100**

Source: 2000 U.S. Census of Population

Table 11 presents educational attainment for the three Somali subgroups. The modal category for those born in Somalia is a high school education, while for the other two subgroups it is 1 to 3 years of college. Relatively high percentages of all subgroups have attended college and many completed four-year degrees. The percentage of those who completed least one year of college ranges from 30% for the Somali born to 47% for both the Somali speaker and Somali ancestry subgroups. Given the young age of the Somali ancestry subgroup, their share of the college educated will likely continue to increase as they mature. When considering those adults who rarely if ever attended school it is obvious that the Somali born are the most disadvantaged. Nearly 24% of the adults born in Somalia completed less than eighth grade and over 13% of this group did not complete a single year of schooling. For the Somali speaker and Somali ancestry subgroups the corresponding figures for those completing less than eighth grade are 14 and 11%, respectively. Thus for all three subgroups a bi-modal distribution emerges. Although there are more individuals in possession of advanced training, the proportion of individuals with limited or no formal education must be a concern to policymakers. The illiterate adults who speak limited English will pose a significant challenge to all who attempt to assist them with their adaptation to a new life in the U.S. Such individuals may find it extremely difficult not only to adapt socially, but also, perhaps more importantly, economically to life in the U.S.

Table 11. Educational Attainment for the Somali Sub-Groups 18 and Over, 2000

	Born in Somalia		Somali Ancestry		Somali Speaker	
Education Level	Frequency	Percent (%)	Frequency	Percent (%)	Frequency	Percent (%)
None or Preschool	3,423	13.3	132	8.4	350	9.3
Grade 1, 2, 3, or 4	490	1.9	13	0.8	0	0
Grade 5, 6, 7, or 8	2,113	8.2	27	1.7	194	5.1
Grade 9	631	2.5	84	5.4	59	1.6
Grade 10	625	2.4	52	3.3	199	5.3
Grade 11	1,068	4.2	65	4.2	168	4.4
Grade 12	9,495	37	457	29.2	1,025	27.1
1 to 3 years of College	4,862	18.9	615	39.3	1,267	33.5
4+ years of College	2,983	11.6	120	7.7	520	13.7
Total	**25,690**	**100**	**1,565**	**100**	**3,782**	**100**

Source: 2000 U.S. Census of Population

A final measure of social assimilation contained in the census data is naturalization status. The adoption of U.S. citizenship bestows not only a U.S. passport to the naturalized individual, but also the right to vote in U.S. elections, as well as complete and unrestricted access to all government benefits. Table 1 utilizes INS data to present naturalization figures by year. These data reveal that as of 2004 approximately 20% of all Somalis admitted had become U.S. citizens. The tendency has also been for more Somalis to naturalize each year.

However, when broken down by subgroups significant variations emerge. While over 32% of the Somali speakers became U.S. citizens, the corresponding figures for the other two subgroups were significantly lower at between 10 and 15%. Part of this difference is because Somali speakers have been in the U.S. longer than the other groups. The other explanation is that many of those born in Somalia, as well as the small children they care for, have not yet naturalized as they continue to hope to one day return to Somalia.

ECONOMIC ASSIMILATION

Economic assimilation is one of the most important aspects of an immigrant or refugee's transition to life in a new country. More specifically, how and to what degree have they been able to integrate themselves into the economy of the host nation? In an attempt to answer these questions various auxiliary tables were created and examined.

The first measure examined monitored labor force status for those 16 and older. Without participating in the labor force, which is defined as either being employed or looking for employment, it is almost impossible to advance economically. In 2000, irrespective of subgroup, between 66 and 69% of the men participated in the labor force. Among women, however, this figure declined to 48% and revealed significant inter-group differences. For instance, among women born in Somalia only 46% participated in the labor force, while over 64% of Somali speaking women did. However, supplemental data reveal that labor force participation rates tend to increase with every additional year of U.S. residence.

Of course, not all people in the labor force are employed as those who are unemployed and looking for work are also counted. In unemployment levels, the Somali ancestry group again fared the best as, irrespective of sex, they had the lowest unemployment levels. For men this figure was less than 3%, which is lower than the national average, while for women it rose to 11%. For Somali born men and women these figures were 12 and 22%, respectively. Somali speakers were between the other subgroups at 7 and 12% for men and women, respectively. These results document the difficulties that foreign-born Somalis, especially women, have in locating U.S. employment. One important consequence of not being gainfully employed is poverty.

Auxiliary tables indicate that 42% of all Somali households fell below the poverty line in 2000. Furthermore, these households accounted for 49% of all Somalis. There was, however, significant inter-group variation. Again the Somali born were the most disadvantaged as 52% of these households lived below the poverty line. This figure declined to 35% for the Somali speaker subgroup. Relative to other U.S. groups these figures are extremely high. For instance, in 2000 the African American poverty rate was 22.1%, while for it was Hispanics 21.2%. As such, a great deal needs to be done to reduce the current level of Somali poverty.

Tables 12 and 13 highlight the ten occupations most commonly reported for men and women, respectively, age 18 and over. The largest category for both men and women is N/A or unemployed. As a mixed category, this grouping contains various types of individuals, including students, the retired, and the disabled as well as those looking for employment. Still, for men of all subgroups this category contains between 34 and 82%. Among women the figures are even higher, ranging from 56 to 83%.

Table 12. Top 10 Occupations among Men for the Somali Sub-Groups, 2000

	Born in Somalia		Somali Ancestry		Somali Speaker	
Occupation	Frequency	Percent (%)	Frequency	Percent (%)	Frequency	Percent (%)
Taxicab Drivers and Chauffeurs	712	10.5	51	11.9	206	21.4
Cashiers	596	8.8	30	7.0	123	12.8
Drivers/ Sales Workers and Truck Drivers	574	8.4	0	0.0	47	4.9
Miscellaneous Assemblers and Fabricators	510	7.5	139	32.3	23	2.4
Stock Clerks and Order Filers	391	5.8	16	3.7	123	12.8
Customer Service Representative	365	5.4	32	7.4	0	0.0
Janitors and Building Cleaners	363	5.3	62	14.4	84	8.7
Cooks, Except Private Household	356	5.2	0	0.0	13	1.4
Other Production Workers	310	4.6	0	0.0	0	0.0
Parking Lot Attendants	283	4.2	0	0.0	0	0.0
Total	**4460**	**65.7**	**330**	**76.7**	**619**	**64.4**

Source: 2000 U.S. Census of Population

Table 13. Top 10 Occupations among Women for the Somali Sub-Groups, 2000

	Born in Somalia		Somali Ancestry		Somali Speaker	
Occupation	Frequency	Percent (%)	Frequency	Percent (%)	Frequency	Percent (%)
Janitors and Building Cleaners	602	10.6	58	15.9	35	4.5
Cashier	531	9.4	11	3.0	70	9.0
Child Care Workers	454	8.0	19	5.2	49	6.3
Retail Salesperson	416	7.3	20	5.5	0	0.0
Miscellaneous Assemblers and Fabricators	394	7.0	41	11.2	77	9.8
Maids and Housekeeping Cleaners	320	5.6	49	13.4	24	3.1
Customer Service Representative	303	5.3	0	0.0	6	0.8
Stock Clerk and Order Filer	258	4.6	38	10.4	15	1.9
Cooks	214	3.8	33	9.0	45	5.8
Receptionist and Information Clerks	214	3.8	17	4.7	64	8.2
Total	**3706**	**65.4**	**286**	**78.3**	**385**	**49.4**

Source: 2000 U.S. Census of Population

Among employed men various patterns emerged. First, the activities of the Somali speakers and those born in Somalia were quite similar and very distinct from those with Somali ancestry. Among the former two groups the most common professions were driving related activities. Of these, cab driver was the most common activity as more than 7% of the Somali speakers and 4% of those born in Somalia worked in this profession. Other common non-driving related professions were cashiers, waiters, laborers, security guards and assemblers. Among those with Somali ancestry the only profession with more than 3% was miscellaneous assemblers and fabricators.

The female subgroups revealed fewer discernible patterns than those observed among the men. The most common professions among Somali born women were data entry keyers, janitors, cashiers, retail sales worker, assemblers, and childcare workers. Among Somali speaking women the most common professions were data entry keyers, cashiers, assemblers, receptionists, nurses or health aides, and cleaners. Thus while some overlap is evident, it is not as pronounced as it was among the men. Among the much younger Somali ancestry subgroup janitor was the most common female profession (1.5%).

These tables indicate that Somalis in the U.S. are having a very difficult time finding their place in the labor market. Not only is the unemployment rate extremely high, but very few individuals with college educations appear to be working in the professions for which they were trained. Instead the portrait presented in Tables 12 and 13 is one where it appears that most Somalis, regardless of education, are working in low-level positions that do not require advanced degrees, and presumably do not pay very well. Perhaps it is too soon to expect much occupational mobility among this group, but as of 2000 apparently little of this had occurred.

This section indicates that the Somali people, although making important strides, still have a very long way to go to become economically assimilated in the U.S. Although some progress has occurred, too many Somalis who desire to work remain unemployed. As a consequence, too many Somalis live below the poverty line. Furthermore, a sizeable component of this population remains outside of the labor force not even looking for employment. In addition, most of those who have found gainful employment are presently working at low paying, entry level positions, irrespective of their educational qualifications. As such, a great deal of work remains to be completed in this area to determine how to best assist this population successfully adapt to life in the U.S.

CONCLUSIONS

This study of Somali residents of the United States is largely an analysis of the data contained in the 2000 U.S. Census of Population. Although these data are national in scope and represent the best survey information available, they provide only a somewhat superficial overview of the population examined. For instance, while they tell us where people live, they do not tell us why they live there nor do they provide detailed information on their experiences in that locale. These are just a few of the reasons that many of the studies in this book have collected and analyzed primary data. Oftentimes that is the only way to address specific research concerns. Nonetheless, the census data analyzed herein have allowed for the development of a detailed socio-demographic portrait of Somali residents of the U.S. This portrait documents the arrival of a new and growing population that has established a few important population centers while at the same time spreading throughout all regions of the U.S. The data also document a growing second generation and clearly demonstrate how their experiences are significantly different from those of the first generation, individuals born in Somalia.

Such census documentation can help explain tendencies observed and documented by smaller data collection projects. For example, many older Somalis express the desire to return to their birthplace once it becomes politically stable, while numerous members of the second generation have no such intention.[13] The latter group knows the U.S. as home, a home they have no intention of trading for a land they do not know. While their parents and elders have many fond memories of Somalia and the way things used to be, they do not. The census data helps us better understand these divergent perspectives. Throughout this study these data have revealed the rather distinct past and present realities of these subgroups. Such documentation provides important insights for understanding these differing viewpoints. They also enable us to predict that the futures of the distinct Somali subgroups will be very different. Some will certainly attain high levels of success in the US, while others will probably be left behind never to achieve the social, occupational or economic status formerly held in Somalia.

In sum, the analysis of census data is extremely useful for documenting important patterns and trends, and even for helping explain tendencies observed with other data. Still, census data will never be able to answer the more specific types of concerns addressed by other studies in this volume. However, when considered together micro- and macro-level studies will help provide a comprehensive understanding of the Somali diaspora and its many experiences and outcomes.

Notes

1. Pagliacolo, E. (2004). Group backgrounds: Somalis. Retrieved September, 2004 from http://www.diversitywatch.ryerson.ca/backgrounds/somalis.htm.
2. Department of Homeland Security (DHS). (2003). *Yearbook of immigration statistics, 2002*. Washington, DC: U.S. Government Printing Office.
3. Immigration and Naturalization Service (INS). (various years). *Statistical yearbook of the immigration and naturalization service, 1995*. Washington, DC: U.S. Government Printing Office. INS, 1997
4. Anderson, M., & Fienberg, S. (1999). *Who counts? The politics of census-taking in contemporary America*. New York: Russell Sage Foundation.
5. Jones, M. (2004). The new Yankees. *Mother Jones*, 29, 64-69.
6. Schaid, J. (2004). Somali immigrant settlement in small Midwestern communities: The case of Barron, Wisconsin. Unpublished manuscript.
7. H. Omar (personal communication, 2005).

   D. Stokes (personal communication, 2005).

   I. Thaci (personal communication, 2005).
8. Community Research Partners (CRP). (2004). Franklin County immigrant and refugee services resource analysis, Interim Report #1. Columbus, OH: Community Research Partners.

H. Omar (personal communication, 2005).

9. I. Thaci (personal communication, 2005).
10. United Nation High Commissioner of Refugees (UNHCR). 2002. America here we come. *Refugees*, 3, 2-8.
11. I. Thaci (personal communication, 2005).
    S. Walker (personal communication, 2005).
12. Goza, F. (1987). Adaptation and adjustment among Southeast Asian refugees in the United States. Unpublished doctoral dissertation, University of Wisconsin-Madison, Madison, WI.
13. Goza, F., & K. Otiso. (2004). Somali refugees in Columbus, Ohio. Unpublished manuscript.

Chapter 12

THE SOMALI DIASPORA IN MINNEAPOLIS: EXPECTATIONS AND REALITIES

Cindy Horst

INTRODUCTION

In recent years, increased interest can be observed within the academic world as well as amongst policy makers and practitioners in the transnational networks of migrants and the role that members of the diaspora can play in various developmental processes. In particular, there is a strong focus on the quantity of remittances sent by migrants, which is compared to, for example, international aid in order to establish that remittances play a central role in local economies within the developing world. Similarly high expectations are expressed by those "left behind" in the region. However, one may ask how those in the diaspora see these issues themselves. What role can and do they want to play in economic and political processes in their region of origin, especially considering their often precarious position as migrants in their host country? Research amongst Somalis in Minneapolis provides an answer to these questions for a particular group of people who may be seen as transnational *par excellence.* This strong transnational orientation is related firstly to the collapse of the nation-state in Somalia: people have had to look beyond common state institutions and borders for solutions to their problems. Secondly, it is linked to the Somali "nomadic heritage" which includes high degrees of mobility, tight social networks and risk-reducing strategies through dispersed investments.[1]

In this chapter, I will first briefly outline the increased international interest in and expectations of the transnational activities of migrants. Then, I will illustrate how refugees in the region also have various high expectations of their relatives in resettlement countries. In a second section, I will describe the situation of Somalis in Minneapolis, first providing some background information on the large Somali community there and then looking at the different activities they engage in that link them to the region, involving flows of remittances, people and information. These various issues will be discussed in order to, in conclusion, analyze how realistic the expectations facing Somalis in Minneapolis are. Findings are based on fieldwork in Kenyan refugee camps and amongst the Somali community in Minneapolis between July 1999 and May 2004. Whereas the Dadaab research involved extensive anthropological field research of well over one year, in Minneapolis information was collected over a one-month period. In both settings, common anthropological methods such as participatory observation, in-depth interviewing, and the collection of life histories, were combined with more interactive, dialogical and participatory approaches. I have actively tried to involve the Somali community in research set-up, data collection and analysis, both in the field and through electronic media.[2]

MIGRANT DIASPORAS CONTRIBUTING TO REGIONAL DEVELOPMENTS: FACING EXPECTATIONS

Over the last decade, interest in the transnational activities of migrants, and in particular their remittance sending behavior, has rapidly increased. Government and UN bodies as well as NGOs are investing much in attempts to understand this aspect of international migration and develop policies that maximize the benefits of remittances. Expectations are so high that they are being dubbed the "new development finance".[3] Other transnational potential is also focused on, including the role of self-organizations in development and the use of knowledge and skills existing amongst diaspora members.[4] Migrant communities have noticed and responded to this increased interest, for example by calling for greater involvement of diaspora members in the development and implementation of policies and projects affecting their regions of origin. Somalis attend discussions and debates organised by NGOs and academia, and are particularly vocal in stressing this need to involve the diaspora. At the same time, members of migrant diasporas remain skeptical of the intentions behind the focus on their transnational activities, stressing the fact that it is entirely up to the remittance sender and receiver to decide how best to use these private funds.[5] But those living in the diaspora are not only confronted with the expectations international actors have of their potential to contribute to positive developments in the region. Far more importantly, refugees in resettlement countries face expectations from their relatives in the region as well.

IMAGES OF LIFE IN REFUGEE CAMPS IN AFRICA

Research in the Dadaab refugee camps in Kenya has revealed that Somali refugees in the camps were able to survive in the camps, despite limited regional livelihood opportunities and insufficient international aid, due to the assistance of their relatives outside Dadaab. Remittances were received from regional urban centres such as Nairobi, Kampala, Mogadishu and Johannesburg, but also through relatives in Europe, the United States and Australia. As a consequence of these remittances, which were received by at least 15% of the population but benefited a much larger number of refugees in the camps, images of life overseas were created that lead to great expectations of those who went there. Van Hear suggests that remittances are not a simple one-way transfer from those abroad to those at home, because migration involves considerable investments, which have often been taken care of within kinship networks.[6] Thus, a kind of exchange is taking place. Amongst Somalis, this may be very true. Before departure, peer groups, lineage members and the community as a whole are all mobilized by the desires of the individual who is leaving to execute his or her plan and keep the dream alive.[7] After the person leaves, the pressures are reversed, with the traveler now indebted and expected to give back what has been received. Those who go carry the responsibility of supporting relatives left behind and possibly facilitating their resettlement to the West.[8]

Marian Abdulahi[9] illustrates how strong the pressures are that some refugees in Dadaab put on their relatives overseas:

> I would never present my situation differently from what it is just to obtain money from abroad. But some refugees, and especially older women, really behave terribly at times. You can hear them complain in the *xawilaad* (money transfer) office, when they, for example, talk to their son: "Ay, we are almost dying in these camps and we hear nothing from you. You are a useless child; you are not my son. I will never talk to you again if you do not send money. How can you forget us like that, when you are living there in such luxury?" When the son tries to explain that he is a student and it is therefore impossible for him to send money, the mother will not accept his excuses and screams: "But you are in America!! Of course, you can get money. We are all suffering here because of you: all our money was spent on you."

As this example illustrates, those who send remittances often do so not only because of feeling a great responsibility but also because of being pressurized by their relatives in the camps. The social pressure increases with time, and the longer someone is abroad, the greater the expectations of remittances, sponsorship for resettlement, or relevant information. After the migrant has lived abroad for some years, he or she is not only supposed to provide remittances and sponsorship but also understand the new country of residence: "To nomads, the exploration of new lands and what they have to offer is of vital importance; the same is expected of refugees and immigrants – they must be thoroughly familiar with the new country".[10] Yet, providing information is a complicated issue, especially when that information may not be what those remaining behind would want to hear.

THE SOMALI COMMUNITY IN MINNEAPOLIS: LIVED REALITIES

Minnesota is amongst the top destinations for Somalis, and in recent years, Minneapolis is said to host the largest number of Somalis in the US. The problem, however, is that there are no precise figures on the Somali population here or anywhere else. One of the difficulties encountered in identifying exact numbers is that Somalis who reside outside their home country fall under several statistical categories. There are those who migrated before the war, for education, job opportunities and a number of other reasons, who hold various types of residence permits or are now nationals of their new country. Then, there are those who fled after the war, some of whom are still registered as asylum seekers, others who hold temporary permits, others with full refugee status and yet others who are nationals. On top of all this, there is a grey mass of unregistered and illegal migrants. As a consequence, estimates of exact numbers vary widely. The 2000 Census data for the state of Minnesota indicated that 11,164 Somalis live in Minnesota or 0.2 % of the total state population.[11] By far the highest concentration can be found in the "Twin Cities" Minneapolis and St. Paul, but small towns like Rochester, Marshall and Owatonna also attracted considerable numbers in recent years. It is likely that official census figures greatly underestimate actual numbers, as many extended Somali families live in one house with larger numbers than allowed, so they underreport their numbers. Public school enrollment and welfare statistics suggest a range of 15,000 to 30,000 Somalis in Minnesota, a number that is still growing.

Thus, it is indeed likely that the Somali community in Minneapolis is larger than the one in Columbus, Ohio and Seattle, San Diego, other towns with major concentrations of Somalis. It is the second largest immigrant community in the city, after the Hmong, who have been in Minnesota since the 70s and 80s. Somalis on the other hand, arrived mainly in the mid-to late-90s.[12] In 1994 and 1995, larger groups of Somalis (amongst whom mainly Benadiri) were officially resettled to Minneapolis. The total number of officially resettled Somalis is estimated at approximately 6,000. But the large majority of Somalis currently residing in Minneapolis, at least 60%, came from other states.[13] Secondary movement within the US largely took place in recent years, from 1998 – 1999 onwards. When asked for the reason for the steady increase of the Somali population in Minneapolis, a number of factors are usually mentioned. Minnesota has a healthy economy with low unemployment rates, so job opportunities are quite good. The Twin Cities were in fact founded by business entrepreneurs from New England as a moneymaking venture, attracting waves of immigrants from early ages.[14] Somalis work there in various low-skilled jobs that require little knowledge of

English and often give the possibility of working many over-hours. Such jobs include work in assembly plants, meat factories, especially many turkey plants in the region, as security guards, parking attendants, cleaners and taxi drivers. Furthermore, higher educated Somalis with excellent English skills work inter alia as teachers, social workers, lawyers, managers, professors or doctors.

A second reason mentioned for the mass migration to Minneapolis is its more open, welcoming climate towards migrants and its better social welfare system in general. Minnesota is a state with a large Scandinavian originated population, and this translates itself as better social security arrangements and services provided, for example in education and health care. Its history of dealing with large groups of migrants also assists in the creation of a welcoming attitude. A further very important reason for the migration flows is the fact that the word about the virtues of Minnesota spreads and that a Somali community has established itself there. A parallel economy was created that enables Somalis nowadays to do everything "the Somali way": there are Somali shops, malls, NGOs, travel agents, hairdressers, restaurants, Quranic schools, mosques etc. For businessmen and –women, providing goods and services to the now well-established Somali community in the area may be a good alternative or addition to having a regular job. And as the community grows, more Somalis move to Minnesota to be near their families.

In order to understand how Somalis are doing in Minneapolis, it is important to realize that the Somali community is not a homogeneous mass. There are single students, young men and women in their twenties who have at least one but more often two or even three jobs and/or operate a business besides their studies. While working very hard, most of them are settling well in town and live a rather comfortable life. There are single mothers with three to six children, who do not speak English and have to work 20 hours and go to school 20 hours in order to be eligible for often insufficient social benefits. Most of the lower income groups in Minneapolis live in the Riverside-Cedar area, in large, run-down flats with cheap rents that are mainly occupied by Somalis. Others, like professionals or successful businessmen and women, live in the suburbs in nicely decorated mansions, driving comfortable family cars. Then, I also met men and women working in poultry factories in small Minnesota towns, single or with families that were left behind in the region or came with them. Most of these men and women spoke highly insufficient English for other types of jobs and often also did not have the required education. They worked many over-hours, doing very filthy jobs, and lived extremely sober lives in empty flats.

REMITTANCE SENDING TO RELATIVES

Whether someone was successful in Minneapolis depended on age, gender, education, English proficiency, length of stay, type of employment, social network and number of dependants. In general, only a small percentage of Somali professionals and top businessmen formed a highly successful elite; then, a reasonably large middle class was formed by social workers, teachers, university students etc.; the group of (non-English speaking) Somalis with low-skilled jobs leading sober lives was similar in size; and finally, a small percentage of the Somali community, mainly consisting of single mothers and some elderly without relatives, were really struggling to make ends meet. Yet, financially stable or not, almost all Somalis in Minneapolis at least sent some money to their relatives left behind. Dahabo Abdulahi, a single mother of four, told me:

> We have to send. We know that life in Somalia and Kenya and those regions is very difficult. So if my mother calls and tells me that she does not have food on the table that night, I will have to send something. I know their difficulties. But it is not easy for me, having four daughters to take care of. At times, I send 50 dollars, at times 100, at times nothing; it depends on the expenses I had that month.

Others are able to send much more, with amounts ranging from $200 up to even $1,000 a month, larger amounts being sent to a number of families. Sending large amounts of money home does not necessarily indicate the wealth of the sender. In particular many of those who send very high amounts seem to be working young men and women whose main aim is to provide an income for their family members left behind. One case that provides good insight into this is a small village close to Minneapolis, where a large group of Somalis had migrated to work in a turkey factory. A tour through the factory gave an impression of the monotonous and filthy jobs people had. Afterwards, we visited a number of men who worked there at their home: an empty apartment ("our table and chairs are in the laundry") decorated with a huge flag of Somalia. I asked them about remittances, and they all informed me they sent $400 home monthly, volunteering to tell me that women usually sent double that amount, because they worked over-hours and did not spend money like men did. Hassan Aden said in this respect: "I thought about working over-hours, but whether I have 1,000 or 400 in my pocket, I will send it anyway. So I might as well send the 400 and not over-work myself."

I wanted to know whether people "back home" knew where the money came from. Hassan told me that he had visited relatives in Kenya recently, telling them he sold mobiles and cars for a living. The contrast between the image being created and the actual life these people lived to me was very shocking. I imagined that on the one hand they created dreams to deal with reality and add to their status as successful migrants, but on the other hand these dreams made the reality of life in "turkey town" much more unbearable. This example illustrates some of the complexities of remittance sending for Somalis in the diaspora. Their life and livelihood choices are to a certain extent determined by the responsibilities they have towards relatives elsewhere. At times, one may get the impression that this transnationalism is indeed "forced," with people having no option but to send to those left behind in far worse circumstances. Yet, at the same time fulfilling family obligations is not only a matter of having no option, but it is also related to the status acquired when assisting others. I will provide some more examples to illustrate these points.

Somalis in Minneapolis make decisions about their lives that are not only determined by local factors, but also by transnational ones. Khadija Osman for example explains how the money she sends to relatives in Somalia is part of her monthly bill and she always pays them before even paying the rent: "If I cannot pay the rent, I will still manage. But if those people do not get the money I send them, life will be too tough for them." Besides affecting patterns of expenditure, family obligations affect migration decisions. I met quite a number of Somalis who had moved from the Netherlands, and one of the reasons they mentioned for their migration was the difficulty of sending remittances from the Netherlands.[15] Others rather indicate how family responsibilities restricted their movements; even if they wanted to, they could not go back to some of the African cities they lived before. Rashid Kasim told me:

> I cannot go back to Cairo, because my family is there and I have to take care of them. No matter how difficult life may be here, at least I can provide for my family. In Cairo, I could not send them anything, now I send money to my sister in Cairo and my parents and siblings in Somalia every month.

Not only do transnational responsibilities determine the migration choices that Somalis in Minneapolis (can) make, but they also influence their lives in other ways. A friend to Abdulhakim Axmed sends \$500 to the Kenyan refugee camps and \$200 to relatives in Somalia every month. He told him that as long as he has that responsibility, he cannot marry. Personally, Abdulhakim does not completely agree with that decision: "Some people give their life to their family; they always work and send everything to their relatives back home. But you do not need to give all your life, you should also think of your own options." Nevertheless, many would agree that marriage does complicate dealing with family responsibilities. Dhofa Abdi told me that a very important condition for marriage would be that her husband would agree for her to continue working so that she can keep sending money to her relatives:

> A number of my relatives are simply dependent on me, so even if I get married I will remain responsible for those back home. Many of my friends stopped working after getting married and they just sit at home. The problem is that the husband has to provide an income for them and maybe children, as well as for his family. He has to work many extra hours in order to pay for everything. If her family calls and needs assistance, she will want them to receive money as well and this might lead to conflicts. Also, she will ask him what he sends to her family in

> comparison to what he sends to his family.[16] Her family will put their stresses on her life, and the husband will never be able to provide for all these people. People get divorced over these issues, and that is why I would really want to continue working.

While family obligations thus can cause great pressures in the personal lives of Somalis in Minneapolis, many feel that this is not sufficiently understood or appreciated by their relatives.[17] Whereas almost all Somalis send monthly or at least occasional remittances, many complain about the way in which relatives often simply expect or even demand to be assisted. Yusuf Abdinoor arrived in Minneapolis only one year ago. He is very disappointed with his inability to find an appropriate job, preferably as a teacher. Still, he sends $500 every month to his wife and children in Egypt. Their expenses are high because the children are going to a private school there. Then, he has 13 siblings, with one sister in Saudi-Arabia, one in Djibouti and a brother in Yemen. All others live in Somalia, and depend on the remittances sent by his brother, who is a doctor in Yemen, and himself. Every other month, he sends the families of his three bigger brothers as well as his stepmother with five younger brothers $150 to $200, bringing the total amount to about $1,000 a month. Yet, as Yusuf says, "I cannot assist all of them all the time, and they do not understand. They will comment 'he is gone, he is in America now,' which means that I no longer care for them. They do not understand my position." Moxamed Hussein similarly sighs: "I wish I was alone. I have worked all my life to assist others, and they are never satisfied. Everybody thinks that life is good here, and that I am rich. A friend of mine just called and asked for $200. I said that I did not have that money right now but will try my best to send it. But they find it hard to believe I do not just have that money."

A further frustration in some instances is caused by the fact that remittances do not appear to be used wisely and may cause dependency. Remittances are mainly sent to families and used for daily survival. At times, the money can be used to start up a small business or send people to school, but others use it to buy *qat* or stop working altogether because of remittances sent. Dhofa Abdi told me how she recently went to Mudug to visit her relatives, and stopped sending $800 a month after that. Now, she only sends $200 to her father, who is taking care of her epileptic brother, and $200 to a cousin of her father who is a sheikh:

I used to send that money to the ex-wife of my brother, but realized the lady is a spender. Some of the children did not even have a bed to sleep in, so I bought them beds while I was there and no longer send the money through their mother. Also, I no longer send money to some of my brothers. The three who stay in Galgacayo chew qat and leave their wives behind. I used to be very sensitive when they call and work on my conscience, saying their condition is so bad. But at least since I went, feelings of guilt have really reduced: They do not work hard like me, having many responsibilities. The problem is that they have become dependent on the money I sent. What if I am no longer around, or am no longer able? I asked them what they did with all the money I had sent them throughout the years. Where did it go? They could not answer me.

COMMUNITY-BASED PROJECTS

Remittance-sending patterns do not only involve responsibilities to family members but also include community development–and emergency aid projects as well as investments in housing and facilities for eventual return. Somalis in Scandinavia and the UK have set up cooperative organizations to enable repatriation to Somaliland through both private and public investments, that might also benefit development in the region.[18] During my stay in Minneapolis, various communal projects were set up, both in response to crisis situations in Somali areas as well as in attempts to contribute to improved livelihoods in the region. These projects were largely organized by region and thus often by clan, though it was stressed that all Somalis were able to and did participate in fund raising efforts; whether from the area or not. The most urgent projects were directed at Sool and Sanaag regions, where serious droughts occurred by the time I was in Minneapolis at the end of 2003. Abdulhakim Axmed informed me about the way that the aid was organized:

> We have various programs, like sending letters to Somalis who originated from Sanaag region and expecting them to contribute twenty dollars until June 2005 or pay the total

> amount of 440 dollars at once. We expect to collect about 6,000 dollars, which will be send to Abu Dhabi, where others involved in the project will buy food, water and other basic needs for nomads in that region. They will send us the receipts, and the goods will be send to Galgacayo, where the receiving families have to sign letters to prove that they received the money.

Communal development efforts were carried out in the field of improved water supplies, education and health care. In the offices of one of the Somali NGOs working in Minneapolis, a poster advertised a fundraising for a primary school, inviting everybody to come and contribute. Suleiman Hashi, who was heading one of the Somali NGOs providing social services for his community in Minneapolis, explained how a good friend of his had set up a High School in Mogadishu. He used to be a lecturer at the University of Mogadishu at the time Suleiman was also working there, and as the director of the school, received very positive reports so far. As it is difficult to run such a school financially at the moment, Suleiman and a number of his friends have agreed to contribute to some of the items he needs, in order to enable him to get additional funding elsewhere. Besides their financial contributions, they are also offering him their advice, as most of them are highly qualified professionals. In these kinds of efforts, it is not uncommon for Somalis to share responsibilities and costs with NGOs or institutions. Another fundraising was carried out for medical supplies in Gedo region, for example, which was organized by the Somali community in conjunction with the Islamic Center of Minneapolis.

However, when I asked Suleiman his views about a more systematic cooperation between the community and NGOs, he told me that they had tried this on a regional level, but he was a bit skeptical about it:

> There are Somalis who set up their own NGO and then tried to get other NGOs to contribute. Some were successful in setting up schools or water projects etcetera. Still, I believe that at times it is better for individuals or the community to set up these projects, as they should

> not always expect things. They should not always think that they will be assisted. Besides, there seems to be more respect for private property than public property. Nowadays, all schools, clinics etcetera are private property. If governments or NGOs get involved, there is a far higher chance that these buildings will be looted.

Such factors are very important to take into account for the NGOs and governments who at present are showing such great interest in the development potential of remittances. Much of this interest is not necessarily only directed towards the situation as it is at present, and the ways migrants are handling remittance sending. Rather, these actors are trying to find ways to get involved in existing practices, gaining control by formalizing transfer mechanisms and having a greater say in the use of remittances, all in order to increase their contribution to development. In the concluding section, I want to discuss these issues in greater detail.

DEALING WITH MIGRATION DREAMS

Those who now live in Minneapolis are frequently confronted with the fact that many others would want to follow their example. These dreams to move to a Western country from Africa or the Middle East in Dadaab were called 'buufis'.[19] In fact, when I started asking questions about *buufis*, I realized that many Somalis in the USA used the word in a different way. Only those who had come from Kenya or Cairo more recently were familiar with the way in which I used it. As Yusuf Abdinoor told me: "In Mogadishu the word was used amongst young people, as a kind of slang, meaning 'suspect'." I then heard it being used in Egypt and realized the person did not mean suspect, so I asked what it meant. I was informed that buufis was related to resettlement." Yet in the US, buufis is far more often used to indicate mental health problems of all kinds. It is fascinating to see the various uses of the term in different places, although there does seem to be a link between the use of the word in Dadaab and Minneapolis. Those who really dream of going for resettlement badly, suffering from serious buufis in the Dadaab sense, are often seen to have mental problems that can only be solved by enabling them to go for resettlement.

Rashid Kasim's brother for example was a serious buufis case. His mother was really worried about her 20-year-old son, as at times he would not talk to anybody, behaving strangely. Rashid realized he really had to help him to move from Mogadishu, as the "symptoms" were getting increasingly worse:

> My brother just finished High school and has extreme buufis because all around him, all people of his age, like neighbors and classmates, have gone or are going. There are simply no opportunities for them in Somalia, and he says that he cannot be in Mogadishu in 2004. His mind is focused on Western countries. I guess it used to be the same for me as well; we used to talk about streets and places in the UK or Canada, about people who went, or as we formulated it '*wuu galay*' (he has entered), as if it was paradise they were entering.

Just before I left, Rashid's brother attempted to go to London through Dubai with an uncle who would move there with his family. Rashid bought the ticket of $2,500 for him, and there was no one to assist him: "Everybody is in the same position; if you do not have your family here, you will have to work towards bringing them over. We tried before and I spent 5,000 dollars on him, but the attempt failed." Unfortunately, I was informed that the second attempt also failed, but they would try again.

This possible loss of money was not the only risk that people were taking while attempting to reach Western countries. Sacadiyo Muse showed me a book that she kept with pictures and stories from and about friends and relatives who stayed with her in Cairo. They were all young people, some living in European countries, some staying in the US, Canada or Australia, some who went back to Somalia, but also three who had died while trying to cross from Libya to Italy by boat, independent from each other. I was informed that on the Internet, one could find the names and clans of those who died there. Somalis take great risks when trying to "enter," and one may wonder whether their relatives in Minneapolis are always ready to assist them in such dangerous attempts. Besides, there are other reasons why some may not be ready to sponsor their relatives. Dhofa Abdi clearly explained this to me:

> My brothers all want me to sponsor them, but how can I sponsor them when they are so irresponsible? How can I sponsor my brother who left his wife with four children? If he behaves so irresponsible in Somalia, what can I expect of his behavior here? I will be responsible for their misbehavior here. What if one of my brothers marries a new wife here? How will my sister-in-law accept that I have assisted him to come to the US?

A further dilemma that Somalis in Minneapolis face is caused by the fact that their relatives have dreams of coming to the US, but as Sacadiyo formulated it, “The America that is there in Africa is not here.” Almost everybody arriving in the US has much higher expectations of his or her life there than reality can offer. Suleiman Hashi, the director of one of the Somali NGOs in Minneapolis, tells me: “When they come to the USA, people expect plenty of money, work, no responsibility and easy access to everything. Then, the reality is that they have to look for a job, some live on welfare and life is very hard. Many people cannot deal with that reality.” Positive images are based on media and communication with relatives and friends already in the USA. Khadija Osman remarks: “They watch TV there and think that life in America is like the Hollywood movies.” Then, pictures that relatives send distort reality, but also the fact that large amounts of money are being sent from the US and people seemingly obtain everything that those “left behind” can only dream of. Abdulhakim Axmed had very clear ideas in this respect:

> We tell horrible stories about life in America, but when they see we have a car, we have housing, we have education and we have an income, all things that they do not have and that thus seem like a dream, it is difficult to make them change their views. A friend of mine is going back to Galgacayo and asked me whether he can do anything for me there. I told him to show people *Bowling for Columbine*, just to make them understand that in the US,

guns are freely available and cause as much problems as in the places they are running from.

So on the one hand, some Somalis in Minneapolis try to explain to their relatives and friends what their lives are really like, but it seems they are not listened to. Yet on the other hand, others do not provide correct information. Yusuf Abdinoor admits that he does not inform most of his relatives of the fact that he has nothing. He simply gives them what he can, and tries to explain his situation only if they complain that he does not send enough. He tells me: "Somalis are very proud people, and they will not tell the truth. If someone was a manager in Somalia and now works as a loader, he will not confess that. He will hide the reality and send money." At the same time, when going to Africa many Somalis engage in a life-style that also portrays a different image, while their relatives will not realize that the life styles they display there for a short period are the result of a hard and difficult life for the rest of the year.[20] For those who are seen to "have made it," keeping up appearances may be just as vital as the dream of a better future is for those in difficult circumstances like in the Dadaab refugee camps.

CONCLUSION

This chapter started off by asking the question whether expectations placed on Somali refugees in resettlement countries by the international community as well as relatives in the region are realistic. Not only do various governments, institutions, and organizations have high hopes in relation to the potential of the transnational activities of various diaspora groups to contribute to positive developments in the region, but resettled refugees are also faced with the expectations of their relatives. These expectations are linked to what Van Hear sees as an exchange process of migration-related investments and remittances, but they are also caused by unrealistically positive images of life in resettlement countries.[21] As this chapter has illustrated, conditions of life in Minneapolis are not easy for Somalis, as they have to face local difficulties as well as transnational responsibilities. Although many refugees do not have well-paying jobs and are struggling with their daily lives, they do take their responsibilities towards relatives in the region very seriously. Not only do they send remittances to relatives, but Somalis in Minneapolis also engage in communal relief and development projects in the region. Besides, they perform an important role in facilitating the migration of others. As was illustrated, this sense of transnational responsibility is partly caused by the high pressures that exist to continue doing this. Thus, it can be concluded that, although Somali refugees in Minneapolis contribute greatly to development in the region, on an individual and communal basis, this contribution is made under great pressure of local conditions and transnational expectations. International organizations focusing on the potential of diaspora engagement should heed this.

Furthermore, additional research would be needed to understand the long-term potential of these transnational activities. In the first place, this potential may be threatened by generational changes. As Abdulhakim Axmed indicated:

> Generations change and the children might not send money to the extent that their parents did. They have to be taught, like I do with my five-year old daughter. I take her to the *xawilaad* and tell her to give the money to the owner, and my daughter can even ask me 'father, when are we going to send them money again?' But many parents do not teach their children, saying that they are working hard for their pensions so that their children do not need to send them money.

Another threat to the continuity of transnational networks is the fact that transnational burdens are often managed with an idea of temporality: eventually, sending remittances may no longer be necessary or at least the amount can be lessened considerably. Initiatives are being developed to enable the development of sustainable livelihoods in the region, yet in many places self-sufficiency can only be envisioned in the long-term and might not be possible without large-scale political-economic changes.

A final concern is that relatives in the region often do not understand the extent to which they burden those now living in places like Minneapolis. Images of life in resettlement countries are still highly unrealistic, leading to extreme expectations of the role of the Somali diaspora. As such, an important step towards a more balanced division of responsibilities, and thus possibly greater endurance, could be an attempt amongst the Somali diaspora to provide more realistic images of their lives "overseas." The increasing availability of electronic media and mobile networks may assist in this process. It is true that providing a more accurate picture of life in resettlement countries may remain extremely difficult as material realities do differ greatly. As Abdulhakim illustrated: "It is like trying to explain to my mother what snow is. You cannot make people understand exactly how cold it is." Yet, part of the problem is caused by the fact that there is still reluctance amongst Somalis in Minneapolis to give up the status and relative power that comes with living in the USA. Some find it unnecessary to burden their relatives with the problems they are facing in Minneapolis. Others are embarrassed to admit to the humble lives they lead. Many would not easily give up their position as wealthy, successful migrants, no matter the difficulties they find in keeping up this image.

Notes

1. Horst, C. (2006a). *Transnational nomads. How Somalis cope with refugee life in the Dadaab camps of Kenya.* Oxford and New York: Berghahn Books.
2. Horst, C. (2006b). Virtual dialogues? The value of electronic media for research amongst refugee diasporas. *Refuge*, 23(1).
3. Wimaladharma, J., Pearce, D., & Stanton, D. (2004). Remittances: The new development finance? *Small Enterprise Development Journal*, 15(1).
4. For example, The UNDP QUESTS programme enables Somali professionals in the diaspora to work in Somalia for a fixed period of time.
5. Carling, J. (2004). Policy options for increasing the benefits of remittances. Paper presented at workshop Remittances and development: beyond increasing incomes. *International Metropolis Conference*, Geneva. Oslo: International Peace Research Institute.
6. Van Hear, N. (2001). Sustaining societies under strain. Remittances as a form of transnational exchange in Sri Lanka and Ghana. In K. Koser & N. Al-Ali, (Eds.), *New approaches to migration? Transnational*

communities and the transformation of home (pp. 202-223). London: Routledge.

7. Rousseau, C., Said, T., Gagne, M., & Bibeau, G. (1998). Between myth and madness: The premigration dream of leaving among young Somali refugees. *Culture, Medicine and Psychiatry*, 22, 385-411. p. 402.
8. Horst, C. (2006a). *Transnational nomads. How Somalis cope with refugee life in the Dadaab camps of Kenya.* Oxford and New York: Berghahn Books. p. 198.
9. Names are changed in order to respect the privacy of my informants.
10. Rousseau, C., Said, T., Gagne, M., & Bibeau, G. (1998). Between myth and madness: The premigration dream of leaving among young Somali refugees. *Culture, Medicine and Psychiatry*, 22, 385-411. p. 395.
11. United States Census (2000). American Factfinder, Quick Tables: P13 Ancestry. Retrieved August 13, 2004 from http://www.census.gov.
12. Layman, A. & Basnyat, A. (2003). Social capital of the Somali and Hmong Communities in Minneapolis - Saint Paul. Minnesota Social Capital Research Project.
13. Mattessich, P. (2000). Speaking for themselves. A survey of Hispanic, Hmong, Russian and Somali immigrants in Minneapolis-Saint Paul. Saint Paul, MN: Wilder Research Center.
14. Adams, J. & Van Drasek, B. (1993). *Minneapolis-St. Paul: People, place and public life*. Minneapolis: University of Minnesota Press. p. 56.
15. Somalis also move from the Netherlands and Denmark to the UK in very large numbers for similar reasons. See also Bang Nielsen, K. (2004). Next stop Britain: The influence of transnational networks on the secondary movement of Danish Somalis. Working Paper No. 22. Sussex: Centre for Migration Research.

    Reek, E. v.d. & Hussein, A. I. (2003). *Somaliers op Doorreis: Verhuisgedrag van Nederlandse Somaliers naar Engeland.* Tilburg: Wetenschapswinkel Universiteit van Tilburg.
16. That this is a very common scene is proved by similar dialogues in the Somali theatre play 'Qaabyo'.
17. This does not seem to be a problem specific to the Somali diaspora, as research amongst Sudanese refugees indicates.

    See Riak Akuei, S. (2004). Remittances as unforeseen burdens: Considering displacement, family and resettlement contexts in refugee livelihood and well being. Is there anything states or organizations can do? UNHCR Livelihoods Network.

18. Kleist, N. (2003). Somali-Scandinavian dreaming. Visions of home and return in Somscan and UK cooperative associations. Unpublished report. Copenhagen: University of Copenhagen.
19. Horst, C. (2006c). Buufis amongst Somalis in Dadaab: The transnational and historical logics behind resettlement dreams. *Journal of Refugee Studies*, 19(2).
20. Compare Salih, R. (2001). Shifting meanings of "home". Consumption and identity in Moroccan women's transnational practices between Italy and Morocco. In K. Koser & N. Al-Ali, (Eds.), *New approaches to migration? Transnational communities and the transformation of home* (pp. 51-67). London: Routledge. p. 58.
21. Van Hear, N. (2001). Sustaining societies under strain. Remittances as a form of transnational exchange in Sri Lanka and Ghana. In K. Koser & N. Al-Ali, (Eds.), *New approaches to migration? Transnational communities and the transformation of home* (pp. 202-223). London: Routledge.

Chapter 13

THE SOMALI DIASPORA IN SMALL MIDWESTERN COMMUNITIES: THE CASE OF BARRON, WISCONSIN

Jessica Schaid and Zoltán Grossman

INTRODUCTION

Tens of thousands of Somali refugees have settled in the Midwestern United States since Somalia's civil war erupted in 1991. Minnesota's Twin Cities of Minneapolis and St. Paul have become the de facto "capital" of the Somali community in North America. Somalis have arrived directly from refugee camps or in secondary migrations from other US cities, drawn by an attractive urban job market and refugee service agencies.

More recently, many Somalis have begun to settle in smaller cities and towns around southern Minnesota and western Wisconsin. This secondary diffusion is creating an "immigration hinterland" that increasingly resembles the ethnic make-up of the Twin Cities. The Somalis have been drawn by meat processing plants (and other industries that do not require advanced English language skills) in small Minnesota cities such as Rochester, St. Cloud, Owatonna, Faribault and Marshall, and in the town of Barron, in northern Wisconsin. Somalis have racial, cultural and religious gaps in these previously monoethnic rural towns, much greater than Latino meatpackers before them.

This study focuses on one such town, the Wisconsin "turkey capital" of Barron, about 80 miles northeast of the Twin Cities. In conducting our research, we have investigated the connections between Somali immigration to the Twin Cities, and subsequent urban-to-rural migration of Somalis to smaller communities such as Rochester and Barron. We sent questionnaires to the mayors and superintendents of several Minnesota cities, along with conducting interviews in Rochester.

Continuing our research, we conducted a series of interviews in Barron with the Somali director of the International Center, Nasra Xashi, and Somali residents, along with the English as a Second Language (ESL) teacher at the Barron High School and the school district superintendent.

There has been a great deal of research conducted on immigrant groups in the rural Midwest from the perspective of the local American population. Therefore we felt that is was important to conduct a study from the perspective of the immigrant group, in this case the Somalis.

There are several theoretical questions that this research set out to examine. The first question revolves around the cultural gap facing Somalis in rural America. The majority of Somalis are war refugees, like many immigrant groups before them. However, the Somalis have a unique culture, and have arrived with little knowledge of English. They are Muslim and African, unlike the predominantly Mexican or Hmong immigrants who preceded them in the rural Midwest. This combination of a minority culture, religion, and race therefore provides for a different type of immigration issue.

Another question revolves around the issue of assimilation. Do the Somalis intend to be absorbed into US society, even in a small town? Do they see their rural US experiences as more positive or negative than their urban experiences? Are the Somalis being educated to "blend" into the local culture, or are the local residents being educated about the culture and religion that the Somalis have brought into the community?

Finally, the question of the urban-to-rural migration comes into play. Barron, WI is located in the Minneapolis/St. Paul metro area's hinterland and has a large Somali population, similar to the Twin Cities. Nearby, Eau Claire, WI, also located in the Minneapolis/St. Paul hinterland, has a large percentage of Hmong immigrants from the highlands of Laos, another immigrant group with a significant population in the Twin Cities. Mexican and other Latin American immigrants have also settled in other nearby rural areas, drawn by meatpacking and "factory farm" jobs from their homelands and the Twin Cities. Rural southern Minnesota and western Wisconsin is becoming an "ethnic hinterland" of the Twin Cities, slowly developing the same Mexican-Hmong-Somali mix as the Minneapolis-St. Paul metro area.

EARLIER IMMIGRANT GROUPS IN THE MIDWEST

In recent years, the rural Midwest has increasingly hosted immigrant workers, particularly in the meatpacking industry. Over the past two decades, the decreasing consumer demand for meat has forced the meatpacking industry to cut costs. One of the simplest solutions is to move to more rural areas, and to hire immigrant workers who are typically willing to work for lower wages than Americans. The firms benefit from the immigrant workers, not only because immigrants work for lower wages, but also because of high employee turnover, and linguistic barriers to labor organizing:

> Plants benefit from turnover in at least five ways: 1) it keeps aggregated labor costs low; 2) it prevents many workers from becoming eligible for health benefits; 3) it allows the plant to use job training funds to supplement the wages of new hires; 4) it provides replacements from injured and tired workers on a continuing basis and fewer workers become eligible for union representation; 5) and unstable workers are less likely to become union activists.

Another way in which the meatpacking plants benefit from high turnover is that fewer employee injuries are reported to regulatory agencies, because the injured worker is no longer an employee; therefore they avoid fines or higher equipment improvement costs.[2] Also, because some of the immigrant employees are undocumented, unions have difficulty organizing within the plant.[3] Many of the immigrant workers are refugees from countries or regions in which governments and companies have harshly repressed unionization.

The meatpacking industry does not hire immigrants only to save money. A plant is often forced to hire immigrants because the local

American youth no longer want to work there.[4] Ironically, immigrants can sometimes provide a more reliable labor pool than local employees. At one point in the 1990s, approximately half of the population in Norwalk, Wisconsin was Mexican, due to the presence of a meatpacking plant, and its continuous need for a workforce.[5]

The meatpacking industry's practice of hiring immigrant workers is not always beneficial to its bottom line. High turnover rates can end up costing plant money due to the costs of new interviews, screening, training, and periodic labor shortages.[6] High turnover rates can create problems in the host community, such as unstable school enrollments.[7] Conflicts between the local population and the immigrant population can also arise. These tensions are exacerbated by issues such as immigrant workers dating local young people, or perceptions that immigrant workers are "taking away" local jobs.[8] Tensions are particularly acute if local American workers have recently been laid off or fired from the plant.

Not only are immigrants attractive employees for the meatpacking industry, but meatpacking is an attractive job for immigrants. Most jobs in the meatpacking plants require few technical skills, and what skills they do require can be learned fairly quickly. Notably, little English proficiency is needed to successfully complete a job on a processing or packing line. Translators are often hired for the training process, but then the employee is left to do the work and not required to learn any English.[9] (Some companies promise English instruction, but do not deliver.) Another positive aspect of working for the meatpacking industry is its flexibility. For example, workers are able to quit their job, take a break, and then be rehired at the same plant or at another nearby plant.[10] This allows the workers to take a break, visit family back home, or move around the area in search of better jobs.

COMPARING SOMALIS WITH OTHER IMMIGRANT GROUPS

Midwestern states have hosted Hispanic (Latino) immigrants from Mexico and Central America since the 1970s. Large meatpacking companies in Iowa, Nebraska, Minnesota, and Wisconsin have recruited and employed Latino immigrants. Latino immigrants were sometimes recruited by the employer in order to break a strike, and in other cases to offset local labor shortages. The Latino immigrant workers were willing to work for lower pay and fewer benefits than the American workers. This allowed the factory to keep its lower wage structure and may have left some local residents unemployed, thus creating a negative feeling towards the immigrant group.

Somali workers employed in meatpacking factories were not brought in to break unions, but were generally recruited to fill empty positions that local workers did not want. This factor, however, does not outweigh the many "negative" aspects that the Somali population has been forced to confront which the Latino immigrant population has not.

For example, the majority of the Latino immigrant population is Christian. The Latinos therefore blend in with the existing religious beliefs of the majority of the American population, and do not have to face the religious gap that the Somali Muslim population faces. Muslim customs and practices are typically not well known in Midwestern communities, and this lack of understanding has created several points of conflict. Somali women's Muslim dress is very different from the attire of the majority population. The Somali women wear brightly colored dresses and head coverings, and so stand out amongst the rest of the population (more so than do Somali men).

Second, the greater contrast in skin color makes Somali immigrants stand out more than Latino immigrants, and make them more easily identified as a foreign "other." The only other distinctively "foreign" immigrant community in northern Wisconsin is the Hmong from Southeast Asia.

Third, due to the longer span of time that the Latino immigrants have been in the US, and the common border with Mexico, Americans are more familiar with Latin Americans then with Africans. Spanish is a much more common language in the US than Somali (or Arabic). This makes finding Somali translators much more difficult, and also makes some of the local American residents feel uneasy because they are not knowledgeable or familiar with the Somali language. Although some Somalis have been exposed to English in the formerly British northern region of Somaliland, or in Kenyan refugee camps, most arrive in the US with little or no knowledge of the language that opens the door to a wider range of American jobs.

WAR IN SOMALIA AND EMIGRATION TO UNITED STATES

Somalia gained independence in 1960, unifying the formerly Italian south and the formerly British north (or British Somaliland). Despite its ethnic and religious homogeneity, Somalia has a history of conflict among its six major clan families and smaller sub-clans. In Somalia, which has an arid environment and limited natural resources, people have long had to depend on their clan for survival. This situation of dependency created strong clan ties, which later developed into political allegiances along the clan lines, often encouraged by national governments that ruled through divide-and-conquer tactics.[11]

In 1969, Mohammed Siad Barre, a member of the Marehan (a sub-clan of the Darod) became president of Somalia. Although he promised a government that would not be clan-based, Barre "systematically replaced top officials with his own clansmen and by 1987 half of the senior officer corps in the army were Marehan."[12] He also waged a war in the late 1970s against Ethiopia, to annex the ethnic Somali Ogaden region, where fellow Darod clan members lived. The US backed Barre against Soviet–allied Ethiopia, and in return received strategic naval bases in Somalia formerly used by the Soviet fleet.

The clan shift in government greatly upset the northern region of Somalia which was mainly inhabited by members of the Issaq clan. In May 1988, an uprising against Barre began in the north and continued as armed opposition spread across the country.[13] Soon the country was embroiled in a civil war among the clans. Barre's army destroyed the northern city of Hargeisa.[14] In January 1991, southern rebel forces fought their way into Barre's residence in the capital city of Mogadishu, forcing him to flee. When Barre and his supporters fled Mogadishu, they left Somalia without any form of government.[15] The weapons Barre had possessed were left in the hands of the clan leaders, who quickly became militia leaders (called "warlords" by the West) ruling over different regions and different Mogadishu neighborhoods.

Chaos overtook Somalia in 1991-92. More than 300,000 Somalis where killed in the war, or from the famine that resulted from militia confiscation and blockade of food shipments. US forces intervened in late 1992 as part of a UN peacekeeping force, but soon took sides in the clan war by hunting the most powerful Mogadishu militia leader, Mohamed Farah Aidid. After losing 18 soldiers in a 1993 Mogadishu battle with Aidid's forces (popularized in the movie *Black Hawk Down*), the US forces withdrew. Refugee camps in Kenya became flooded with Somali refugees fleeing the violence and famine. These refugees were soon on their way to cities in the United States. The majority of the refugees settled in large cities (such as Minneapolis or Atlanta), but also moved to smaller communities such as Lewiston, Maine.

LEWISTON, MAINE

In 2001-02, more than 1,000 Somalis moved into Lewiston, a small working-class city of 36,000 in southern Maine. The initial group came in a secondary migration from Atlanta, drawn by Maine's low crime rate. Most of the local American residents only knew of Somalia from the Hollywood film *Black Hawk Down*, which was not a realistic presentation of Somalia or its people. Within a short time, rumors about the Somalis began to spread around Lewiston. The rumors contended that the Somalis had access to free cars, air conditioners, and groceries, along with US government grants of $10,000. While these rumors where false, they still created a negative feeling among the local residents towards the Somali newcomers.[16]

These negative feelings in Lewiston escalated when Mayor Laurier T. Raymond Jr. wrote an open letter to the Somalis in Lewiston asking them to stop other Somalis from coming to Lewiston. Somalis quickly responded with their own letter accusing the mayor of being an "ill-informed leader who is bent toward bigotry."[17]

Soon Lewiston, Maine became the center of national protests against immigration, and at the same time a center for protests supporting immigration. At least two white supremacist groups (one led by the Illinois militant Matt Hale) quickly turned Lewiston into a national rallying cry against immigration. Petitions began circulating and rallies were held against and in support of the Somali immigrants.[18] A January 2003, pro-immigrant rally drew 4,000 people. Since then, the situation has calmed down in Lewiston, but some of the Somali residents have also left for other cities.

MIGRATION IN AND OUT OF THE TWIN CITIES

There are currently between 10,000 and 30,000 Somalis residing in Minnesota's Twin Cities of Minneapolis and St. Paul. The ambiguous number is partly a result of continuously shifting populations, but mostly due to the amount of error in census data regarding Somali refugees (as the US Census notoriously minimizes other recent immigrant populations).[19] This large Somali population makes the Twin Cities the *de facto* Somali "capital" of North America.

There are several "pull factors" that drew Somalis to the Twin Cities, including an initially attractive job market, and experienced refugee social service agencies. More recently, the presence of a large Somali community allows newer Somali immigrants to feel at home, and the presence of Somali restaurants and shopping centers makes meeting Somalis' everyday cultural needs much easier than living elsewhere.[20]

However, large American cities also have their drawbacks. The Twin Cities has a higher crime rate than elsewhere in the state. A larger city is much more expensive in which to live, and the unemployment rate is higher. Also, the school system in the poorer neighborhoods of the Twin Cities is not as well funded as the school systems in other communities. Therefore, Somalis have experienced some major "push factors" to leave the big city and move to smaller communities. Although the lower crime rate draws some to small cities such as Rochester, MN,[21] the prospect of employment attracts most Somalis to even smaller rural communities.

Manufacturing jobs in St. Cloud, technical and janitorial jobs at IBM in Rochester, and the Jennie'O Turkey Store in Barron are just a few of the employment opportunities that have pulled the Somalis away from the Twin Cities to the surrounding hinterland. These jobs have many similarities including a low level of required English proficiency required, and immediate on-the-job training.

Yet employment was not the only attractive aspect of the smaller communities for the Somalis. The school systems in general are much better in the smaller communities than in the Twin Cities neighborhoods where most of the Somalis were living. Smaller towns are small enough that Somalis could walk to work and school without driving--a major attraction for immigrants without drivers' licenses.

A smaller community is also quieter and safer than the large city, with a slower lifestyle that is more familiar to Somalis. These "pull factors" were major reasons for Somalis moving to small communities in both Minnesota and Wisconsin.

MINNESOTA COMMUNITIES

Saint Cloud, Minnesota

St. Cloud, Minnesota is a small city located 75 miles northwest of the Twin Cities, with a population of 59,200. Somalis arrived in St. Cloud in 2000-01. The number of Somalis residing in St. Cloud is in the 2,000-3,500 range, with 135 Somali children enrolled in the public school system in 2003. As in Barron, WI, the majority of Somalis work in either poultry or manufacturing factories, and have yet to be employed outside these types of jobs.

St. Cloud has one of the only local governments to act prior to the arrival of the Somali immigrants, in order to prepare the local community. First, the city acted to educate and train public service providers and the general community about the Somali population, culture, and Islamic beliefs. Second, the city identified the housing needs of the Somalis, and was able to negotiate housing opportunities with providers. Next, the city set aside funding and space to encourage and allow the Somalis to practice their culture and religion.[22]

The policies that the city of St. Cloud implemented helped to proactively address many conflicts with the local community before they arose. There were, however, some areas that needed to be addressed after the Somali population arrived in St. Cloud. First, a basic curriculum was developed to educate the Somali population on American culture, community norms, laws, and general resources. Second, panel presentations were organized to provide educators, religious communities, service providers and the general community with information about Somali culture and Islamic beliefs. Next, cultural awareness training was provided for City administrators, and human rights and housing brochures were translated into Somali.[23] Also, the Mayor's office set aside funding for local nonprofit Somali organizations, "to directly serve immigrants and refugees."[24]

There were many positive interactions between the Somali immigrants and St. Cloud's American population. Several Somalis sought to become involved in the St. Cloud community, and the St. Cloud population was eager to learn about the Somali culture. However, after September 11, 2001, there were some negative interactions between Somali and American employees at one of the factories. Also, in the fall of 2002 a Somali community center was vandalized with hate graffiti, and again in late 2002 a Somali-owned and an Ethiopian-owned business were both vandalized with hate graffiti. The city reacted very quickly to "denounce the hate crimes and discrimination of any kind."[25] Several community members contributed to a fund to remove the graffiti and the community sent letters of support, made personal contacts and developed business relationships with the Africans who were impacted by hate crimes.

Rochester, Minnesota

Somali students arrived in the Rochester School District in the summer of 1997; therefore the schools where forced to put programs in place before the school year began in September. The most difficult issue for the Rochester School District was the language barrier between the Somali students and the English-speaking staff. The main struggling point within the ESL program was that most of the Somali students had grown up in refugee camps in Kenya, where a limited amount of education was available in either English or Somali. The refugees were not literate and sometimes not even fluent in Somali. Instruction in English became even more difficult because the teachers did not have a base language to teach from. Also, many of the students had never had experience in a formal educational system and were not accustomed to the school structure. This made the learning environment even more tense between the students and teachers.[26]

Because most of the Somali youth had grown up in a war-torn country or in refugee camps, they were accustomed to a more turbulent living situation, and were therefore more easily provoked. Therefore, an innocent bump in the crowded hallways could easily turn into a physical fight. Also, *qat* chewing was popular among some Somali students. The qat leaf is commonly used in Somalia and is taken ingested by chewing. However, the use of qat is illegal in the US, and therefore prohibited in the schools.

There were also a few instances of Somali students taking advantage of the cultural and religious misunderstandings present in the school staff. For example, some of the students would use prayers as an excuse to skip school. However, after meeting with some of the elders in the local mosque, the school district was able implement policies regarding prayer in school.

All of the students in the Rochester Public High Schools are of the traditional student age, or under 18. The Rochester School District has the Adult and Family Literacy Programming at Hawthorne Education Center. The Adult Literacy Program is an educational system through the Rochester Public Schools that is set up specifically to educate adults of all ages in many different programs. Adult Basic Education not only teaches immigrants English, but also reading, math, writing, and computer skills. There are staffed homework rooms and one-on-one tutoring sessions with volunteers, and daycare and preschool provided for the children of the adult students. The adult education program allows adults to learn in an environment with other adults, which provides not only childcare, but also a schedule that is flexible around work schedules.

Since 1997, there have been several policy changes made in the Rochester School District to accommodate Somali cultural and religious practices, and also to help diminish the language barrier. For instance, prior to 1997 it was a policy violation for any type of head covering to be worn inside a school building. This policy needed to be changed to accommodate the Somali cultural and Muslim religious practice of the woman wearing a *hijab,* or head covering. The school district's policy was changed to allow head coverings for religious or medical reasons (therefore also allowing students undergoing chemotherapy for cancer treatment to cover their heads).

Another policy change was implemented to encourage Somali parents to become more involved with their child's education. Previously, teachers had contacted parents with a letter if there had been any academic or behavioral trouble with the student. This practice, however, was not advantageous for the Somali students, because oftentimes the parents could not read English and would depend on the student to translate the letter. A new policy was implemented to allow translators to contact the parents with any concerns that the teachers may have about the students.

The Rochester School District has adopted a Cultural Responsive Program, with a series of activities to enhance cultural understanding. All staff within the school district will take part in the program, first looking at their own culture and then comparing it with other cultures in the school district. After staff members have gone through the program; they will begin passing on their instruction to the students. A major focus of the program is correct name pronunciation. The superintendent of the Rochester School District feels that correct name pronunciation is a very important part of the program, because it shows respect for the students.[27]

Owatonna, Minnesota

Owatonna is another small community in southern Minnesota that is home to a large Somali population. Owatonna is 42 miles west of Rochester, and has a total population of 22,400. The Somali immigrants first arrived in Owatonna in 1995. They have since continued to move into Owatonna, but often move out to follow different opportunities afforded to them in other towns.

The 2002 census estimate of approximately 1,400-1,500 Somalis does not truthfully represent the number of Somali immigrants that reside in Owatonna (or for that matter anywhere in Minnesota).[28] The majority of Somalis are employed by factories; however, some have begun to find jobs outside of the factories. For example, several women are employed in health care jobs and in nursing homes, and Somali youth can be found working in the local supermarket. There is also a *halal* market that is owned by a local Somali.[29] The halal market not only provides jobs for Somalis, but also provides the Somalis a local place to buy their food rather than through driving to the Twin Cities.

As of 2003, there were not any policies adopted by the Owatonna city government that specifically addressed the new Somali population. This is largely due to Owatonna's past experience with other immigrant groups, such as Vietnamese, Hmong, Bosnians, and other groups. Past experience with non-English speaking immigrant groups prepared the community and the city government to be open to different ethnic groups. However in 1996, Mayor Peter Connor developed the Cultural Diversity Network, which helped supply Somali immigrants with furniture, clothing, food, and other basic needs. Today the Cultural Diversity Network continues to help the community, but through "emphasis on helping to create an environment of understanding and mutual respect."[30] Many long-time residents and local church groups have helped the Cultural Diversity Network by helping welcome the Somalis and also supporting the English as a Second Language (ESL) and English as a Learned Language (ELL) programs.

The reaction to the Somali immigrants has not been wholly positive. Beginning in 2001, the Steele County Coalition for Immigration Reduction formed and began lobbying Congress to reduce the number of legal immigrants to pre-1970 levels.[31] Members have also lobbied to completely close US borders and prevent undocumented immigrants from entering the country. Although the group's direct objective may appear national in scope, the Mayor sees as its indirect objective "to make Owatonna an unwelcome place for those who are racially and culturally different."[32]

The Mayor contends that the vast majority of Owatonna's population, about 80%, is still fairly neutral in its feelings toward the Somali immigrants. He asserts that the other 20% is divided equally into 10% who welcome the Somalis and the 10% who want the Somalis to leave Owatonna.

BARRON, WISCONSIN: A CASE STUDY

Barron is a small community in northwestern Wisconsin with an estimated 2003 population of 3,250 residents. Of the 3,250 Barron residents, approximately 400, or 13% of the population, are Somali immigrants. Somalis first began to move to Barron in 1999 when the Jennie'O Turkey Store experienced a labor shortage in its poultry processing plant. The younger generation of Barron residents was moving out of Barron, or had no interest in the meatpacking business. The Turkey Store was forced to look to a larger pool of potential employees in Minneapolis-St. Paul. Many Somali immigrants who were living in the Twin Cities took jobs in Barron, and moved 90 miles to the small Wisconsin community. The Turkey Store offered employment that required little formal education, little English proficiency, and provided a steady job with overtime hours available.

The state of Wisconsin had a strong appeal to Somalis who were interested in attaining their high school diploma. Minnesota requires each high school student to pass a graduation standards exam, which is very difficult to pass if the student is not highly proficient in English. Therefore, many young Somali students moved across the state boundary to Barron, WI, in order to attain their high school diploma without having to take the Minnesota graduation standards exam. The employment option at the Jennie'O Turkey Store also guaranteed that the students could afford to live in Barron while attending school.[33]

As the Turkey Store began to provide jobs to Somali immigrants, the community was not prepared for the sudden increase in the numbers of non-English speaking residents. The plant did not initially offer English classes, but later funded classes at a nearby service agency. Although Barron had small numbers of Mexican and Hmong residents, the schools and medical facilities were caught off guard and did not have the necessary staff for translation needs. Some residents among the Christian majority were unprepared for a large Muslim minority. The Somalis were not only foreign immigrants, but were racially, religiously and culturally more distinct than previous immigrants.

COMMUNITY NEEDS IN BARRON

Due to the uniformity of the Barron population prior to the arrival of Somali immigrants, the stores and public services in Barron were not prepared to provide for the needs of the Somalis. For example, the grocery stores in Barron were not aware of the special food needs of Somali Muslims. They did not stock halal meats, or the seasonings that the Somalis use in their food preparation. Even though there would be a considerable profit to be made from selling these items to the Somali community, the stores still do not supply the items, and the Somalis are forced to drive to the Twin Cities to buy their groceries.[34]

Somalis in Barron have also had a difficult time organizing and finding a building to start a community center and mosque. Although a mosque would be well attended and the community center would provide the Somalis a place to gather rather than the park, the Barron community has not supported the proposal, and the Somalis are forced to also drive to the Twin Cities to attend a formal mosque.

BARRON SCHOOLS

There have been only a few incidents of conflict between the Somali students and the local Barron students. In October 2001, after the September 11th attack and the arrival of more outspoken urban Somalis from the Twin Cities, there was a short period of name-calling between the local students and the Somali students. A Somali flag was desecrated by small groups of American students, who later as restitution met with members of the Somali community. This problem was addressed and the verbalization ended, but the negative feelings persisted. In April 2002 there was a physical fight between five American students and five Somali students, all of whom were expelled due to the school district's strict no-tolerance of violence policy.

After the violent breakout it became more difficult for the teachers to motivate Somali students, due the students' lack of trust stemming from the expulsions. There has been no outward conflict between the American and Somali students since April 2002. There are still, however, some tensions around racial and cultural differences and the American students' perception of the Somali students' "special treatment." Some of the American students are jealous, for example, that the female Somali students are allowed to cover their heads, but that American students are not allowed to wear hats in school (American students wore banned hooded sweatshirts as a protest). However, the conflict in the school during the 2002-03 school year appeared to occur more among Somalis than between the Somali and American students.[35]

The largest problem for the Barron schools was the language barrier between the Somali students and the English-speaking staff and students. The Barron School District had very little experience with non-English-speaking students. In the past there had been a few students in the public school system who were Mexican immigrants. However, the number of non-English-speaking students had never been great enough to form an ESL program.[36] In 2001, there were suddenly 28 non-English speaking Somali students at the high-school level who enrolled in the Barron public school. This number was clearly great enough for an ESL program to be initiated.

Once the ESL program was put into place, there were other key issues facing the Barron High School, as pointed out by Kim Frandsen, ESL coordinator/teacher for grades K-12 in the Barron Area School District. Most of the Somali students attending the school were not traditional students, but somewhat older. Some Somali students who had enrolled in the Barron High School had moved from Minnesota to Wisconsin to take jobs at the Turkey Store and by doing so--according to Frandsen--avoid taking the newly stringent Minnesota Graduation Standards test. This test was put in place in Minnesota in 1996 to ensure that all students receiving a diploma from a Minnesota public schools where meeting specific standards in English, math and science. Some Minnesota high school students who were unable to pass this exam (sometimes due to lack of English proficiency) moved to Wisconsin in order to obtain their high school diploma. Therefore, many students that move to Barron to complete their education are older students struggling with mastery of English. These students require additional help from instructors in order to earn their diploma, and this situation has put great demand on the ESL teachers and other staff at Barron High School.

Since most Somali high school students in Barron are over the age of eighteen, they no longer live with their parents, but with relatives, friends, or each other. They often lack the parental guidance so their teachers have no parents to contact for additional help. According to Frandsen, the students have a lack of guidance in career goals, due to the absence of parents. Many Somali students do not have goals after receiving their high school diploma. Although there have been efforts made by the ESL teachers to set up mentorships with community members, only a few mentors have volunteered for the numerous Somali students.[37]

The students are dependent on themselves not only for their education, but also for their economic livelihood. After completing a full day of school, most of the students head directly to the Turkey Store to work the second shift from 3:00 p.m. to 11:00 p.m.[38] This demanding work schedule leaves little time for homework or extracurricular activities.

Despite these obstacles, the Barron School District has made some major advances. The faculty within the school district has been required to undergo diversity education. For example, a panel of Somali students volunteered their time to educate the faculty and staff about Somali culture, religion and language, and to answer any questions. Videos on intercultural understanding have been produced under the direction of Superintendent Monti Hallberg. Through Hallberg's fortuitous previous teaching experience in Saudi Arabia, Pakistan, and Kenya, he learned about Islam and speaks Arabic. (He had coincidentally visited the same Somali refugee camps in Kenya that housed the district's future students.) The school district has developed a way to test the Somali students' English proficiency before they attend school in order to better place them in classes, using school transcripts from refugee camps in Kenya.[39] Hallberg also initiated Boys and Girls Soccer teams at the high school level. Since soccer is a very popular sport among the Somali, American, and Mexican students, the creation of a soccer team helped bridge the gap between them.[40] One of the American students involved in the Somali flag desecration went on to play on the soccer team and make Somali friends. These conflict resolution strategies continue to be developed by the school district.

HOUSING IN BARRON

In Barron there is currently a shortage of affordable housing. This limitation has forced many Somalis to reside in one of two apartment complexes on the outskirts of town. Because of their low rent, these apartments were initially the only housing options for the Somalis who work at the Turkey Store. The two apartment complexes are owned and operated by two Mennonite sisters who have been very responsive to the needs of the Somalis. Somalis typically live with their extended family, and it is not uncommon for several young single adults to live together, if their family is not present. The employment and educational situation in Barron has drawn many young adults to the area who live with friends or distant relatives.

The apartments were intended to be rented to one or two tenants per apartment; however, while only 1-2 names were on the lease, the Somalis were living with five or six people per apartment. This situation initially caused misunderstandings, however the cooperation of the tenants and the landlords has allowed for five of six people to live in one apartment, as long as all of their names are on the lease and they do not break the lease. (In 2004 some Somalis began to rent their own apartments in the community, potentially easing the housing shortage).

Even with five or six people residing in one apartment, the housing shortage has caused Somalis to search in other small communities around Barron, such as Rice Lake and Cameron, for housing options. This simple housing shortage in Barron has begun to affect the surrounding towns. For example, while adults might commute to work in Barron, the children attend school in the smaller communities in which they live, thus creating the need for ESL classes and other language and cultural services in the communities surrounding Barron.

Most Somalis moving into surrounding Wisconsin communities continue to commute to work at the Turkey Store plant. But a few have begun to diversify their seasonal employment options, such as taking jobs at a vegetable canning plant in Balsam Lake, a computer manufacturing plant in Chippewa Falls, and a furniture plant in Cumberland. The contagious diffusion of Somalis from Barron means that neighboring communities are starting to face the same questions that Barron faced at the start of the decade. The lessons of Barron can be a resource for these communities, to learn how to make Somalis feel welcome, and how to educate the local American community to prepare for Somali immigration.

SURVEY OF BARRON SOMALI COMMUNITY

In the summer of 2003 we distributed an extensive survey to the Somali community in Barron, through the International Center and the ESL program at Barron High School. Upon collection of the survey we determined that the survey was too complex, and developed a shorter, simpler survey to target more specific areas of interest. This simpler survey was distributed in spring 2005, and is yielding ongoing results.

The survey was designed to target the specific areas of migration to and within the United States, and the different push and pull factors affecting Somali migration from large cities, such as Minneapolis, MN, and smaller communities, specifically Barron. While the survey is still in circulation, the preliminary results (approximately 10% of the Somali population in Barron) are as follows.

The first section of the survey traced the migration from Somalia, to the US, and then within the US There was space to record up to six migrations; however, no more than five were used on any of the returned surveys. Preliminary results show that of the Somali immigrants entering the US 42% settled in Minneapolis, MN upon arrival. Of the remaining immigrants 10.5% settled in California, and other states listed as first arrival points were Ohio, Tennessee, New York, and Massachusetts.

Migration to Barron also showed results similar to those we predicted. Of the Somali immigrants settling in Barron, 76% arrived directly from the Twin Cities. The remaining 24% were equally distributed between Ohio, Tennessee, Virginia, and Washington State. The survey also asked how Somali immigrants heard about Barron, and the responses indicated only two sources: family members (56%) and friends (44%).

Survey participants were also asked to rate their first experience in Barron as Very Positive, Positive, Negative, or Very Negative. While the majority reported their experience as Very Positive, or Positive, there were some individuals who felt their experience was negative. The results are presented in Table 1.

TABLE 1. FIRST EXPERIENCE IN BARRON, WI

First Experience	Percentage
Very Positive	44%
Positive	37.5%
Negative	12.5%
Very Negative	6%

The final section of the survey asked participants to compare and rank different aspects of the larger cities, such as Minneapolis, in comparison to smaller communities, such as Barron. The responses to these questions (in the form of numerical rankings from 1 to 5) were then averaged in order to evaluate the push and pull factors affecting migration from the larger cities to smaller communities. The preliminary results showed little difference in several categories.

However, when comparing the averages, there were some which showed a difference of greater than half a unit. For example, the larger city ranked higher for having more jobs available. However, the smaller community ranked higher as a safer place to live, and as an easier place in which to support a family, to overcome regional and clan differences among Somalis, and to provide a closer knit community. These categories should be taken into consideration for the preliminary results, with the hope of more conclusive results shown after more surveys have been returned. The averages of this section of the survey are presented in Table 2.

TABLE 2. COMMUNITY ASPECTS COMPARISONS BETWEEN LARGER CITIES AND SMALLER COMMUNITIES; BASED ON THE AVERAGE OF NUMERICAL RANKINGS FROM 1 (STRONGLY DISAGREE) TO 5 (STRONGLY AGREE).

Community Aspect	**Average for Large City** (rounded to two decimals)	**Average for Smaller Community** (rounded to two decimals)
Less Prejudice	3.67	4.00
More Welcoming	4.07	4.19
Better Schools	4.19	4.14
More Jobs	4.14	3.35
Safer Place to Live	3.57	4.25
Easier to Support a Family	3.56	4.21
More Accepting of Religious Differences	3.88	4.21
More Accepting of Cultural Differences	4.06	4.29
Stronger Sense of Somali Identity	3.81	4.14
Have Overcome Regional or Clan Differences	3.17	3.67
Closer Knit Community	3.60	4.20
Better Working Conditions	4.31	4.00

SURVEY METHODS

The process of conducting this survey was not without difficulty, as several factors impeded the process. The first difficulty was the language barrier. The majority of Somalis in Barron are not highly proficient in English, so the survey was a bilingual survey printed in English and Somali. The original survey was translated by the Intercultural Mutual Assistance Association in Rochester, MN, and the changes to the secondary survey (and written remarks) were aided by a Somali student at the University of Wisconsin-Eau Claire, Abdirahman Ahmed.

However, a bilingual survey was not enough to overcome the language barrier. The majority of Somali immigrants in Barron were raised in refugee camps in Kenya, and therefore do not have strong literacy in Somali. Therefore, the surveys must be completed with the aid of an individual who can read either Somali or English; this can be accomplished in ESL classrooms at the High School or International Center. As a result, completing even a short survey can be very time consuming. The majority of Somalis in Barron work at least full time, go to school, and travel to the Twin Cities on the weekends, so they have very little free time to complete the survey.

In addition there are no major gathering points for Barron Somalis, so distributing the survey has been limited to the High School and International Center. Translators have had to clearly communicate the purpose of the survey, since some in the community are on guard after post-9/11 FBI raids on several Somali businesses in the Twin Cities, and recent attempts to expatriate Omar Jamal, a Somali leader in Minnesota. These barriers make the survey process more difficult and time consuming, but they do not make it impossible. With ample time and patience it is still possible to obtain results.

CONCLUSION

Through the interviews that were conducted in Barron, the questionnaires that were returned from the Minnesota communities, and the interviews conducted in Rochester, MN, it is apparent that the most of the educational efforts in these communities are directed at the Somali immigrants, to ease their transition into Midwestern American society. In general, the education that the Somalis received appeared to be aimed at assimilating them into the local culture and the American way of life. There have been relatively few efforts, however, to educate the American community about the Somalis.

Somali grocery items, a mosque for worship, English-language classes, and other basic needs can go a long way in making Somalis feel welcome, and keeping them in town on the weekends, when socializing with Americans is the most possible. Invitations to participate in weekend festivals can also keep Somalis from leaving for the Twin Cities, at the same time as educating local Americans. But even these basic needs are not a substitute for educating local Americans about Somali history, culture and religion, in order to open the doors of understanding between the communities.

While there have been some programs directed at the local population, the majority were passively advertised, and only attended by individuals that had a previous interest in cultural diversity. Without a concurrent program to educate Americans--in their schools, social clubs, and places of employment--the programs to educate Somalis can become irrelevant when confronting by local assumptions, fears, and prejudices.

In a small community of 2,000 or 3,000 people, it is possible to develop educational curriculum, videos, and speaking tours that can systematically reach all American adults and young adults in the community. Generalized appeals to "respect diversity" or experience ethnic dances or foods at an annual multiethnic event are not a substitute for education on more difficult aspects of war, refugee status, family structures, customs, language, and religious beliefs. State agencies such as the Wisconsin Department of Public Instruction have in the past developed educational curriculum on intercultural understanding (such as the "Act 31" legislation of 1989, requiring instruction in fourth and eighth grades on Wisconsin American Indian history and culture).

Somali immigrants will not go away in western Wisconsin, even if future moves toward a peace agreement are finalized in Somalia, and some refugees return home. Over the past decade, an "ethnic hinterland" has been growing around the Twin Cities. The Minneapolis-St. Paul area is home to a large number of Somalis, Hmong, and Latinos. Many communities in the hinterland around the Twin Cities also now contain a high percentage of these same immigrant groups.

Barron, WI, for example, is home to a large Somali population that came mainly from the Twin Cities, and which is slowly diffusing into neighboring towns. Eau Claire and La Crosse,WI have been home to a large Hmong population since the 1970s. Strum, Merrillan, and Curtiss, WI are home to a growing Latino population. Large communities, such as Rochester, MN, have large and mixed Somali, Hmong, and Latino populations.[41] While the push and pull factors may vary for individuals, the push factors of crime and increased job competition tend to press people to leave the larger city, and the pull factors of employment, good schools, and a safe, smaller community tend to draw them into rural communities in the "ethnic hinterland" around a metro area.

The development of this "ethnic hinterland" means that communities that have not yet experienced ethnic or racial diversity may have to deal with it in the very near future. Proactive education of local Americans, to help them to ease the transition for the immigrants, and to view immigration as a potential gain rather than loss for their community, can prevent some of the problems that have beset unprepared communities.

Notes

1. Stanley, K. (1992). Immigrant and refugee workers in the Midwest meatpacking industry: Industrial restructuring and the transformation of rural labor markets. *Policy Studies Review*, 11(2), 106-117.
2. Grey, M. A. (1999). Immigrants, migration and worker turnover at the hog pride pork packing plant. *Human Organization*, 58(1), 16-27. p. 17.
3. Ibid. 20.
4. Martinez, R. (2001). *Crossing over: A Mexican family on the migrant trail*. New York: Metropolitan Books.
5. Hart, J. (1997, November 26). Blood, sweat, and supper: One week on the evisceration line. *Scrawl Winter Books Issue*, 18, 866.
6. Martinez, R. (2001). *Crossing over: A Mexican family on the migrant trail*. New York: Metropolitan Books. p. 241.
7. Grey, M. A. (1999). Immigrants, migration and worker turnover at the hog pride pork packing plant. *Human Organization*, 58(1), 16-27. p. 17.

   Ibid, 18.
8. Martinez, R. (2001). *Crossing over: A Mexican family on the migrant trail*. New York: Metropolitan Books. p. 253.

9. Grey, M. A. (1999). Immigrants, migration and worker turnover at the hog pride pork packing plant. *Human Organization*, 58(1), 16-27. p. 22.
10. Ibid, 24.
11. Peterson, S. (2000). *Me against my brother: At war in Somalia, Sudan and Rwanda*. New York: Routledge. p. 8.
12. Peterson, S. (2000). *Me against my brother: At war in Somalia, Sudan and Rwanda*. New York: Routledge. p. 13.
13. Peterson, S. (2000). *Me against my brother: At war in Somalia, Sudan and Rwanda*. New York: Routledge. p. 14.
14. Ibid.
15. Sahnoun, M. (1994). *Somalia: The missed opportunities*. Washington, DC: United States Institute of Peace Press. p. 9.
16. Belluck, P. (2002, October 10). Mixed welcome as Somalis settle in Maine city. *New York Times*.
17. Ibid.
18. As depicted in Ziad Hamzeh's documentary film, *The Letter*.
19. Black, E. (2002, August 3). From Mogadishu to Minneapolis. *Minneapolis Star Tribune*.
20. Lourdes Medrano, L. (2002, June 4). Sights, sounds of Africa increasing. *Minneapolis Star Tribune*.
21. Nigon, J. (personal communication, Rochester, MN, July 22, 2003).
22. Ellenbecker, J. D. (2003, July 9). Mayor, City of St. Cloud. letter to authors.
23. Ibid.
24. Ibid.
25. Ibid.
26. Williams, J. (personal communication, Rochester, MN, July 22, 2003).
27. Ibid.
28. Connor, P. W. (2003, July 12). Mayor, City of Owatonna. letter to authors.
29. Ibid.
30. Ibid.
31. Ibid.
32. Ibid.
33. Frandsen, K. (personal communication, Barron, WI, June 5, 2003).
34. Xashi, N. (personal communication, Barron, WI, June 5, 2003).

35. Frandsen, K. (personal communication, Barron, WI, June 5, 2003).
36. Ibid.
37. Ibid.
38. Ibid.
39. Hallberg, M. (personal communication, Barron, WI, June 5, 2003).
40. Ibid.
41. US Census Data, 2000.

ABOUT THE AUTHORS

EDITORS

Stephanie R. Bjork, co-editor, is an independent scholar who resides in Phoenix, Arizona. She received her Ph.D. in Anthropology from the University of Wisconsin-Milwaukee. Her dissertation, *Diasporic Moments: Practicing Clan in the Somali Diaspora,* is an ethnography of everyday life which explores how Somalis in Finland use clan. Her dissertation fieldwork in Finland, 2003-2004, was supported by the American-Scandinavian Foundation and the Wenner-Gren Foundation for Anthropological Research. Her interest in the Somali diaspora developed during her Rotary exchange in Finland, 1990-1991. This period coincided with the arrival of the country's first Somali asylum seekers. A Fulbright Fellowship to Finland, 2000-2001, culminated in her master's thesis which focused on the production, transnational circulation, and viewing of Somali wedding videos. She is a member of the 10th Triennial Somali Studies International Congress program committee.

Abdi M. Kusow, co-editor, is Associate Professor of Sociology at Oakland University in Michigan, USA. He has written extensively on transnational migration and racial identities in North America and Somali society. His work appears in leading sociology and international migration journals: *Symbolic Interaction*, *Journal of Ethnic and Migration Studies, and Ethnic and Racial Studies*. He edited *Putting the Cart Before the Horse: Contested Nationalism and the Crisis of the Nation-State in Somalia*, Red Sea Press, 2004. His article, "Contesting Stigma: On Goffman's Assumptions of Normative Order," has ranked in the top 20 most read articles in *Symbolic Interaction* since 2005. He is the recipient of the 2005 Tenth Annual Oakland

University Faculty Research Recognition Award. He is 2007-2010 Vice Chair of the Somali Studies International Association and Vice Chair of the Organizing Committee for the 10th Triennial Somali Studies International Congress, Columbus, Ohio, 2007.

CONTRIBUTORS

Mulki Al-Sharmani is Assistant Research Professor at the American University in Cairo's Social Research Center. She also teaches for the University's Forced Migration and Refugee Studies Program. She received her Ph.D. in Anthropology from Johns Hopkins University. Her recent publications include "Living Transnationally: Diasporic Somali Women in Cairo," *Journal of International Migration*, February 2006 and "The Livelihood and the Identity Constructions of Somali Refugees in Cairo," Working Paper 2, Forced Migration and Refugee Studies Program, American University in Cairo, 2003. Her research interests are the integration of diasporic communities, citizenship, transnational families and communities, child protection policies and practices in Egypt, and the interplay between gender and law in family courts in Egypt.

Rima Berns-McGown is a lecturer in diaspora studies with the Historical Studies Department and the Centre for Diaspora and Transnational Studies at the University of Toronto. She is the author of *Muslims in the Diaspora: The Somali Communities of London and Toronto*, as well as numerous articles in edited books and refereed journals. Born in South Africa, she completed her Ph.D. in International Politics at the University of Wales at Aberystwyth and her M.A. at Johns Hopkins School of Advanced International Studies (SAIS) in Washington, DC. Her research interests include diaspora and migration; the interrelationships between culture, religion, and politics; and political culture as it concerns the integration of immigrants and minorities. She is currently writing a book on Toronto's diaspora communities.

Francesca Decimo is Assistant Professor of Sociology at the University of Trento, Italy where she teaches sociology of migration and sociology of ethnic relations. Decimo is currently studying migration flows in Italy, particularly networks and migration processes, and fertility and social reproduction issues among minorities. These issues are investigated through a socio-anthropological approach. Her main publications are *Quando emigrano le donne. Percorsi e reti femminili della mobilità transnazionale* [When women migrate. Female paths and networks of transnational mobility] Bologna, il Mulino, 2005 and *Stranieri in Italia. Reti migranti* [Foreigners in Italy. Migrant networks], with G. Sciortino (Eds.), Bologna, Il Mulino, 2006.

Mohamed A. Eno received his Ph.D. in Social Studies Education from St. Clements University and M.A. in TESOL (Teaching English as a Second Language) from the University of Sunderland, United Kingdom. He taught at the University of Nairobi and the Somali National University. Mohamed is a linguist, poet, composer, journalist and the director of the Eno School of Languages. He speaks six languages and the distinct Somali dialects of Af-Maay and Af-Maxaa. His essay, "Understanding Somalia through the Prism of Bantu – Jareer Literature," was published in *The Road Less Traveled: Reflections on the Literatures of the Horn of Africa* (2006). He also published articles in the HEEGAN, an English weekly newspaper circulated by the former Somali Ministry of Information and National Guidance. He has presented on various subjects: peace and reconciliation; conflict resolution; ethnic minority and marginalization; refugees and social stratification; and education. Mohamed's research interests include sociolinguistics, social culture, teacher education, oral tradition, and ethnic studies.

Omar A. Eno is Ph.D. Candidate in African History at York University, Toronto. He is Director of the National Somali Bantu Research Project at Portland State University where he also serves as a faculty member. He has written extensively on Somali history and culture. Recent publications are "Landless Landlords, and Landed Tenants…" in *Putting the Cart Before the Horse: Contested Nationalism and the Crisis of the Nation-State* (2004); "The Abolition of Slavery and the Aftermath Stigma," in *Abolition and its Aftermath in Indian Ocean Africa and Asia* (2005); "Somalia's city of the

Jackals: politics, economy, and society in Mogadishu, 1991-2003," in *African Urban Spaces: In Historical Perspective* (2005), and "The making of a modern Diaspora: The resettlement process of the Somali Bantu refugees in the United States," in *African Minorities in the New World* (2007). Eno's research interests are East Africa and the African diaspora in Africa and the Middle East.

Franklin Goza is Professor of Sociology and Director of Demographic Studies at Bowling Green State University, Ohio. He received his Ph.D. in sociology from the University of Wisconsin-Madison where he began his research on refugees. His dissertation examined the experiences of Southeast Asian refugees in the United States. For the past three years, Goza has studied the incorporation experiences of Somali refugees in the United States and Canada. His fieldwork and data collection projects have been funded with grants from the Canadian Government, the Center for Family and Demographic Research, and the Office of Sponsored Programs and Research at Bowling Green State University. He was the recipient of a Senior Fulbright Scholar award and a Rockefeller Social Science Fellowship, both of which he served in Brazil. His research has been published in leading academic journals: *International Migration Review, International Migration, Population Research and Policy Review, Critical Sociology, Social Biology, Journal of Biosocial Sciences,* and *Journal of Aging Studies*.

Zoltán Grossman is a member of the Faculty in Geography and Native American and World Indigenous Peoples Studies at the Evergreen State College, Olympia, Washington. He received his Ph.D. in Geography from the University of Wisconsin-Madison. From 2002 to 2005, he taught geography at the University of Wisconsin-Eau Claire. Grossman has a background in research and community service around interethnic conflict and cooperation in North America and globally. His faculty website is http://academic.evergreen.edu/g/grossmaz.

Petri Hautaniemi is a researcher in the Finnish Youth Research Network and the Institute of Development Studies at the University of Helsinki. He received his Ph.D. at the University of Tampere, Finland and his M.A. in Social Anthropology at the University of Stockholm. His dissertation focused on young Somali boys in Helsinki growing up in a transnational family network. He previously worked in the field of immigrant education in Helsinki and conducted a study on street children in Nepal. Hautaniemi also carried out a short-term EU research project on family policies, fertility, gender equality and aging in contemporary Finland. Hautaniemi's current project on St. Petersburg street children looks at transnational governance with special attention to the position of children who have fallen out of the safety networks of families and educational institutions. Significant publications include a monograph, *Pojat! Somalipoikien kiistanalainen nuoruus Suomessa* [Lads! Contested childhood of Somali youngsters in Finland], and "Episodic Memory – Life narratives of young Somali boys in Finland," *Anthropological Journal of European Cultures,* no 2/2006.

Cindy Horst is Senior Researcher at the International Peace Research Institute, Oslo (PRIO). She previously worked as a lecturer on forced migration at the University of Amsterdam and as a moderator for the Refugee Livelihoods Network, UNHCR. Horst is a social anthropologist specializing in forced migration studies. She has extensive fieldwork experience among Somalis in Kenya and the wider diaspora. Her main research interests focus on assistance practices, cultures of migration and interactions between forced migrants and the refugee regime. Her most recent publications include *Transnational Nomads. How Somalis Cope with Refugee Life in the Dadaab Camps of Kenya* (2006), an edited volume of the *Refugee Survey Quarterly* on refugee livelihoods (2006), and *Buufis amongst Somalis in Dadaab: The Transnational and Historical Logics Behind Resettlement Dreams*, *Journal of Refugee Studies* 19(2), 2006.

Anu Isotalo (Salmela) is Ph.D. Candidate in the School of Cultural Studies at the University of Turku, Finland. She is working on her Ph.D. dissertation, *What are good girls made of? An Ethnographical Study of Somali Girls in the city of Turku* at the Department of Comparative Religion. Recent publications include "Constancy in Change, Change in Constancy. Somali Women as Mediators of Islam and Community Tradition in Turku" (2004) and "Somali Girls, Socio-sexually Defined Space, and Ways to Talk about Sexuality" (2006). Her research interests include the socio-cultural meanings of gender, body, space, ethnicity, communality, religion and cultural tradition.

Nauja Kleist is Project Researcher at the Danish Institute for International Studies. A Danish migration researcher, she received her Ph.D. in Sociology at the University of Copenhagen. Her dissertation analyzes struggles for recognition and diasporic mobilization in Somali-Danish associational involvement. Kleist has worked as a junior lecturer at Roskilde University and the University of Copenhagen. She has published on Somali transnational involvement as well as issues concerning inclusion and exclusion, gender relations, repatriation, and home and belonging. Kleist has edited two special issues in the Danish journal *Kvinder, Køn & Forskning* focusing on migration and citizenship, and war.

Gudrun-Katharina Kroner is Research Associate at the Austrian Academy of Sciences. She received her Ph.D. and M.A. in Cultural Anthropology from the University of Vienna. She currently works on a project related to identity constructions of Somali and Palestinian refugees in the Arab world. She also is a lecturer at the University of Vienna and a research fellow at the American University in Cairo. For her master's thesis, *Stages of Expulsion: Somali Refugee Experiences in East-Africa and the Western World*, she carried out fieldwork in Austria, Kenya, Ethiopia, and Canada. For her Ph.D. dissertation, *Beyond Local Contexts: A Comparative Analysis of Female Refugee Experience in the Arab-Muslim World*, she conducted two years of fieldwork among Somali refugees in Egypt, and 15 months among Palestinian refugees in Gaza and Jordan. She published articles on this topic in English and German. Her present research focus is on refugee studies, identity constructions, and survival strategies (especially in the Arab world).

Jessica Schaid received her B.A. in Political Science with a minor in Anthropology from the University of Wisconsin-Eau

Claire in May 2005. She is currently working on her Master's Degree in Curriculum and Instruction at New Mexico State University. Upon completion of her degree, she plans to work with disadvantaged students and to work for educational equity for all students in the public education system.

Marja Tiilikainen works as a researcher for the Department of Sociology at the University of Helsinki, Finland. She completed her Ph.D. in Comparative Religion in 2003 at the University of Helsinki. Tiilikainen's dissertation, *Arjen islam: Somalinaisten elämää Suomessa* [Everyday Islam: Life of Somali women in Finland], was published in 2003 and based on extensive ethnographic fieldwork among Somali women in metropolitan Helsinki. Her postdoctoral research deals with suffering and transnational healing practices among Somalis in the diaspora. Tiilikainen has lectured widely and published in both national and international journals and books about Somali migrants in general and Somali women and health in particular. Tiilikainen also worked as a manager for a project against female circumcision at the Finnish League for Human Rights. She is a founding member of the Nordic research network *Diaspora and State Formation in the Horn of Africa*, funded by the Nordic Africa Institute, Sweden. She recently served as an organizer of the network's first international conference, "A Double Heritage of Democracy".

INDEX